The Unusable Past

Theory and the Study of American Literature

RUSSELL J. REISING

METHUEN

New York and London

First published in 1986 by
Methuen, Inc.
29 West 35th Street, New York, NY 10001

Published in Great Britain by
Methuen & Co. Ltd
11 New Fetter Lane, London EC4P 4EE

Photoset by Rowland Phototypesetting Ltd
England
Printed in the United States of America

Library of Congress Cataloging in Publication Data
Reising, Russell.
The unusable past.
(New accents)
Bibliography: p.
Includes index.
1. American literature – History and criticism –
Theory, etc.   2. Criticism – United States – History.
I. Title.   II. Series: New accents (Methuen & Co.)
PS25.R44 1986   810'.9   86-5372

ISBN 0-416-01311-2
ISBN 0-416-01321-X (pbk.)

British Library Cataloguing in Publication Data
Reising, Russell
The unusable past: theory and study of
American literature. – (New accents)
1. American literature – History and
criticism   2. Criticism
I. Title   II. Series
810.9   PS55

ISBN 0-416-01311-2
ISBN 0-416-01321-X Pbk

NEW ACCENTS

General Editor: TERENCE HAWKES

Unusable Past:
Theory and the Study of
American Literature

IN THE SAME SERIES

* Not available from Methuen, Inc., in the USA.

To the memory of
Phoebe MacDougall Reising

Contents

General editor's preface

It is easy to see that we are living in a time of rapid and radical social change. It is much less easy to grasp the fact that such change will inevitably affect the nature of those disciplines that both reflect our society and help to shape it.

Yet this is nowhere more apparent than in the central field of what may, in general terms, be called literary studies. Here, among large numbers of students at all levels of education, the erosion of the assumptions and presuppositions that support the literary disciplines in their conventional form has proved fundamental. Modes and categories inherited from the past no longer seem to fit the reality experienced by a new generation.

New Accents is intended as a positive response to the initiative offered by such a situation. Each volume in the series will seek to encourage rather than resist the process of change; to stretch rather than reinforce the boundaries that currently define literature and its academic study.

Some important areas of interest immediately present themselves. In various parts of the world, new methods of analysis have been developed whose conclusions reveal the limitations of the Anglo-American outlook we inherit. New concepts of literary forms and modes have been proposed; new notions of the nature of literature itself and of how it communicates are current; new views of literature's role in relation to society flourish. *New Accents* will aim to expound and comment upon the most notable of these.

In the broad field of the study of human communication, more and more emphasis has been placed upon the nature and function of the new electronic media. *New Accents* will try to identify and discuss the challenge these offer to our traditional modes of critical response.

The same interest in communication suggests that the series should also concern itself with those wider anthropological and sociological areas of investigation which have begun to involve scrutiny of the nature of art itself and of its relation to our whole way of life. And this will ultimately require attention to be focused on some of those activities which in our society have hitherto been excluded from the prestigious realms of Culture. The disturbing realignment of values involved and the disconcerting nature of the pressures that work to bring it about both constitute areas that *New Accents* will seek to explore.

Finally, as its title suggests, one aspect of *New Accents* will be firmly located in contemporary approaches to language, and a continuing concern of the series will be to examine the extent to which relevant branches of linguistic studies can illuminate specific literary areas. The volumes with this particular interest will nevertheless presume no prior technical knowledge on the part of their readers, and will aim to rehearse the linguistics appropriate to the matter in hand, rather than to embark on general theoretical matters.

Each volume in the series will attempt an objective exposition of significant developments in its field up to the present as well as an account of its author's own views of the matter. Each will culminate in an informative bibliography as a guide to further study. And, while each will be primarily concerned with matters relevant to its own specific interests, we can hope that a kind of conversation will be heard to develop between them; one whose accents may perhaps suggest the distinctive discourse of the future.

TERENCE HAWKES

Acknowledgments

I would like to thank those people and agencies that have helped me in my work. An Arts and Sciences Summer Research Fellowship from the University of Oklahoma assisted my work on *The Unusable Past*. I am very grateful to Mary McClain and her staff at the Information Processing Center of the University of Oklahoma for preparing my manuscript. I would also like to thank the departments of English at the University of Oklahoma and at Marquette University for providing me with moral support and research assistants. Diana Osetek of Marquette University provided excellent editorial and research assistance.

The following people have read, discussed, and improved *The Unusable Past* in many and important ways. Janice Price and her colleagues and readers at Methuen provided support and stimulating suggestions. Donald Daiker, Wayne Falke, Jerome Rosenberg, and Jack Wallace (all of Miami University) figure largely, though indirectly, in *The Unusable Past*, and have each contributed to my thinking about American literature and culture. Robert Con Davis, Robert Murray Davis, and Clayton Lewis (all of the University of Oklahoma); T. H. Breen, Barbara Foley, Harrison Hayford, Gregory Meyerson, and Carl Smith (all of Northwestern University); Herbert Tucker (of the University of Michigan); Robert Jones (of Rice University);

xii The Unusable Past

and Joseph DeFalco (of Marquette University) all read sections of this manuscript and offered significant insights, most of which have found their way into my book.

I would like to express special and continuing gratitude to Gerald Graff, whose work, example, and friendship have inspired and challenged me over the past decade. He urged me to undertake this project, and his contributions to *The Unusable Past* have been numerous and important.

My deepest thanks to Alma A. MacDougall, my editor, colleague, and wife, for her untiring and expert editing and advice, and for her sustained encouragement. My daughter, Margaret MacDougall Reising, provided invaluable assistance in aligning my paragraphs and my priorities over the past three years.

Introduction

In a book on theories of American literature, it is prudent, perhaps, to clarify some difficult terms at the outset. The field is so large – conceivably all texts construable as American literature and all secondary texts, histories, reviews, critical studies, and more, taking American literature as their subjects – that the possibilities for analysis seem endless. This present work must admit of being tertiary – it is very obviously not a work of imaginative literature, no matter how broad I argue that term must be, and it purports to offer no new definition of what American literature means, what its Ur-theme(s) may be, or what makes it 'American' as distinct from any other geographic, political, social, or cultural category. My subject is a relatively small yet well-known and influential body of critical studies of American literature taking, in one way or another, the definition of American literature as their subjects. More specifically, my interest here is in how those theories define the canon of American literature and how those definitions influence our understanding and teaching of that canon. Some early figures such as V. L. Parrington, Yvor Winters, and Perry Miller enter into the discussion in a variety of ways – as precursors, as founders of traditions, and as antagonists against whom later critics defined their field – but most of the critics I study wrote after World War II, in the midst of social crises from the

McCarthy era through Vietnam and the social rebellions of the sixties and up to the present.

I am using the phrase 'theories of American literature' to refer to a specific group and type of texts – book-length studies of American literature by such critics as Sacvan Bercovitch, Richard Chase, Charles Feidelson, Jr, Leslie Fiedler, John T. Irwin, R. W. B. Lewis, Leo Marx, F. O. Matthiessen, Richard Poirier, Lionel Trilling, and Yvor Winters. While the methods and scopes of their works vary, these theorists have taken up the task either of describing what makes American literature distinctively 'American' or of defining what *the* American tradition is, what the 'best' American literature is or does. Some critics are more ambitious, others more modest in their claims, but they tend to advance essentialist theses about what American literature is all about. Richard Chase, for example, sets out to identify 'the *originality* and "*Americanness*" of the novel' and 'to define some of [its] leading qualities' (Chase 1957, 7, 12). Leslie Fiedler argues that 'the quest which has distinguished our fiction from Brockden Brown and Cooper, through Poe and Melville and Twain, to Faulkner and Hemingway is the search for an innocent substitute for adulterous passion and marriage alike' and that a 'bargain with the Devil' is '*the essence of American experience*' (Fiedler 1960, 339, 433). Leo Marx's *The Machine in the Garden* addresses 'the *classical* canon of our literature,' 'our *best* writers,' and defines its theme as 'a great – in many ways *the greatest – event in our history*' (Marx 1964, 10, 11, 27). For Lionel Trilling, 'the fact is that *American writers of genius* have not turned their minds to society' (Trilling 1950, 212). R. W. B. Lewis claims that his thesis accounts for '*the best of our fiction*' and suggests that 'the future of American literature depends in some real part upon the durability of the image of the hero as Adam' (Lewis 1955, 90, 152). Yvor Winters asserts that 'the Puritan view of life was allegorical, and the allegorical vision seems to have been strongly impressed upon the New England literary mind,' a claim he argues influences subsequent American literature (Winters 1938, 4). Sacvan Bercovitch's readings of Puritan rhetoric and the rhetorical constitution of the 'American self' assume that 'the myth of America is the creation of the New England Way' (Bercovitch 1975, 143). F. O. Matthiessen argued that the '*one common denominator*' among writers of the American Renaissance 'was their devotion to the possibilities of democracy' (Matthiessen 1941, ix); Charles Feidelson later replaced Matthiessen's thesis with the claim that 'it is more likely that the *really vital common denominator* is precisely their attitude toward their medium – that their distinctive quality is a devotion to the possibilities of symbolism' (Feidelson 1953, 4). For Richard Poirier, 'the *great*,' the '*most exciting*,' and the '*most interesting*' American books, those which 'constitute *a distinctive American tradition* within English literature . . . resist within their pages the forces of environment that otherwise dominate the world' (Poirier 1966, 36; all italics added). This is, of course, only a sampling of such grand statements, but it communicates the totalizing impulse behind these studies.

One of my assumptions in this study is that these claims are *significant*, that they are not merely the posturings of critical imperialism or moments of critical bravado attempting to validate the worth of certain critical approaches. It is conceivable that they are nothing more, but the interconnections, the shared assumptions, and the mutually reinforcing inertia that link these works – even when they seem antagonistic – suggest otherwise. That the actual accomplishments of these works are less monumental (though no less important) than their *claims* does not detract from what they have revealed about certain themes in certain admittedly great books. Their expressed intentions, the implications of those intentions, and the strategies for supporting those intentions, however, pose some of the problems this inquiry will examine. I should also note that, though I use the term 'theorist' for convenience, I have focused only on certain works by these critics, those explicitly concerned with defining the American literary tradition, rather than on the critics' entire range of criticism. Theorists such as Trilling, Miller, Matthiessen, and Fiedler have obviously worked on American literature in much broader terms than those by which they are represented here, some of which – especially in the cases of Trilling and Miller – are eminently compatible with my own preferences. This study in no way claims to exhaust the significance of any of its subjects.

The theorists I will examine have been instrumental in defining the field of American literature and in generating a dazzling array of studies of individual writers, texts, and genres. Though other critics, notably Henry Nash Smith, Joel Porte, Harry Levin, and Richard Slotkin, have also offered major theses on American writing, I discuss them only briefly. Nor do I discuss extensively critics from 'the great tradition' of Granville Hicks, Maxwell Geismar, V. L. Calverton, and V. L. Parrington, though they are important to my account. It was, after all, *against* the politicized criticism of Parrington and the others that more recent theorists of American literature have written, and a thorough history of American criticism would need to address their work. They are, however, marginalized by the group of critics I do discuss, and I regard that act of exclusion as the primary ideological brace for the prevailing theories. These early Marxist scholars are no less important for contemporary Americanists than are Richard Chase, Leslie Fiedler, or Leo Marx.

Also conspicuously absent are theories written by women and minorities. The recent work of Annette Kolodny may well have a positive impact on subsequent theorists of American literature, but it is too early to tell. The fact is that the most influential theories have all been written by white males. Of course, literally hundreds of other scholars and critics have been involved in the enterprise of describing, defining, and criticizing American literature and culture, and I in no way mean to ignore their contributions. The American studies work being conducted in Japan, the GDR, the USSR, France, and Italy, as well as that done by the MELUS group here in the US, is rich and diverse. I have narrowed the field on the assumption that the twelve or fifteen theories I do examine not only constitute a representative selection but are also the most widely read and assigned, most often praised as pioneering insights or lambasted as narrow, provincial, or ineffectual shots in the dark at an invisible, perhaps nonexistent, subject. Whether they are praised or ridiculed, the influence of such texts as Matthiessen's *American Renaissance*, Lewis's *The American Adam*, Fiedler's *Love and Death in the American Novel*, Chase's *The American Novel and Its Tradition*, Marx's *The Machine in the Garden*, and Bercovitch's recent work is undeniable, an assertion partly substantiated by the prominent place they occupy in the Kartiganer and Griffith anthology *Theories of American Literature*. Even more remarkable a testimony to their enduring power is the fact that, with the single exception of Yvor Winters's *Maule's Curse*, all of these critical theories of American literature are still in print, ten, twenty, thirty, and even forty years after their first publication. Their leads have been followed, disputed, and expanded, but whether one agrees or disagrees with their insights, the fact remains that they have pushed the study of American literature in new, provocative, and often exciting directions. Perry Miller's work on Puritanism has been often attacked since his death, but where would American literary and cultural studies be without his lifetime of research? One may be (or have been) scandalized by Leslie Fiedler's daring thesis on homo-eroticism in American novels, but Fiedler is a crucial figure in the history of American literary studies. So are most of the critics in this study.

I have chosen to classify these theorists according to their methods and assumptions. They have frequently been discussed in reviews, prefaces, and critical discussions of the canon (see, for example, Nina Baym's 'Melodramas of Beset Manhood: How Theories of American Fiction Exclude Women Authors'). I believe, however, that this is the first extended study and categorization of their works. The three 'schools' I posit are 'Puritan origins' or historical theories, including the work of Miller, Winters, and Bercovitch; cultural theories, including studies by Lionel Trilling, R. W. B. Lewis, Richard Chase, Leslie Fiedler, and Leo Marx; and self-reflexive theories by critics such as Charles Feidelson, Jr, Richard Poirier, and John Irwin. I have not granted separate categories to frontier theses or to psychological theories, primarily because while insights gained from both approaches have influenced all other 'schools,' they have not generated a tradition of studies. Such a division is meant to suggest a particular theorist's *primary* theoretical orientation (whether historical, cultural, or linguistic), and is not meant as either absolute or exhaustive. Several of these critics could have been discussed under each category, as in fact a few here are. For instance, I discuss Richard Chase and Leslie Fiedler at length as cultural theorists and briefly as historical theorists. Charles Feidelson, Jr, anchoring his theory in Puritan Ramistic rhetoric, could have been addressed as a historical critic, but I place him in the self-reflexive chapter because of his emphasis on the self-referentiality of American symbolism. On the other hand, I situate Bercovitch (conceivably a linguistic theorist) as a historical critic partly because of his scholarly lineage as a student of Perry Miller, but primarily because of his own stress on the historical continuities from Puritan rhetoric to contemporary ideology. Within each category, I also posit an early figure as the 'founding father' (the sexist terminology is unfortunately descriptive) of a tradition – Yvor Winters and Perry Miller of Puritan origins theories, Lionel Trilling of cultural theories, and F. O. Matthiessen of self-reflexive theories – and trace the influence of these seminal thinkers on later practitioners. This division reflects my own view of the traditions of American literary study and is offered as one of several possible schemes.

In addition to classifying these works, I also debate them on several fronts. I am particularly concerned with the way they narrow the American canon and discourage us from viewing literature as a form of social knowledge or behavior. Literary study in the United States has been moving in the direction of social and ideological criticism, as any review of journal articles or Modern Language Association papers on 'The Politics of . . .' will testify. *The Unusable Past*, then, is an attempt to review and revise the major theories of American literature in light of these new directions in critical practice. Many other critics have called for a revision (sometimes revolution) of the canon of American literature. In chapter 1 I discuss some of these early critics, such as Van Wyck Brooks (whose well-known quest for 'a usable past' informs my own title), Norman Foerster (whose 1928 *The Reinterpretation of American Literature* triggered a renewal of critical interest in the status of American writings), F. O. Matthiessen, and Malcolm Cowley. More recently, critics have questioned the prevailing notions of American literature on any number of fronts, from Martin Green's eccentric *Re-Appraisals: Some Common Sense Readings in American Literature* to the charges of racism and sexism leveled by H. Bruce Franklin, Paul Lauter, Nina Baym, and the Feminist Press project *Reconstructing American Literature*. William C. Spengemann, too, has recently asked 'What Is American Literature?' and has challenged Americanists to expand their conceptions of both crucial terms in that question, 'American' as well as 'literature.' Each of these attempts contributes to the project of revising, enlarging, and democratizing, if you will, our conception of American literature.

I am not sure that Green's suspicion of any literary criticism influenced by political, economic, historical, or psychological considerations or his 'common sense' attempt to replace Faulkner with J. D. Salinger points in very promising directions – in fact I argue antithetical positions throughout this study. Nor do I think, as Spengemann seems to, that a definition of American literature is possible (or desirable) if we only break through the geographical, cultural, and national provincialism limiting many theories of American literature. Lauter and Baym are, I think, more accurate in going directly to forms of political exclusion in the racist and sexist *practice* (if not theory) informing some of the reigning theorists' studies. But the problem as I describe it is at once larger and more deeply (if less obviously) ideological than these critics have presented it. Each of these critics, though, has influenced my own thinking, and I offer my own analysis of the state of American literary studies in the same spirit that motivates theirs.

One persistent shortcoming of many discussions of theorists of American literature is a harsh, often strident, tone. Some discussions are, of course, more virulent than others. See, for example, any of the numerous attacks on Perry Miller (Thomas 1952 is representative); also excessive attacks on Lionel Trilling (Hirsch 1966; Schwartz 1953); 'Radicalism for Rotarians' on Richard Chase (Green 1958); or, more recently, the criticism of Sacvan Bercovitch (Hirsch 1977); as well as the charge that Richard Poirier must have 'dropped' some 'mind expanding verbs' while writing *A World Elsewhere* (Trachtenberg 1967). Even the more modulated discussions by recent critics such as Nina Baym and Paul Lauter, though incisive and important, tend toward monolithic criticisms rather than more cautious analysis and exposition. While I often share the views, if not the impatience, of these critics, I have attempted to explore each theorist's method on its own terms and to grant the positive implications of a project first, only *then* going on to speculate on its shortcomings. I may not have been successful in all cases, and may be overly critical at times, but I have at least attempted to avoid an overly thesis-ridden and formulaic discussion.

Something more also needs to be said about my relationship to my primary materials – American literary texts and the theories purporting to describe them as a cultural whole. As is most likely the case with other scholars educated during the sixties and seventies, my education in American literature owes a tremendous debt to the theorists I discuss in this study. I, like many, wrote my share of Millerian, Feidelsonian, Fiedlerian, and even Bercovitchian seminar papers. If I pay less attention to the strengths of these theorists than to what I perceive as their ideological biases or limitations, it is because their positive contributions are so well known, their insights more or less canonical. Having worked from the inside of their studies, I now step back and comment on their assumptions. I am more sympathetic with some, less tolerant of others, but my aim is to be part of a dialectical inquiry, a project of assessments, qualifications, and revisions that has been going on for most of this century and should continue to be pushed toward newer, more synthetic comprehension.

As many of my own insights were formulated during my debates with the critics I discuss, I claim no perspective immune from the same ideological blindness that I uncover, and I offer no panacea for further studies of American writing. I offer, in short, no new theory of American literature. I do offer a theory of the theories we now have, pointing to continuities linking theorists of otherwise opposing methods, and situating their theories in a historical and political context.

It might seem a blindness in my own method to use as test cases such canonical texts as the *Magnalia Christi Americana*, *The Scarlet Letter*, and *Huckleberry Finn* in a study so critical of the narrow canon of masterpieces most theorists endorse. Should I not read Phillis Wheatley, Black Elk, Jane Addams, and Richard Wright rather than Hawthorne and Twain? Probably. In fact such revisions are implicit in my method, as in chapters 5 and 6 when I read Melville in the light of Frederick Douglass (and vice versa) and Hawthorne through those 'scribbling women' (and vice versa). I resort (I think the term is penitent enough) to canonical test cases more out of necessity. Since the theorists I discuss themselves study a relatively small and homogeneous group of texts, I chose to argue with them using exactly those texts which they claim to have contained in a definition of American literature. Many examples of the more historicized and socialized literary method I advocate do, of course, exist in monographs, journals, and elsewhere – I am not inventing a new hermeneutic, only noting the pervasive denial of such readings by those critics positing definitions of American literature. I draw on the work of H. Bruce Franklin, Marcus Klein, Carolyn Porter, Carolyn Karcher, Michael Wilding, and a host of others whose perceptions of American writing synthesize political, historical, even economic perspectives. That my own study is more a work of theory than of practical criticism stems from my perceived need to address the theorists of American literature thoroughly and directly rather than from any unwillingness to reread American texts.

While an important part of my program insists on the integration of the many noncanonical (regarded as subliterary by the most vociferous defenders of the canonical status quo) writers, texts, and genres, I discuss only Frederick Douglass to any great extent. The reason for so seemingly contradictory a lapse is, quite simply, that I don't regard it either necessary or valuable to prove that Douglass or, say, Richard Wright, Tillie Olsen, or any other writer could also be read as a romancer, as a forger of 'complex pastoralism,' or as a creator of worlds elsewhere. Such an imposition of a pre-existing ideology or theory would reveal little beyond the fact that marginal figures can always be made to conform to the literary standards of what are seen as more homogeneous cultural traditions. The inclusion of excluded writers is unimportant unless the ideological – aesthetic, political, philosophical, etc. – basis of the entire canon is revised. It is the principles of selection and rejection that concern me.

The ideology of the American canon naturally involves both questions – who is in or out, as well as the rationale for any inclusions and exclusions – and it may appear that I conflate the issues. However, my criticism of the 'narrowness' of the canon, while an important project in its own right, is here abbreviated in favor of an analysis of the assumptions common to many theorists. I argue that the problems are interrelated and symbiotic – the types of theories that critics such as Chase, Marx, Poirier, and Bercovitch have advanced necessitate the rigorous selectivity that excludes masses of more directly 'social' or mimetic writers in favor of the more oblique fictionists, say Hawthorne or Melville, whose social vision seems less restrictive than the so-called realists or naturalists, and certainly less than many minority writers who address the social contexts of various forms of oppression and inequality. That theorist after theorist can discover newer traditions in the same group of writers obviously testifies to something resilient about the writers of the American Renaissance and testifies as well to the exploratory powers of the theorists. They are in no way imposing specious or arbitrary models onto the American literary past, but rather rewriting that past under the inspiration of various historical, social, and aesthetic changes. The theories they have written are, in this sense, important indexes to the state of literary criticism, as they only slightly belatedly test the insights of critical methods – whether Matthiessen with the New Criticism, Feidelson with Ernst Cassirer and Susanne Langer's symbolist dynamism, or John Irwin with the poststructuralisms of Jacques Lacan and Jacques Derrida. For the purpose of this investigation, however, I attempt to address the narrowness (what I call the 'major authors' approach) that underwrites many theories, primarily in the first chapter. I return to that exclusivity (or freedom from it) in particular theorists briefly, especially when that theorist's definition of the canon or principle of selection is noteworthy, as in the case of Leslie Fiedler's resilient and expansive work.

I would like to clarify one final working assumption. I do not believe that there is a 'thing' one can call American literature. It does not exist in the abstract. It does not offer itself for our scrutiny. It does not present itself in or as a unified phase or tradition in American writing. Furthermore, any thorough attempt to define American literature would have to recognize the fact that American literature is a startlingly different body of works and set of priorities for readers in France, Italy, Japan, the USSR, and elsewhere. I address only American responses here for the sake of a focus. Thus my remarks on the existing canon and suggestions for revising it are posed with the awareness that the task of criticizing the canon is always a relative, problematic, and ultimately international project. When I discuss the possibility of a revision process for American criticism, I invoke M. M. Bakhtin's notion of 'dialogism' as one possible strategy for literary scholarship to take, not as an absolute or panacea. I will advance a hypothesis that what we call American literature is the product of two separable, yet interrelated areas of practice: *what* texts we teach at any given time, and *how* we teach them. These two forms of activity, furthermore, exist in a complex relationship with the marketplace and affect as well as respond to what books are in print (and how they are marketed) at any given time. Many of us have probably been shocked to be informed that a particular text we desire to teach is no longer in print. I was recently dismayed (shocked, perhaps) to be told that a major publisher of classroom paperbacks had ceased publishing two texts I wanted for one semester: Dreiser's *The Genius* and selections from Thoreau's journals. These works are, in one obvious sense, works of American literature, but because of what we are teaching and how we are teaching it, they are no longer available (at least they were not available at the time of writing) in classroom format. On the other hand, we now have a good choice of Kate Chopin's *The Awakening* and Frederick Douglass's *Narrative*, again because of a greater demand for those particular commodities. So, a subtheme of this work involves not only the political and aesthetic but also the economic reclamation of diverse strains of American writing.

The unused past:
theorists of American
literature and the
problem of exclusivity

An unusable past?

> The present is a void and the American writer floats in that
> void because the past that survives in the common mind is a
> past without living value. But is this the only possible past? If
> we need another past so badly, is it inconceivable that we
> might discover one, that we might even invent one?
>
> Van Wyck Brooks, 'On Creating a Usable Past'

Van Wyck Brooks's famous call for a reevaluation of American
literature stands, along with his other works, at the beginning of
modern criticism of American literature.[1] As studies such as
Howard Mumford Jones's *The Theory of American Literature*
demonstrate, the status of American literature was a matter of
controversy long before Brooks formulated his own prescription
for American letters. Early calls for a national literary identity
urged America to declare her intellectual independence,
while later, after the establishment of English departments,
Anglophiles ridiculed the very idea of a distinctively 'American'
literature. Most of the major statements from Emerson's 'The
American Scholar' to Whitman's '1855 Preface' to calls for the
'great American novel' all advocated an American literature
commensurate with America itself, a literature which could
communicate the power and diversity of life in the United

States. As early as 1835, Alexis de Tocqueville perceived the
American people as a 'motley multitude' whose heterogeneous
educations, desires, feelings, and fortunes would produce a
literature antithetical to conventional notions of order, skill,
style and form – a literature of a 'rude and untutored vigor.'
Many recent critical attempts to define and to reevaluate
American literature have followed the leads of such expansive
thinkers.

Since World War II the study of American writing has
flourished and has generated many theoretical attempts to
locate the characteristically American element in American
literature. Partly out of a renewed sense of nationalism following the war and partly out of the need to defend the study of
American literature against skeptical factions within English
departments, scholars set out to legitimate the study of
American literature as a distinct and valid discipline. The
best-known and most influential of these works include: Yvor
Winters's *Maule's Curse* (1938), F. O. Matthiessen's *American
Renaissance* (1941), Henry Nash Smith's *Virgin Land* (1950),
Charles Feidelson's *Symbolism and American Literature* (1953),
R. W. B. Lewis's *The American Adam* (1955), Richard Chase's
The American Novel and Its Tradition (1957), Marius Bewley's *The
Eccentric Design* (1959), Leslie Fiedler's *Love and Death in the
American Novel* (1960), Leo Marx's *The Machine in the Garden*
(1964), Roy Harvey Pearce's *The Continuity of American Poetry*
(1965), Richard Poirier's *A World Elsewhere* (1966), and Sacvan
Bercovitch's *The Puritan Origins of the American Self* (1975).

These modern theorists of American literature and the
canons they endorse signal a great change from earlier literary
histories and their canons. In fact, the twentieth century has
witnessed three major paradigm revolutions with respect to the
American canon. Around the turn of the century, studies such
as Henry A. Beer's *Outline Sketch of American Literature* (1887),
Francis H. Underwood's *Builders of American Literature* (1893),
Henry C. Vedder's *American Writers of Today* (1894) and Barrett
Wendell's influential *Literary History of America* (1900) promoted
the 'genteel tradition,' canonizing a literature of high ideality,
Anglophilism, and, according to its detractors, benign irrel-
evance to the realities of American life. It was against this 'weak
and fluffy' period, as Ambrose Bierce called it (Brooks 1951,

322), that a new approach to American literature emerged. Responding to the phenomena of immigration, urbanization, and industrialization, critics such as Brooks, Floyd Dell, Randolph Bourne, Granville Hicks, and V. L. Parrington defined American literature from a frankly social and political perspective. Hicks's 'great tradition,' for example, rejected the

> genteel *litterateurs*, with their correct sonnets and their polite essays, . . . [who] preserved their readers from sordid contacts with the facts of the fierce industrial struggle; [and who] somehow made those facts vanish and the real world yield to a world of respectable, sentimental, lily-white ladies and gentlemen.
>
> (Hicks 1933, 30)

In place of a genteel literature of polite manners and conventional morality (both of which were associated with a prohibition against looking critically at American society), Hicks and others studied the literature of politics, business, and labor, as well as the progressive impulse in American literature. Though Brooks, Bourne, and Parrington did not share Hicks's explicit Marxism, they too studied literature as an expression of American material culture, of life as lived in America by common men and women.

During the thirties, however, even in the midst of proletarian art and socially based literary criticism, a recoil from the social study of literature took place. Initially and most clearly represented by the Agrarian/New Critics, a new critical paradigm emerged and, after protracted struggle, triumphed both theoretically and pedagogically over the sociological mode. The New Critics altered the grounds of literary thought in two distinct ways. First, they declared historical and social considerations (the very essence of the previous aesthetic) 'extrinsic' and therefore ancillary to literary study, often denying or devaluing the referential nature of literary discourse. Second, they excluded from study as serious literature most texts and genres which did explicitly refer to social questions. Alexander Karanikas offers a historical analysis of these trends:

> The Agrarian-New Critics and their methods of evaluation became the most exciting subject of comment on the literary

scene. Their textbooks were adopted by colleges and universities. They and their followers published voluminously.
They have since taught, lectured, judged writing contests,
taken part in conferences, reviewed books, and reaped all the
rewards reserved for the highest authorities in literature.
More important perhaps, they have greatly influenced the
standards by which all literature, past and present, is judged.
In general, those standards have been such as to denigrate
the democratic and popular authors of the past, and to
discourage such writers in the present. No Whitman, Dreiser,
or Sandburg, for instance, has been deemed worthy of consideration as a genuine artist by the New Critics.

(Karanikas 1966, 209–10)

In their earlier Agrarian phase, John Crowe Ransom, Austin
Warren, and the others did try to precipitate a cultural revolution consistent with their rightist politics in the South, and as
New Critics 'they succeeded in doing what they had failed to do
as Agrarians: to denigrate the democratic content in American
literature, to smother its traditional note of social protest, and to
elevate in its stead new literary gods and canons more acceptable to the rightist tradition' (Karanikas 1966, viii).

Such a wholesale revision of values had a historical side as
well. Karanikas argues that the purging of historical considerations from the valuation of literature provided a rationale for
the Agrarians to abandon their previous sociological thrust. His
position, however, imputes an ahistorical and apolitical essence
to New Critical aesthetics. The shift to an aesthetic *program* can
more accurately be accounted for as an aestheticization (and
eventually an institutionalization) of a deeply conservative
interpretation of history. To argue that the New Critics either
attempted or succeeded in depoliticizing literary thinking is to
miss the profoundly political recoil from history and politics
implicit in their work. While less obvious and explicit, the
politics of the Agrarian/New Critics were no less central to
their project, as their virulent rejection of the leftist tradition in
American criticism suggests. In their declared program, however, and this is the importance of their influence, the New
Critics did reverse the popular 1930s conceptions of both
literature in general and American literature in particular. This

series of revisions in the canon and conception of American literature has remained inadequately examined. The theories we have are still, for the most part, within the New Critical paradigm, even as they deny some of its central tenets. So far-reaching was the New Critical aesthetic that later theorists of American literature have failed adequately to approach American texts in a specifically cultural and social context.

Each modern theorist claims to have defined an American tradition, if not *the* tradition. However, a static and exclusive conception of American literature frustrates these ambitious studies. This is not to deny that each of these works, from Matthiessen's *American Renaissance* (1941) to John Irwin's *American Hieroglyphics* (1980), has made an important contribution to our understanding of American literature. Their value, though, is of a more limited nature than the expressed intentions of their projects suggest. In fact, the very idea of a comprehensive theory of American literature, like that of the great American novel, may be an impossibility.

The various attempts to circumscribe American literature under a theoretical framework – obscurantism, symbolism, complex pastoralism, and others – pose two specific problems. First, the 'representative' or 'major' American authors tend to be a fairly predictable and very small group of white, male writers, for the most part those canonized by Matthiessen in *American Renaissance*. Second, these theorists project a vision of American literature as an isolated body of texts, estranged from, or only vaguely related to, American social or material reality. This inadequately social notion of American literature, perhaps the most significant residue of the critical rebellion against the overtly sociological assumptions of the thirties, takes two forms. The theorists either grant that there is an important socially mimetic element in American literature but devalue it as they privilege the aesthetic, symbolic, or linguistic elements (which they maintain are separable from social considerations), or they deny the possibility (sometimes the desirability) of studying American literature as a vehicle of social knowledge, regardless of how oblique that expression may be. What we get are operationally asocial critical theses not only inspired, but verified as well, by a limited approach to a small group of writers. As a result the same authors, the same books, and often the same passages are summoned time after time to support a tautological reading which proves what it assumed in advance, that is, that the writers under investigation are truly our 'major' figures.

Such exclusivity, Raymond Williams argues, is common to any tradition which 'has in practice to discard whole areas of significance, or reinterpret or dilute them, or convert them into forms which support or at least do not contradict' a particular point of view (Williams 1977, 116). The American tradition, as represented in these theories of American literature, has indeed been deprived of whole 'areas of significance.' There is bound to be a certain amount of excluding and condensing in any study of American literature. But a tradition so selective and so exclusive needs to be reexamined precisely because of the large areas of significance it neglects or flimsily appropriates and because an undeniably large and heterodox range of American writing is available for inclusion and analysis. In the quest to define American literature, recourse to the huge 'unusable,' or, more precisely, 'unused,' past is not only quite clearly possible, but necessary as well.

What is an American author?

Crèvecoeur posed the troublesome question 'what is an American?' in 1782. After noting that Americans 'are a mixture of English, Scotch, Irish, French, Dutch, Germans, and Swedes,' he concluded that 'from this promiscuous breed, that race now called Americans have arisen' (Crèvecoeur 1957, 37). Since we now need to account for millions of Central and Eastern European, African, Asian, Hispanic, and native American peoples, no definitive answer to his question seems forthcoming. Our question, 'what is an American author?', has been equally troublesome and has, in theories of American literature, been answered unsatisfactorily.

The essential tradition for theorists of American literature is still, following Matthiessen, the New England tradition, a lineage of six to ten American writers from the Puritans through the transcendentalists to such twentieth-century figures as Henry Adams, Henry James, T. S. Eliot, and Wallace Stevens, most of whom are studied, properly enough, in light of their traditional New England heritage. A variation of the New England tradition is the romance tradition, best characterized by Richard Chase in *The American Novel and Its Tradition*. The romance tradition includes, with a few differences, the same figures as does the New England tradition, notably Poe, Emerson, Hawthorne, Thoreau, Melville, and Whitman. The New England tradition is not new; it has dominated American literature since the nineteenth century. Edward Eggleston's preface to *The Hoosier Schoolmaster* is a particularly lucid criticism of the pervasiveness of the New England approach to American writing, a problem he felt acutely as early as 1871.

> It has been in my mind since I was a Hoosier boy to do something toward describing life in the back-country districts of the Western States. It used to be a matter of no little jealousy with us, I remember, that the manners, customs, thoughts, and feelings, of New England country people filled so large a place in books, while our life, not less interesting, not less romantic, and certainly not less filled with humorous and grotesque material, had no place in literature. It was as though we were shut out of good society. And, with the single exception of Alice Cary, perhaps, our Western writers did not dare speak of the West otherwise than as the unreal world to which Cooper's lively imagination had given birth.
>
> (Eggleston 1957, xiii)

Eggleston's West now, of course, has literary representation in anthologies and the classroom, but rarely by theorists of American literature. At a time when American literary scholarship has generated theme studies, source studies, biographies and interpretive works on scores of other American writers, studies of Puritanism, realism, naturalism, the western novel, the local color movement, the southern novel, the black novel, the frontier novel, the radical novel, and others, critical theories of American literature have remained impervious to these studies and have contracted all the more to a small handful of canonical figures.

Dealing with only Poe, Emerson, Hawthorne, Thoreau, Whitman, Melville, and James, Floyd Stovall's *Eight American Authors* (1963) suggests the narrowness of the American canon according to the literary establishment. Stovall justified his select group by asserting that 'doubtless most readers will agree that at this time and for the purpose of this volume they are the most important American writers' (Stovall 1963, vi). Stovall's edition, now over twenty years old, did, given its historical context and its intent, lend important recognition to American writing. The subsequent persistence of the 'eight American authors' approach, however, raises new problems. For one, Stovall's time is no longer our time. The transformations of American culture by the Vietnam War and by the struggles of women and minorities for equality highlight the necessity for a revised American canon.

Despite attempts to expand our conception of American literature, the 'usable past' for many of these theorists of American writing is a very limited past indeed. F. O. Matthiessen's *American Renaissance*, although admittedly dealing with a limited phase in American literature – 'art and expression in the age of Emerson and Whitman' – established the core of the present American canon. Matthiessen studies the works of Emerson, Hawthorne, Melville, Thoreau, Whitman, Eliot, and James in detail, referring to others – Poe and Cooper, for example – only in passing. D. H. Lawrence had earlier singled out a similar group of 'classic' American writers: Franklin, Cooper, Poe, Hawthorne, Dana, Melville, and Whitman. These two figures, Lawrence even more than Matthiessen perhaps, are acknowledged as the most influential fathers of modern American literary theory, and many other critics accept the canon as defined by them. No doubt they were both responding to something capacious and compelling about the American Renaissance, but their lead needs to be expanded, not just followed.

Follow, however, is just what most later theorists have done. Feidelson, Bewley, and Harry Levin don't diverge at all from the 'eight American authors' canon except to limit their studies even more. Others depart only slightly. In addition to including the standard figures, Chase adds Brockden Brown, Faulkner, and Norris, along with Fitzgerald, Cable, and Howells to a lesser extent. Fiedler adds Brown, Faulkner, and Hemingway in detail, and a score of others in passing. Marx adds Henry Adams; Poirier includes Wharton, Dreiser, and Howells; and Bercovitch gives several Puritans, especially Cotton Mather and Jonathan Edwards, and Benjamin Franklin more attention than they receive elsewhere. Only R. W. B. Lewis ranges widely outside the canonical parameters into lesser-known authors (such as Horace Bushnell, Francis Parkman, and George Bancroft) and texts (including *The Marble Faun* and *Billy Budd* rather than more commonly cited Hawthorne and Melville works). Even these deviations from the standard canon, however, are deceptive, since they serve merely as anticipations of what is seen as the major mode. Thus many theorists discuss Brockden Brown's nightmarish vision, for instance, as a prototype of Poe, Melville, and other masters of 'American gothic.'

After the success of *Eight American Authors*, *Fifteen Modern American Authors* (Bryer 1969) granted fifteen new names (decided by Modern Language Association ballot) official recognition. Still, of the fifteen additions, only Dreiser, Eliot, Faulkner, Hemingway, and Stevens have been discussed in any of the theories listed above. In addition to the virtual exclusion of the remaining ten figures from the dominant theoretical definitions of American literature, scores of others are conspicuously absent. Such a list of exiles could cover pages, but most notable among them are many colonial writers, especially southern figures like William Byrd; major political writers from all periods of American history, especially eighteenth-century thinkers such as Thomas Paine and the Connecticut Wits; and numerous nineteenth- and twentieth-century writers, including George Ade, Jane Addams, James Baldwin, George Washington Cable, Winston Churchill, John Dos Passos, Frederick Douglass, Ralph Ellison, James T. Farrell, Henry Blake Fuller, Hamlin Garland, William Dean Howells, Langston Hughes, Sarah Jewett, Joseph Kirkland, Upton Sinclair, Harriet Beecher Stowe, Richard Wright, and others. Sinclair Lewis, Pearl Buck, John Steinbeck, and Saul Bellow all have won Nobel Prizes in literature, yet all fall outside the prevailing theories. Of course, the schoolroom poets, the dethroned giants of the so-called genteel tradition, are excluded from all but a few studies. Many of those excluded from serious consideration have played critical roles in the development of American writing. Garland, Crane, and Howells, for instance, helped revolutionize American literature at the turn of the century. Upton Sinclair's *The Jungle*, a powerful work in its own right, even had a direct impact on American life by precipitating legislation regulating the meat-packing industry. Perhaps most conspicuously absent from these theories are women and minority writers, especially blacks, native Americans, and Hispanics, many of whom have been instrumental in breaking through sexual and racial prejudice and articulating the problems of oppressed peoples. Yet none find treatment in the principal theories of American literature.

The American canon according to these theories has implications which extend well beyond the theoretical confines of literary criticism. The 'eight American authors' approach has resulted in a monopoly of sorts over not only which authors and texts we study, but *how* we study them as well. A survey of influential anthologies of American literature reveals the extent to which this approach affects classroom study. Donald Emerson has dubbed anthologies the 'Dun and Bradstreet volumes' of American literature, suggesting that they 'reflect the decline of once successful ventures and the establishment and consolidation of new enterprises' (Emerson 1972, 45). Emerson may well attribute too much power to anthologies and does, I feel, underestimate the market pressures and audience demands that influence their constitutions, though his market metaphor *does* hint at them as telling indexes for the state of American literary studies. My emphasis, however, is on theories of American literature, and I do not intend to conflate questions peculiar to them with the very different questions and problems posed by anthologies, their markets, and their economics, nor do I suggest a necessary causal relationship between the theories and the anthologies. Moreover, if we add to these two specific areas of *practice* the more abstract question of the 'canon' of American literature, three distinct areas of inquiry present themselves, each deserving a full study. The canon represented by the anthologies does reflect trends seen also in the theories, and it is likely that an overarching conception of American literature informs both practices.

A new type of anthology which, like most theories of American literature, devotes most, if not all, of its pages to traditional masters and masterpieces (the sexist terminology is, again, descriptive) has come to dominate anthology production and consumption. Another coincidental trend abandons thematic or topical subdivisions of literature in favor of a purely chronological organization, ostensibly to grant teachers freedom for their own approaches. Both developments signal a movement away from the historical understanding of literature by emphasizing individual authors, who are presented as so many isolated subjects, and by minimizing their thematic significance. Whereas Hicks's *The Great Tradition* (1933) subordinated, say, James Russell Lowell and Walt Whitman under the historical heading 'Industrialism after the Civil War,' the editors of the 1979 *Norton Anthology of American Literature* 'have dropped the traditional period names and have discontinued the practice of organizing writers according to "influences" or "schools,"' opting, instead, for a simple chronology based on the authors' dates of birth (Gottesman *et al.* 1979, xxiv). We should return, however, to the exclusivity which characterizes these collections.

Best known and, perhaps, most influential of these anthologies was the Gay Wilson Allen, Henry A. Pochman collection, *Masters of American Literature* (1949). In the later introduction to their collection, the editors comment on the rationale behind their project:

> The two-volume Pochman-Allen anthology . . . caught the crest of popularity during the late forties when the demand for fewer authors and more complete coverage put the scattergun kind of anthology virtually out of business. The wide adoption of this major-authors book underscored the soundness of the idea and, in turn, helped prepare the way for the substitution of inexpensive paperback editions of individual authors or single works for bulky, expensive anthologies. This revolution in the teaching of American literature brought about by paperback texts confirmed the soundness of our design, namely, that the most effective teaching can be accomplished by concentrating on the 'literary masters,' whose writings are read either uncut or at least in large chunks.

(Allen and Pochman 1969, v)

The editors justify their selections on pedagogical advantages, economy, and convenience, all of which criteria seem justifiable. They fail to consider, however, that reducing the scope of classroom studies affects students' conceptions of American literature and its range of concerns. Such an approach also simplifies the teaching of American literature, relieving the teacher of the need to consider the fullness of history and culture.

In recent years anthologists have tried to move beyond the 'major authors' principle by including more materials and more writers. Even the most expansive of these collections, however, reveal a continuation of the 'major authors' philosophy. The following statistics represent the space allotted to seventeen 'major' American authors in selected anthologies. These authors include Edward Taylor, Jonathan Edwards, Franklin, Poe, Emerson, Hawthorne, Thoreau, Melville, Whitman, Dickinson, Twain, James, Crane, Pound, Eliot, Stevens, and Faulkner, and roughly represent contemporary critical tastes. In Leon Howard's 1955 *American Heritage*, these writers represent 8 percent of 190 authors and occupy 30 percent of 1600 pages. In Richard Poirier and William Vance's 1970 *American Literature*, the same authors represent 14 percent of 120 authors and occupy about 45 percent of 2300 pages. In the 1979 *Norton Anthology of American Literature*, these seventeen writers represent 12 percent of 131 authors and occupy half of 5000 pages.

Several important trends present themselves: (1) the anthologies themselves have grown from 1600 to 2300 to 5000 pages; (2) the number of authors has dropped from 190 to 120 and 131 (the later two anthologies, written fifteen and twenty-four years after Howard's, could conceivably have included substantially more modern and contemporary figures); (3) the ratio of 'major' authors to all others increased from 8 percent to 14 and 12 percent; and (4) the proportion of the pages they occupy grew from 30 percent (or 500) of 1600 pages to 45 percent (or 1065) of 2300 pages to a startling 50 percent (or 2500) of 5000 pages.

The *Norton Anthology*, because of its currency and circulation, presents the most interesting problem. Intended to 'close the ever-widening gap between the current conception and appraisal of the American literary heritage' by redressing the long neglect of many authors, especially women and blacks, the collection sets out to rectify the vast imbalance I have been studying. To do so, the editors have chosen to expand the entire format in order to allot more space to writers commonly underrepresented. But they have not changed the proportion of pages allotted to 'minor' figures in a manner commensurate with their editorial intentions. The format of the *Norton Anthology* actually frustrates those goals both by granting 88 percent of the anthologized authors only half of the total pages and by adopting a purely chronological arrangement which eliminates period, group, and topical divisions that the editors feel 'encourage students to prejudge the literature.' Such a *laissez-faire* compendium appears to escape exclusivity, but really does not. In one obvious sense, the 2500 pages devoted to a small core of writers already biases the anthology toward the major figures. Since these writers have more or less monopolized classroom and critical attention, we can assume they are the best known and, despite obviously complex ideas and styles, the most easily taught.

In an essay on reclaiming 'neglected literature,' Stephen E. Tabachnick grants the quality and worth of canonical texts, but suggests that 'the canon is simply too seductive' and that 'canon-worship' is not merely fun, but 'easy, safe, and required' for university intellectuals (Tabachnick 1981, 36–8). The problem is that we are also 'seduced' into ignoring volume after volume of important noncanonical writing while practicing scorched-earth criticism on a handful of masterpieces. Tabachnick adds 'literary nationalism' in his anatomy of our canon-worship malaise, and offers insightful correctives for integrating little-known writers and texts into our teaching. While his analysis is important, we need to be aware of some limitations. Merely including other authors without providing adequate information concerning their historical contexts, their influence by and on other figures, or their thematic concerns and how they anticipate, reflect, or contradict those of other writers hardly compensates. Their position in the new *Norton* parallels, in some disturbing way, the cultural status of many minority groups in the United States, who, though 'recognized' in institutional ways such as housing projects, welfare programs, and job quotas, still remain outside the mainstream of American culture. Sandwiched between 150 pages of Edgar Allan Poe and 300 pages of Thoreau, Frederick Douglass, 'represented' by ten pages, may well, like Ellison's hero, still remain invisible – separate *and* unequal.

The exclusion of minority writers raises deeper problems

than the ones we have been considering. The specter of racism in American literary studies has not, however, gone unnoticed. In his survey of the problem Robert E. Morsberger concludes with Mark Twain's remark that 'there is no basic difference between burning books and leaving them unread; the result is the same' (Morsberger 1970, 8). So extreme a conclusion is largely validated by the statistics and insights Morsberger brings to bear on surveys of American literature and their exclusion of black authors. Heading a National Council of Teachers of English 'Task Force on Racism and Bias in the Teaching of English,' Ernece B. Kelly introduced *Searching for America*, its collection of evaluations of anthologies:

> Because the twelve books reviewed here are typical and so can be viewed as a microcosm of the range of collections of American literature and criticism, these critiques can lead to an understanding of the general character of current American literature anthologies with respect to their several traditional biases. Revealed here is the ethnic racism. Revealed here is the emphasis on the Atlantic frontier, the Puritan spirit, and the Cavalier tradition. Revealed here is the pattern of reprinting what has been printed before and shunning the otherwise meritorious writer because he [*sic*] has not been previously anthologized.
>
> (Kelly 1972, iv–v)

Believing that 'American literature anthologies today give students only a skewed and deceptive portrait of American life and letters,' Kelly and other contributors compare economic and social oppression with the cultural oppression resulting from inadequate or demeaning representation of minorities in the anthologies. *Searching for America* lists crucial deficiencies in the representation of minority writers and offers specific criteria for redressing the problem of biased anthologies. The critiques of anthologies themselves are varied, citing flaws ranging from pretending to comprehensiveness while actually offering a very limited, though traditional, canon, to unintentional dismissals of racist attitudes in American writers, to overt racism. *Searching for America* is an important collection, practical and compassionate, yet uncompromising in its demand for equality in the study and teaching of American literature. More recently, the Rutgers

Newark College Colloquium on 'Ethnicity in American Literature' (1982) brought scholars together to discuss the exclusion
of minorities from the study of American literature. The opening statement from their program addresses this problem
succinctly:

> It is a monumentally sad fact that American literature, about
> 50 years old as a discipline, has been taught and perceived as
> a literature central to the existence of Anglo-Saxon Prot-
> estantism in the United States. Therefore, it has ignored or
> dismissed, in its haste to emulate European literature, the
> many older ethnic contributions to its heritage. These con-
> tinue. Where the contributors have not been dismissed or
> ignored, they have been treated as oddities, examples of
> exoticism or as literary cuteness. Yet, there is hardly a period
> in American history when some writers did not consider those
> outsiders as throbbing with life, vision and perhaps even as
> metaphors of America itself.[2]

Perceiving minorities as 'metaphors of America itself,' a tactic
anticipated by Ellison in *Invisible Man* as well as by Pynchon in
The Crying of Lot 49, seems not to offer a very potent corrective to
the malaise the colloquium addresses, but this description of the
problem is accurate. In all the theories of American literature
we are considering, minorities and women are for the most part
missing. Richard Poirier discusses Edith Wharton in *A World
Elsewhere* (though he believes she demonstrates the *defeated*
American imagination succumbing to environmental determination), and Roy Harvey Pearce devotes sections of
The Continuity of American Poetry to Anne Bradstreet, Emily
Dickinson, and Marianne Moore. Only Leslie Fiedler, who has
consistently advocated 'opening up the canon,' addresses literature by both women and black writers.

A number of recent studies and the Feminist Press project
Reconstructing American Literature have confronted the exclusion of
minority writers from American literature and, for that matter,
from the idea of 'America' in general. In *Foreigners: The Making
of American Literature, 1900–1940*, Marcus Klein notes that by
1930, following the two great waves of immigration, 'between 40
and 50 percent of the entire population of the United States
consisted of persons who had at best an ambivalent relationship

to any such essentialized, mainstream American tradition as anybody might propose' (Klein 1981, 14). These statistics, however, failed to prevent previously entrenched 'Americans' from defining the very idea of the American tradition in anachronistic (and racist) terms. T. S. Eliot, for instance, addressed the question of tradition in his 1933 lecture series at the University of Virginia:

> You have here, I imagine, at least some recollection of a 'tradition' such as the influx of foreign populations has almost effaced in some parts of the North, and such as never established itself in the West; though it is hardly to be expected that a tradition here, any more than anywhere else, should be found in healthy and flourishing growth. . . . Yet I think that the chances for the reestablishment of a native culture are perhaps better here than in New England. You are farther away from New York: you have been less industrialized and less invaded by foreign races.

Eliot added, 'what is still more important [to the establishment of a homogeneous tradition] is unity of religious background; and reasons of race and religion combine to make any large numbers of free-thinking Jews undesirable' (Klein 1981, 14). Klein interestingly defines the literary generation of a dispossessed American gentry as a 'social class,' which, though themselves exiled in America, 'still owned and could define civilization. The property was plainly posted: No Irish Permitted. Jews Not Welcome. Caucasians Only' (Klein 1981, 18).

H. Bruce Franklin similarly calls the prevailing narrowness of academic criticism into question on racial and ethnic grounds. In *The Victim as Criminal and Artist* (1978), Franklin inverts the received notion of American literature:

> Insofar as American literature is in fact a unique body of creative work, what defines its identity most unequivocally is the historical and cultural experience of the Afro-American people. . . . When we grasp the significance of this truth for American literature as a whole, we will be forced to change radically our critical methodologies, our criteria for literary excellence, and our canon of great literature – or perhaps even the entire notion of a canon.
>
> (Franklin 1978, xv–xvi)

Rejecting the period of New Critical hegemony (the 1940s and 1950s) during which 'the American literature taught in our colleges and universities was as lily-white as the faculty club at Johns Hopkins or Stanford,' Franklin adds an important qualification to the charge of overt racism implicit in such a remark:

> I am in no way suggesting that after the late 1940s Black literature was consciously excluded from the canon of American literature because of the skin color or physiognomy of its authors. It simply no longer matched up with the prevailing literary criteria. Certainly since 1964, those professors who edit the anthologies, survey the literary history, and decide the curriculum have been actively searching for Black authors who fit their notion of excellence. That is precisely the point, for the criteria they apply are determined by their own people and social class, and most Afro-American literature conforms to criteria determined by a different people and a different social class. And thus any large-scale inclusion of Afro-American literature within what we call American literature forces a fundamental redefinition and a complex process of reevaluations.
>
> (Franklin 1978, xxi)

Franklin's discussion of a sweeping shift in literary criteria recalls our earlier remarks on the abrupt paradigm changes that have characterized American criticism in the twentieth century. The most recent shift (from a realist tradition to that ushered in by the influence of New Criticism) defined as out of consideration not only Afro-American literature but the realist or social traditions as well. We should remember that only a short time ago the critical realists, such as Dreiser and Lewis, were the heroes of American literature. One now gets the feeling from reading theories of American literature that they hardly existed.

Despite their various biases and interests, the remarks of these critics of the American canon all point to the fact that the question 'what is an American author?' cannot be adequately addressed in isolation from that of 'what is American literature?' Kelly, Tabachnick, Klein, and Franklin all trace the aesthetic rationales of the American canon to an underlying ideological bias, whether ethnic, racial, sexual, or political. As suggested above, the canon is intimately bound up with a definition of literature seemingly derived from those few canonical authors.

It would, however, be both naive and unproductive to suggest either that the canon is a consciously exclusionary apparatus controlled by some abstract group of canonizers (teachers, anthologists, historians, theorists, and others) to manipulate our notion of American literature *or* that the mere addition of names – the inclusion of previously excluded geographic, ethnic, racial, or sexual perspectives – offers a panacea for transcending the limitations of a national canon. The first accusation assumes both that canonizers (whoever they may be) fully grasp the ideological implications of their choices and that they know what their interests are and how to promote them. Post-structuralism's lesson on the decentered subject and the frequently self-contradictory presence any of us can have toward our own interests is pertinent here. Granting a transcendental (and malicious or conspiratorial) awareness to canonizers suggests too simplistic an attempt to rectify a complex problem. Canons *may* support specific ideological interests, but to argue that individuals consciously assemble such an effective ideological tool seems extreme. We need to look beyond individual motives, biases, morals, and politics to understand the canon of American literature.

The second issue – the suggestion that *expansion* is itself the key to a limited canon – also needs more clarification. The inclusion or exclusion of writers by theorists, historians, or anthologists is not simply a quantitative concern. Quite the contrary, the exclusion or devaluation of diverse perspectives within any tradition results in a qualitative diminution of our understanding. Any writer of any ideological thrust (assuming that such a perspective could be stable and discernible) could arguably be appropriated to any view, however narrow, of American literature. The common view that the river, whether great brown god or road to larger imaginative experience, is the crucial issue in *Huckleberry Finn* (positions advanced by T. S. Eliot, Lionel Trilling, Richard Chase, and Leo Marx, among others) is just one example of how an eminently social and political fiction can be denatured to fit an asocial paradigm, a problem which we are about to address (see chapter 3). It is no less likely that Wright's *Uncle Tom's Children* could be canonized for the mythic pattern of individual/community and for its balanced working of natural processes rather than for Wright's frankly Communist politics. As with the narrow view that canonizers are co-conspirators in a monumental sexist or racist coup, the notion that more is necessarily better is too simple.

A third possibility sometimes advanced – the replacement of one canon with another – is equally unsatisfactory. To make fun of Henry James as both V. L. Parrington and Granville Hicks bordered on doing, or to exclude him from a version of 'the great tradition' can't possibly produce a deeper sense of American literature. Nor, of course, could Trilling's attempt to replace Dreiser with James. Casting James aside as a sterile aesthete is little different from excluding Wright for his politically committed writing. Both deny the complexity and heterogeneity of literary production in the United States. As this study suggests, a more comprehensive view of American literature probably will not generate a theory of American literature, but it can at least demonstrate the inadequacies of various readings which deny the heterogeneity of American writing in the name of some theory or tradition. There is no need to argue, as Bruce Franklin does, that prison literature represents the *real* American tradition, only that that literature needs to be accounted for by any theoretical definition of an American tradition.

American literature: out of space – out of time

> Moonlight, in a familiar room, falling so white upon the carpet, and showing all its figures so distinctly, – making every object so minutely visible, yet so unlike a morning or noontide visibility, – is the medium the most suitable for a romance-writer to get acquainted with his illusive guests.
>
> Nathaniel Hawthorne, 'The Custom House'

> Poets who write mostly about love, roses and moonlight, sunsets and snow must lead a very quiet life. Seldom, I imagine, does their poetry get them into difficulty. . . . The moon belongs to everybody, but not this earth of ours. That is perhaps why poems about the moon perturb no one, but poems about color and poverty do perturb many citizens.

Social forces pull backwards or forwards, right or left, and
social poems get caught in the pulling and hauling.

Langston Hughes, 'My Adventures as a Social Poet'

Since the phrase American literature already situates the general term 'literature' within the cultural context of the United
States, the enterprise of defining *American literature* is inherently
cultural. However, and here is the paradox, the cultural aims of
many theorists are often attenuated by formalist, though not
necessarily New Critical, residue in their methods. I refer to this
as paradoxical because the residual (probably undesired) formalism frequently dilutes the explicitly social and cultural
intentions of many of these theorists. This is not to suggest that
each of the works from Winters's *Maule's Curse* to Irwin's
American Hieroglyphics purports to offer a frankly 'political' or
'radical' perspective on American literature and culture, or
even that such a politicization of an entire field is necessary or
desirable. I am more interested in the ways that essentially
cultural projects such as Matthiessen's *American Renaissance*,
Lewis's *The American Adam*, Fiedler's *Love and Death in the American Novel*, Chase's *The American Novel and Its Tradition*, Marx's
The Machine in the Garden, and Bercovitch's *The Puritan Origins of
the American Self* – all at least implicitly political – reduce the
scopes of their projects by adhering to aesthetic assumptions
that deny or highly qualify literature's ability to mediate
American social reality.

In some cases these theorists posit American literature as
playing an adversary role to a shallow and affirmative, almost
'genteel,' American culture that adheres to obsolete notions of
self and society. Lionel Trilling accurately defined the oppositional mode of American criticism in 'On the Teaching of
Modern Literature.' 'Any historian of the modern age,' he
asserts,

> will take virtually for granted the adversary intention, the
> actually subversive intention, that characterizes modern
> writing – he will perceive its clear purpose of detaching the
> reader from the habits of thought and feeling that the larger
> culture imposes; of giving him a ground and a vantage point
> from which to judge and condemn, and perhaps revise, the
> culture that produced him.
>
> (Trilling 1965, xii–xiii)

While Trilling here addresses the ideological thrust of modern literature in general, his remarks characterize equally well the ideological thrust of theorists of American literature (who tend to stress the *modernity* of American writing). Trilling's own assault on the simplistic assumptions of the liberal tradition, Yvor Winters's contempt for flaccid moral and aesthetic values, Charles Feidelson's undermining of a stable epistemology with a symbolist aesthetic, Leslie Fiedler's exposé of the homoerotic constant in American fiction, Harry Levin's stress on the powers of blackness that American fictionists confront, and John T. Irwin's recasting of questions of selfhood all pose such oppositional theses. In other cases theorists claim that it is American literature and literature alone that is capable of synthesizing the antagonisms that polarize culture in the United States. Richard Chase's elevation of romance as the essential American literary mode, F. O. Matthiessen's reading of a unified sensibility among writers of the American Renaissance, who shared the conviction that 'there should be no split between art and other functions of the community, that there should be an organic union between labor and culture' (Matthiessen 1941, xiv–xv), and Leo Marx's vision of American writers seeking a dialectical transcendence of the timeless debate between machine and garden all posit the possibility of a unified culture and see literature as able to fulfill that task. Finally, some critics analyze the political ramifications of and pressures on literary language. Richard Poirier demonstrates how American writers attempt to create linguistic worlds capable of housing enlarged notions of freedom incompatible with existing material environments, and Sacvan Bercovitch traces rhetorical constructs which have bolstered various components of a distinctive American exceptionalist ideology.

Whatever their strategies, these theorists all work toward a cultural (be it moral, philosophical, psychological, or political) apprehension of American literature. Most would deny the validity of rigorous New Critical formalism, with its stress on literary autonomy and its banishing of extrinsic historical considerations. They insist in one way or another on seeing life and literature whole, on perceiving literature as adequate to the task of social and cultural criticism. Some of them would even argue for the centrality of politics to literary production and consumption.

However, whether their declared interests are historical, linguistic, cultural, or psychological, what these prevailing perspectives on American literature tend most consistently to exclude or to marginalize is no longer simply a geographic region, but what can be understood, for lack of a better term, as a 'social' tradition. By social tradition I refer to three specific areas of literary practice: (1) writers, texts, and even genres that reflect a direct, often critical apprehension of the historical, social, economic, and political contexts of American culture; (2) the broader assumption that all literature mediates social reality; and (3) criticism that grants the importance, if not the centrality, of such social concerns, one that takes itself seriously as a form of social knowledge.

Recent theorists of American literature tend to minimize such social and historical contexts in one or both of two ways. First, they devalue, often suppress, writers and varieties of writing that do reflect interest in a historically determined social milieu. Second, they either deemphasize what social reference exists in the writers and works they study, or they turn them into non- or even anti-referential elements. Myth critics, such as Chase and Fiedler, may discuss scores of texts by numerous writers with diverse ideological assumptions, but they actually minimize the scopes of their studies by subsuming the literature they investigate under an archetypal or mythic rubric that explicitly negates the importance of differences among the writers' historical, cultural, or political perspectives. This bias is more pervasive than the simple exclusion of proletarian literature or of obviously social writers like Sinclair Lewis or Theodore Dreiser suggests. 'Obviously' is, perhaps, the wrong word. Many of the theorists deny the importance or relevance of *The Scarlet Letter* or *Moby-Dick* as social documents, yet those works are no less 'obviously' social than *Main Street*, *An American Tragedy*, or *One Flew over the Cuckoo's Nest*. As Tocqueville announced in his usual lucid and prophetic manner, 'There are always numerous connections between the social and political condition of people and the inspiration of its writers. He who knows the one is never completely ignorant of the other' (Tocqueville 1945, II, 63). An important problem for theorists of American literature is to elucidate *how* American texts refer to American social forms, and *what* that mode of reference means. What theorists have done in the past is to skirt the issue by declaring social and historical questions ancillary to their projects.

Just as they contribute diversely to our understanding of American literature, so do these theorists minimize its referential status differently. Some, like Lionel Trilling and Yvor Winters, argue that American literature simply *is*, in Trilling's term, tangential to American social life. Trilling is representative when he issues his now commonplace dictum, 'the fact is that American writers of genius have not turned their minds to society' (Trilling 1950, 212). Richard Chase similarly associates 'the originality and Americanness' of American fiction with its 'freedom ... from the conditions of actuality' and with its disinterest in 'the immediate rendition of reality' (Chase 1957, vii, x). Other critics, notably Charles Feidelson, grant that American literature does have social and historical importance, but maintains that we *shouldn't* dwell on such extrinsic matters. Feidelson chooses, instead, to address the literary text as an autonomous literary structure:

> To consider a literary work as a piece of language is to regard it as a symbol, autonomous in the sense that it is quite distinct from both the personality of its author and from any world of pure objects, and creative in the sense that it brings into existence its own meaning.
>
> (Feidelson 1953, 49)

Marius Bewley, too, asserts: 'The only commitment I am interested in is the commitment of the original artist to the integrity of his own creative act' (Bewley 1959, 11). Feidelson and Bewley both acknowledge history in their studies, but limit that sense of historicity to a history of verbal forms. Still other critics, such as Leslie Fiedler and Richard Poirier, suggest that American literature *can't*, and sometimes *shouldn't*, be a direct reflection of material reality. For Fiedler, 'our fiction is not merely in flight from the physical data of the actual world. . . . It is . . . nonrealistic and negative, sadist and melodramatic – a literature of darkness and the grotesque in a land of light and affirmation' (Fiedler 1960, 29). Poirier argues that literature can be compelling 'without paying strict attention to alternative inventions co-existing under the titles of history, life, reality, or politics' (Poirier 1971, 31). Furthermore, 'to be "outside American society" is, of course, to be in the great American literary tradition' (Poirier 1966, 237). Such an apparent transcendence of material and social contingencies (though Poirier acknowledges the impossibility of the quest) constitutes, according to Poirier and Fiedler, a radical impulse in American texts, a willingness to reject bourgeois conventions. Though these theorists do tend to agree that American literature is peripheral to American society, they differ as to the value of that imputed quality. Yvor Winters, for instance, argues that the allegorical vision of Puritanism has crippled American rationality with a legacy of obscurantism, while Feidelson maintains that American literature's symbolist core constitutes its greatest contribution to world literature.

These and numerous other remarks about American literature are often qualified theoretically, but, in practice, they represent a unified and influential, if not intentional, literary program which valorizes the non- or anti-social. I agree with Gerald Graff that this derealization of literature is symptomatic of much contemporary critical thought and should be understood, in part, as indicative of contemporary aesthetic trends.[3] However, in the context of a body of criticism intent on defining *the* American tradition, this derealization poses a specific problem separable from critical chic. This asocial bias, together with the restriction of the American canon to a few 'major' authors, has resulted in a circular conception of American literature. What constitutes 'majorness' for many theorists is derived from the already canonical writers. Since that majorness is frequently defined as either the rejection or the transcendence of social concerns, the many authors, texts, and genres which *do* express a frank and explicit involvement with social questions are either domesticated to the prevailing critical paradigm (Richard Chase, for instance, studies Frank Norris primarily as a romancer), or they are excluded from study altogether. It is unlikely that the dominant definitions of American literature could account for an American canon that included John Woolman, Thomas Paine, Harriet Beecher Stowe, O. E. Rolvaag, Sinclair Lewis, Tillie Olsen, and Langston Hughes. Furthermore, the inclusion of such writers would affect our readings of

Hawthorne, Melville, James, and other accepted American writers, once their works were seen in the context of more obviously social writers.

The consolation of criticism

These abstract definitions of American literature result, for the most part, from the historical situation of criticism, only recently emerging from the confines of New Critical textuality. Although we now attempt to get beyond the New Criticism or to figure out what, if anything, can come after it, critics like Gerald Graff, Frank Lentricchia, and Terry Eagleton have demonstrated that the New Critical aesthetic is a malleable thing, which, like Melville's Confidence Man, reappears in changing guise, still declaring social contexts as ancillary to 'literary' study. Discussing the flurry of postwar theoretical writings on American national literature, the Soviet critic A. N. Nikolyukin offers the following analysis of this asocial bias:

> New theories explaining the establishment of an American literature are continually appearing. Quite frequently, these theories reflect a subjective-idealistic conception of literary development – Freudian, mythic, existential, and so forth. Their common tendency is to confirm the estrangement of American literature from the sociohistorical conditions of its formulation.
>
> (Nikolyukin 1973, 575)

While Nikolyukin's assessment of the practice of these theorists is justified, he seems not to grant their expressed intentions and the contradictory status of their contributions to American criticism. Part of that contradictory status of many theories of American literature is a pervasive hostility toward social or political criticism that eludes simple historical explanation.

James L. Machor has addressed this issue in 'Tradition, Holism, and the Dilemmas of American Literary Studies.' Machor examines the theories of Matthiessen, William Carlos Williams, R. W. B. Lewis, Leo Marx, and Richard Poirier, all of whom attempt to fuse cultural history and literary analysis. Machor, correctly I believe, defines the common imperative behind these studies to be 'the desire to find the nexus of literature and culture in America' (Machor 1980, 100). Personal fears that no such unity exists, however, frustrate each of the theorists he studies, resulting in the various critics imposing a nostalgic and holistic model onto their field of study. Faced with the dilemma of trying to synthesize poles which they feel may not finally be reconciled, these critics, Machor argues, resort to a 'tragic desire to master history.' They all succeed at recapturing history, but 'each critic offers only a tradition of a cultural inability to resolve the dialectic between ideal and reality' (Machor 1980, 118). In other words, each theorist offers a fragmented vision of American literature and culture which actually reconfirms the dissociation they had originally set out to rectify. Machor concludes that all five of these thinkers

> find that their own desire to rediscover and recapture history has been, paradoxically, a struggle to escape history as a record of the past. The holistic approach, which is an attempt at spatial and temporal unification, is itself symptomatic of this desire, since holism as practiced in all five works becomes a method which tries to redeem time by obliterating it.
>
> (Machor 1980, 118)

Thus each critic locates the source of literature's failure to unify American culture in the historical development of a culture which has marginalized writers of creative genius, a situation that causes them to 'deny any chance of success for the literature to illuminate the value in our culture at large' (Machor 1980, 118).

Machor's focus parallels the paradox I perceive at work in many theories of American literature. Whereas Machor traces the theorists' desire to reclaim history to their self-consuming, ahistorical conclusions, I would suggest that similarly self-contradictory assumptions hamper theorists from situating American literature in the larger social contexts which they all agree are essential to their projects. Machor's provocative essay could have traced this anxiety before historical time to any number of social or political causes. Since any definitive analysis of such causal relations must remain speculative, Machor's reluctance to pursue those issues might be the prudent course to steer. With this realization, however, I would like to suggest a possible (albeit speculative) historical scenario to account in part for the failure of theorists to situate American literature more squarely in a social and political context.

I would like first to restate what I perceive as the paradox of theories of American literature. While many of them attempt to define the 'radical' or 'oppositional' nature of American literature, or, as in Bercovitch's case, its complicity in the history of American exceptionalist rhetoric, the theorists tend to separate literary significance and reflection from social and political significance. They begin with social, sometimes political, theses and often conclude by denying the possibility, the compatibility, even the desirability of viewing literature as a type of social knowledge or behavior. By declaring literature autonomous they tend to deprive it of its capacity to reflect critically on issues of social and political significance. The strategies of each theorist will be examined in detail in chapters 2 through 4, and, as those readings should demonstrate, most critics attempt to argue for a cultural apprehension of American literature, but for one reason or another end up qualifying, sometimes denying outright, the ability of their approaches to do so. The problem is complex and, in most cases, a matter of historical and academic inertia rather than of individual 'failure.' Briefly stated, the contradictions informing theories of American literature can be seen as a historical and political problem – one of a political and intellectual milieu which inhibits truly critical thinking on matters of political significance.

The case of American studies is particularly interesting. Howard Mumford Jones states the issue in refreshingly direct terms:

> It has been urged, usually as a reproof, that American Studies are in fact a branch of propaganda. I think this is not wholly bad, and I think the allegation perhaps puts us on the right track. American Studies are propaganda because they are an attempt to explicate and make persuasive a set of values satisfactory to the American people; and because the American people believe these values, or some of them, may benefit other nations, they are engaged in a mighty effort to make these values comprehensible both at home and abroad.
>
> (Jones 1967, 7)

Such an honest admission of the imperialistic function of American studies is a sobering reminder that not all literary criticism does or should play an adversarial role within American culture. However, it fails to account for the work produced by critics who may not subscribe to the mission of American literary studies. Possible answers to their dilemma are more complex, but have been a matter of concern among American literary intellectuals for almost a century.

One would have to rely on a truly naive belief in the freedom of academic inquiry from political and economic pressures to posit an unhampered and relatively autonomous position for literary studies within the American system. And yet, the extent of 'outside' interference in university thinking and the implications of that encroachment are more profound than many are willing to admit. It was already a critical commonplace when Frank Lentricchia pointed out the 'quietistic' resignation of Paul de Man's brand of deconstruction and when Barbara Foley anatomized the extent to which the Yale School and Derrida in general provide a crucial ideological brace for the American status quo.[4] Historians of the profession trace the infiltration of American universities by 'big business' or some other looming presence well back into the nineteenth century, usually precipitated by some crisis over academic freedom. In the middle 1880s, for example, Henry Carter Adams was fired from Cornell for offending a powerful benefactor with a pro-labor speech. By the nineties, such firings were commonplace and generated concerted, Populist-tinged reaction.[5] Of course, Thorstein Veblen's *The Higher Learning in America* (1918) outlined in strong polemics the desecration of academic ranks by corporate interests. Veblen labels as 'captains of erudition' the capitalists who influenced, often to the point of domination, the ideological parameters of all academic disciplines early in the twentieth century. The nature of this influence was often starkly obvious. For example, when President Andrews offended the trustees and some potential benefactors of Brown University, a newspaper reminded him that 'he was only a servant; and a servant must do as his employers wish, or quit their service.' At Northwestern University, a trustee (also a patent attorney and officer of the Western Railroad Association) announced:

As to what should be taught in political science and social science, they [professors] should promptly and gracefully submit to the determination of the trustees when the latter find it necessary to act. . . . If the trustees err, it is for the patrons and proprietors, not for the employees, to change either the policy or the personnel of the board.[6]

With the outbreak of World War I, the form of outside influences on academic study changed and was often welcomed from within the university as an exciting relief from a life of arid intellectual impotence. In Stuart Sherman's case, the war effort precipitated both a renaissance in his social and political development and his decision to rediscover American literature. As Richard Ruland notes:

> The war and the attendant shattering of Sherman's academic calm had led to a burst of undiscriminating patriotism, and the writing and thinking which followed the Armistice reflected his growing realization of America's role as a world leader and his consequent 'fresh interest' in American life and letters.
>
> (Ruland 1967, 73)

In other words, Sherman welcomed the war as a liberating force within academic circles. George Santayana had by 1915 diagnosed the plague on American culture as the genteel tradition, which separated the life of the mind from the life of commerce and industry. World War I, it seems, was perceived by some as the right medicine to help American intellectuals escape their putative marginality and ineffectuality.

Not everyone, however, embraced that moment of liberation so enthusiastically. Randolph Bourne begins his 1917 essay, 'The War and the Intellectuals,' with a lament for lost freedom:

> To those of us who still retain an irreconcilable animus against war, it has been a bitter experience to see the unanimity with which American intellectuals have thrown their support to the use of war-technique in the crisis in which America found herself. Socialists, college professors, publicists, new-republicans, practitioners of literature, have vied with each other in confirming with their intellectual faith the collapse of neutrality and the riveting of the war-mind on a

> hundred million more of the world's people. . . . An intellec-
> tual class, gently guiding a nation through sheer force of ideas
> into what other nations entered only through predatory craft
> or popular hysteria or militarist madness!
>
> (Bourne 1956, 205–6)

The mistake of entering the war may not be as obvious to
contemporary readers as it was to Bourne, but the important
issue, as he so clearly states, is the unanimity and enthusiasm
with which literature professors and writers joined the war
effort, right or wrong, and how winning the American public
was more a rhetorical (ideological) than an obviously militar-
istic accomplishment, and one which, at least to Bourne's mind,
seduced an entire profession.

Recent critics and historians have pursued the implications of
this merger between literary intellectuals and big business, the
state, and so forth. In *Mars and Minerva: World War I and the Uses
of the Higher Learning in America* (1975), Carol S. Gruber recounts
the process of co-optation that accompanied the war effort.
According to Gruber, the singularity of the American university
system is characterized primarily by its emergence and association with the needs of a democratic, industrializing society, and
by its functions being defined in terms of service for that society.
While there has never been a clear consensus about just what
needs are to be served and how the university should serve
them, the ideal of social service and the willingness of faculties to
lend their expertise to governmental agencies at all levels did
smooth the transition which saw American universities gear
up for World War I on the technical, as well as the ideological
level (Gruber 1975, 28, 95). The war effort, Gruber suggests,
branched out well beyond the academic disciplines into a form
of discipline itself. According to the 'Report of the Committee
on Academic Freedom in Wartime,' professors were expected to
'refrain from public discussion of the War; and in their private
intercourse with neighbors, colleagues, and students . . . avoid
all hostile or offensive expressions concerning the United States
or its government' (Gruber 1975, 160). What Gruber outlines in
her study is a system of coercion and intolerance that rivals
even the most biased visions of contemporary Soviet oppression. The 'Great War Crusade' grew to be so popular on
American campuses, she claims, 'that those professors who did

not share the prevailing enthusiasms were suspected of being mentally or morally deficient, or even dangerous. The climate of opinion on the American campus was so conformist that neither tolerance nor respect was allowed for differences of opinion about the war' (Gruber 1975, 210). As Bourne registered in 'The War and the Intellectuals,' the patriotic rage was variously received. Cephas Allin of Minnesota complained 'the truth is that we will be a military institution this coming year,' but granted that 'there is some small satisfaction in feeling useful.' Edward Corwin expressed similar ambivalence at Princeton: 'Princeton . . . is not Princeton just now – only a cog of the military machine, and we professors are cogs within cogs. Of course it's nice to feel useful' (Gruber 1975, 232, 237).

Gruber doesn't limit the scope of her study to the signing of the Armistice. In an equation that seems common to anyone familiar with cold war rhetoric or with Ronald Reagan's 'Evil Empire' speech of 1983, Gruber points out that 'after the war was over, the theme of absolute good versus absolute evil was retained by simply putting the Bolshevik in place of the Hun as the menace to democracy everywhere,' a simplistic and falsely moralistic interpretation that many American professors subscribed to (Gruber 1975, 241, 253). Furthermore, at the time of her own writing, Gruber could caution:

> Even though America's participation in the First World War was of relatively short duration, the articulation of interest between the higher learning and the world of power that took place during the war's span was not an ephemeral experience; established and exposed then were assumptions, attitudes, and expectations that would flower in the decades to come.
>
> (Gruber 1975, 258–9)

Gruber is careful to avoid crude assertions of conscious complicity or hypocrisy, and one of the major strengths of her work is its cautious, though bold, delineation of an academy won to interests antithetical to its declared and sincerely held values.

Critics from a variety of ideological perspectives have elaborated on Gruber's themes. Tracing the *'embourgeoisement'* of the American intellectual to the purging of leftist politics from the American intellectual scene during the fifties, Philip Rahv criticized university professors who found it 'altogether easy to put up with the vicious antics of a political bum like Senator McCarthy' and who grew less tolerant of 'any basic criticism of existing social arrangements' (Rahv 1957, 225–6). In his political anatomy of American intellectual life, Rahv identifies the rout of left-wing politics as the cause of depoliticized literary thinking. He grants that an adequate substitute for political orthodoxy could serve an equally vital purpose, but bemoans the rise of a 'neo-philistine tendency' that accepts the status quo as it rehearses anticommunist clichés. The general malaise, Rahv observes, is best defined as 'a kind of detachment from principle' and a fragmentation characteristic of literary life (Rahv 1957, 228). The result is a trivialization of literary production and literary inquiry in American universities.

Christopher Lasch has addressed the same problems as did Gruber and Rahv in much of his work over the past twenty years, focusing particularly on the failure of critical thinking in American universities. During the 1950s and 1960s, he argues, larger universities were more or less bought off and implicated so fundamentally in the national defense and the entire 'military-industrial complex' that they came to depend on the government and private foundations for their support. As a result, 'they lost their character as centers of independent learning and critical thought and were swallowed up in the network of "the national purpose"' (Lasch 1967, 316). University intellectuals (Lasch also adds the mass media to his discussion) then ceased to function as voices of criticism and analysis, and became semi-official apologists for and diffusers of official governmental attitudes. Lasch suggests that this commodification of culture led to academics conceiving of their function as the 'propagation of culture rather than the criticism of it' (Lasch 1967, 318). In a more specific analysis of the Congress for Cultural Freedom, Lasch focuses his critique on the impact of national politics (the McCarthy era in this case) on American intellectuals. Lasch understands the willingness of academics to abandon 'their true calling – critical thought' as nothing less than a 'defection,' with all the political intrigue and duplicity fully intended. In the course of his discussion, Lasch defines the climate of universities in the United States in stark terms:

The infatuation with consensus; the vogue of a disembodied 'history of ideas' divorced from considerations of class or other determinants of social organization; the obsession with 'American Studies' which perpetuates a nationalistic myth of American uniqueness – these things reflect the degree to which historians have become apologists, in effect, for American national power in the holy war against communism.

(Lasch 1968, 323)

Lasch's remarks here are also pertinent to the general political tone of theorists of American literature – their stress on American uniqueness, their holistic theories, and their relatively abstract theoretical models. Echoing Howard Mumford Jones, Lasch refers to the de-politicization of cultural criticism as 'propagandistic,' but adds an important qualification when he notes that, as propaganda, American scholarship rarely takes crude or obvious forms and is frequently difficult to penetrate as propaganda. Surveying the activity of the Congress for Cultural Freedom, the editorial policies of journals such as *Encounter*, and, briefly, even the career of Leslie Fiedler, Lasch comes to conclusions that reiterate his thinking in *The New Radicalism in America*, namely that 'academic freedom' as we know it in the United States has not led to intellectual independence and critical thinking. 'It is a serious mistake,' he warns, 'to confuse academic freedom with cultural freedom' (Lasch 1968, 347). The university is free, he grants,

but it has purged itself of ideas. The literary intellectuals are free, but they use their freedom to propagandize for the state. What has led to this curious state of affairs? The very freedom of American intellectuals blinds them to their unfreedom. It leads them to confuse the political interests of intellectuals as an official minority with the progress of intellect. Their freedom from overt political control . . . blinds them to the way in which the 'knowledge industry' has been incorporated into the state and the military industrial complex.

(Lasch 1968, 347)

Gerald Graff would later apply a Laschian analysis to recent posturings of literary and critical radicalism, pointing out similarities between strategies for literary emancipation and antithetical strategies for containment characteristic of advanced capitalism and Madison Avenue. The essential point for both Lasch and Graff is that American intellectuals have, wittingly and willingly or not, been co-opted by a bourgeois culture that entertains the proliferation of radical chic while undermining, often through those very 'political' positions, any grounds for radical thinking.

Terry Eagleton has made these points from an overtly Marxist position. Critics are not just analysts of texts, he reminds us, 'they are also (usually) academics hired by the state to prepare students ideologically for their functions within capitalist society' (Eagleton 1976b, 59). In the same vein, Eagleton situates writers squarely *within* commodity culture, 'hired by publishing houses to produce commodities which will sell' (Eagleton 1976b, 59). One needn't perceive literary production and criticism in terms so starkly commodified as do Lasch, Graff, or Eagleton. Lasch's reminder that the brand of propaganda which he sees American intellectuals producing is subtle and difficult to detect would be an adequate caution to those too eager to pin down the state of literary criticism with some conspiratorial model.

Even this brief account of the politics of 'critical thought' in the United States should make clear how complex a situation theorists of American literature occupy within the larger tradition of American cultural thought. As far back as the 1880s the status of American university intellectuals was troubled. Exacerbated by two world wars, several economic crises, and any number of other pressures – the cold war, Vietnam – literary thinking in the United States has been so caught up in social and political change that any distinctions between literary theory and social or political pressures are difficult to identify, let alone evaluate decisively.

I would not attempt to suggest any direct connections between the cruder manifestations of political power addressed by Veblen, Gruber, and others and the theorists of American literature who are the focus of this study. It would be absurd to argue that any of them would have been fired for writing more uncompromising political or social criticism. Insisting that any or all of them consciously attenuate the depth of their social criticism for any reason seems equally simple. It would be equally reductive, however, to claim that these critics could wholly transcend the subtle pressures and general political drift of American society away from radically critical thought since the late thirties. My assumption is precisely that in the act of attempting to forge literary theories in opposition to trends in American bourgeois culture the critics I address register the pervasive hegemony of those very trends. In attempting to clear a space for American literature as a reformist or revolutionary voice against American society, critics have failed to purge their theories of crucial aesthetic and political assumptions which stifle their objections. What I am suggesting is a scenario similar to that offered by Graff in *Literature Against Itself*. According to Graff, the radical posturings and rhetorical bravado of recent literary theory have obscured the extent to which recent literature and theory has been absorbed by a consumer dynamic that trivializes and denatures such seemingly threatening alternatives. Theorists of American literature have, I would argue, been caught up in a similarly paradoxical position, but one already inherent in the theoretical methods, vocabularies, and more subtly, priorities of the critical program commonly known as New Criticism. Here, I agree with Frank Lentricchia and Terry Eagleton that our claims to be beyond the New Criticism are sorely premature. While I am obviously in agreement with critics like Lasch, Graff, Eagleton, and others about the status of much recent literary scholarship, I would insist on placing within the context of American history the accomplishments and limitations, and on granting the expressed intentions (realized or not), of theorists such as Matthiessen, Feidelson, Trilling, Poirier, and Bercovitch.

In the chapters that follow I will discuss three different approaches to American literature: those which locate the unity of American literature in a historical continuity from Puritanism to the present, those which study American literature in light of various interpretations of American culture, and those which find a peculiar 'Americanness' in the language or style of American literature.

That theorists of American literature have not situated that tradition in sufficiently social a terrain is the major argument of this study; its major part is spent discussing how their mythic, symbolic, rhetorical, romantic, or psychological rubrics deflect the social and political significance of American literature. For the purpose of this work, I focus primarily on their critical texts, but any complete assessment of their position in American literary and cultural history will have to account for their specific historical place. A critique of these theorists should also offer readings capable of correcting their derealization of American literature. I have offered a few such readings, but I have also, I hope, suggested the direction a more comprehensive social and aesthetic theory should follow.

The problem of
Puritan origins in
literary history and theory

Theorists of American literature have consistently viewed the influence of Puritanism on American thought as a critical issue, but they have sharply debated the precise nature of that influence. As early as 1891, Barrett Wendell, one of the founders of American literary studies, wrote, 'To understand the America of to-day, we must know the New England of the fathers' (Wendell 1891, 305). But as Henry May documents, 'young radicals' such as Emma Goldman, H. L. Mencken, and others in the first decades of the twentieth century denounced Puritanism 'for every crime from prostitution to the American Sunday' (May 1957, 308). The search for the 'Puritan origins' of American culture and of the American Self gained momentum during the twenties, receiving a kind of official recognition in 1928 when Norman Foerster's *The Reinterpretation of American Literature* specified Puritanism, along with the frontier spirit, romanticism, and realism, as one of the determining influences on American writing. The debate over the significance of Puritanism, however, had been raging since the turn of the century, when Puritanism became a touchstone for discussions of the merits and defects of American culture. Early versions of Puritan origins scholarship by writers such as Paul Elmer More, H. L. Mencken, Stuart Sherman, and William Carlos Williams demonstrated that Puritanism could be appropriated as the root of any number of different American traditions. These critics and others used Puritanism, however, more than they sought to understand it. They simplified it in order to make it serve as the source of everything right or wrong with twentieth-century America, typecasting the Puritans as heroes or villains in the drama of American history and identity.

Puritan origins scholarship has progressed far beyond the simplified, polarized views of the early theorists. Nevertheless, scholars have continued to simplify Puritanism, reflecting different critical paradigms rather than depicting Puritan culture with historical accuracy. My main purpose here is to explore theories of more recent and sophisticated literary historians and critics, including Perry Miller, Yvor Winters, and Sacvan Bercovitch, and more briefly some works of Richard Chase, Harry Levin, and Leslie Fiedler. Understanding their works, however, requires a review of some early Puritan origins theories. In addition to the colorful polemic that characterizes their writing on Puritanism, the most striking feature of works by early critics such as More, Babbitt, Sherman, and Williams is their fervid disagreement over what Puritanism actually was. None of these thinkers pursued an adequate historical understanding of Puritanism; instead they contented themselves with selective views supporting an *a priori* interpretation of American culture. As Richard Ruland has demonstrated in his analysis of the Stuart Sherman/H. L. Mencken debate over Puritanism, many of the early arguments were never resolved because the antagonists worked at cross purposes, failing to grasp either the other's points or the historical reality of Puritanism.[1] In more subtle fashion, the same failure continues to pervade later studies.

For several early theorists, Puritanism was a positive force in American culture, one which America needed to revive. More and Babbitt, for instance, valued Puritanism both for its vigorous moral sense and its stern 'inner check' against extremism. For them, American Puritanism granted historical legitimacy to their religious or secular conservatism. Similarly, for Stuart Sherman, Puritanism represented a peculiarly 'American' standard of conduct. In a wartime essay, Sherman criticized anti-war sentiment, arguing that it betrayed everything positive in American culture, especially 'the Puritans who since the seventeenth century have constituted the moral backbone of the nation' (Sherman 1918, 7). A few years later in 'What Is a Puritan?' (1923), Sherman identified the 'eternal Puritan' with such American virtues as

> dissatisfaction with the past, courage to break sharply from it, a vision of a better life, a readiness to accept a discipline in order to attain that better life, and a serious desire to make the better life prevail – a desire reflecting at once his sturdy individualism and his clear sense for the need of social solidarity.
>
> (Sherman 1923, 35)

Much of what Sherman attributes to Puritanism is accurate enough, but hardly confined to Puritanism. Sherman finds a usable past in Puritanism, but only by identifying timeless values as peculiarly Puritan.

If Sherman and others celebrated the 'eternal Puritan' in the image of their own ideals, hostile critics were no less biased. The Puritan as villain, as the embodiment of everything wrong with American culture, came under frequent attack in the works of those thinkers whom Henry May, in *The End of American Innocence*, classed as amoralists, liberators, intellectuals, and radicals. For Sherman's arch-adversary, H. L. Mencken, as for William Carlos Williams and Ludwig Lewisohn, Puritanism represented moral cowardice. Ignorant, oppressive, and idealistic, Puritanism was the essence of all that was hypocritical and squeamishly conservative in Victorian America. Striking out against America's wholesale 'sacrifice of aesthetic ideals,' Mencken observed:

> It is no wonder that the typical American maker of books became a timorous and ineffectual fellow, whose work tends inevitably toward a feeble superficiality. Sucking in the Puritan spirit with the very air he breathes, and perhaps burdened inwardly with an inheritance of the actual Puritan stupidity, he is . . . kept upon the straight path of chemical purity. . . . The result is a literature full of mawkishness that the late Henry James so often roared against – a literature almost wholly detached from life as men are living it in the world.
>
> (Mencken 1917, 274)

Mencken's style, the purity of his rhetorical rage against Puritanism, appeals to our appreciation for literary bravura, but the
historical accuracy of his ideas is shallow. Mencken's criticism
of a literature detached from life as lived echoes Santayana's
and anticipates Van Wyck Brooks's attacks on the genteel
tradition; it also levels the same charges against idealism as
those issued by exponents of literary naturalism and realism. It
has, however, little historical proof.

In William Carlos Williams's theory of American history, as
elaborated in *In the American Grain* (1925), the Puritan remains a
figure detached by his narrow and false morality from real
existence in a real environment. Williams divides pivotal figures
in American history into opposed camps: those who came to
America open and receptive to the possibilities of a new land
versus those intent on possessing it and imposing upon it a rigid
set of old ideals. For Williams, the Puritans typify this latter
camp with a vengeance. Driven to the New World by their
emptiness and dogmatism, the Puritans closed the sensuous
world out:

> Having in themselves nothing of curiosity, no wonder for the
> New World – that is, nothing official – they know only to keep
> their eyes blinded, their tongues in orderly manner between
> their teeth, their ears stopped by the monotony of their hymns
> and their flesh covered in straight habits.
>
> (Williams 1925, 112)

Williams's Puritans, it is clear, embody the popular stereotype
of Puritans as prigs and killjoys. Their infamy, furthermore,
survives into the present: 'The trail of Puritanism is the direct
cause of the growth of the Catholic Church with us today, this
dehumanization' (Williams 1925, 128). Williams does differ
from other debunkers in that he cites actual Puritan documents,
primarily Cotton Mather's account of the witch trials, but
his choice of sources guarantees that Puritans will damn
themselves.

Similarly, Ludwig Lewisohn's Freudian theory of American
literature discovers in Puritanism the same repressive denial of
experience as do the views of Mencken and Williams, though he
sees the essence of American literature as a backlash against,

rather than an outgrowth of Puritanism. In *Expression in America* Lewisohn states,

> The true history of literature in America is the history of those poets and thinkers who first in mere theory, later in both theory and practice, denied the Puritan division of experience from expression, broke the moulds of the artificer, and brought their countrymen first freedom of perception and of thought, next flexibility of conduct in pursuit of each man's idea of the good life.
>
> (Lewisohn 1932, 459)

We find here again echoes of Santayana's critique of the genteel tradition, with Puritanism as the source of the split between expression and experience, of 'polite letters unintegrated with life until almost the other day' (Lewisohn 1932, xxxi). While these critics' express purposes are to judge literature by its fidelity to experience, they actually replace the historical reality of Puritanism with abstract models. Oddly, both Williams's and Lewisohn's perceptions of Puritanism exemplify the very rigidity for which they indict Puritans.

Puritanism as tragic vision: Perry Miller

Perry Miller's more thorough and disciplined reexamination, appearing first in the late thirties, restored the complexity of Puritan thought and exposed the inadequacies of these simplistic views of Puritanism. The range and sensitivity that Miller brought to the study of Puritanism have inspired many later scholars, fruitfully provoking even those who strongly disagree with his work. As Miller's work has been thoroughly scrutinized, I will simply attempt to situate Miller in the lineage of Puritan origins theorists of American literature as a catalyst and disseminator of ideas pursued by subsequent literary critics.[2] Miller himself saw his career as a polemical reaction against early Puritan-baiters like Williams and Mencken as well as against such Progressive historians as Carl Becker, V. L. Parrington, and Merle Curti. In his preface to *Orthodoxy in Massachusetts, 1630–1650* Miller remarks:

> I had commenced my work within an emotional universe dominated by H. L. Mencken. My contemporaries and I

came of age in a time when the word 'Puritan' served as a comprehensive sneer against every tendency in American civilization which we held reprehensible – sexual diffidence, censorship, prohibition, theological fundamentalism, political hypocrisy, and all the social antics which Sinclair Lewis, among others, was stridently ridiculing.

(Miller 1933, xviii)

Among historians, established opinion also told Miller that as a field of inquiry Puritanism 'was exhausted, all that wheat had long since been winnowed, there was nothing but chaff remaining' (Miller 1956, viii). Miller none the less set out on a career that was to rehabilitate the Puritans, freeing them from the old stereotypes of Victorian gentility and opening the doors to a historical enterprise of great importance. As Nina Baym notes, 'the great work of Perry Miller . . . sprang significantly from the wish to demonstrate the strangeness of the Puritans, their unlikeness to the bourgeois figures of popular Thanksgiving iconography' (Baym 1979, 349). Another way to view Miller's work is to understand his project as a rebellion against the shoddy historical sense of earlier critics.

Yet Miller's approach has limitations, owing chiefly to his polemical context. Concentrating exclusively on Puritan ideas, he abstracts them from the complex social fabric in which they found their articulation and thus does not adequately show how Puritan 'ideas' grew out of and influenced specific economic and political circumstances. For Miller and many of his followers, ideas assume a mythic or symbolic potency. Miller himself unabashedly stressed the asocial nature of his enterprise. In *Orthodoxy in Massachusetts, 1630–1650*, he boasts, 'I have attempted to tell of a great folk movement with an utter disregard of the economic and social factors' (Miller 1933, xi); in *The New England Mind* he 'deliberately avoided giving more than passing notice to the social or economic influences' (Miller 1939, viii); and in *Errand Into the Wilderness* he reminds us, by way of criticizing social or economic historians, that he has 'difficulty imagining that anyone can be a historian without realizing that history itself is part of the life of the mind; hence I have been compelled to insist that the mind of man is the basic factor in human history' (Miller 1956, ix). Miller also assures us that such a methodological position is not arbitrary or a 'personal predilection,' but a response to what he believes to be the 'inner logic of the research' (Miller 1956, ix). In other words, Miller defends his relatively abstract project on two fronts: as a necessary corrective for the Puritan-baiting scholarship of the teens and twenties; and as a scholarly inquiry coherent with the 'inner logic' of Puritanism itself.

Miller's work illustrates the tension between 'reality' and 'ideas' that Lionel Trilling was soon to address in more literary terms (see chapter 3). We can, in fact, best understand Miller's work as a voice in the debate over 'Reality in America,' that is, between literary realists and nonrealists, and between economic and intellectual historians. Both Miller and Trilling set out to rescue the life of the mind from the crassness of the then-prevalent social materialism. To some extent, then, Miller's polemical context resulted in his using the Puritans, as did More, Williams, and others, for his own argumentative purposes. Whereas Trilling would object to V. L. Parrington's crude definition of 'reality,' which neglected the importance of the 'literary idea,' Miller saw that Puritan ideas had been defamed by 'historians [who] were apt to slide over these [theological] concepts in a shockingly superficial manner simply because they had so little respect for the intellect in general' (Miller 1956, ix). Miller was doubtless right that 'neither the friends nor the foes of the Puritans have shown much interest in their intellects, for it has been assumed that the Puritan mind was too weighted down by the load of dogma to be worth considering in and for itself' (Miller 1939, 64). Before Trilling coined the phrase, Miller believed that 'the liberal imagination' had minimized not only the importance, but also the power of ideas.

In order to challenge their liberal readers to regard ideas more seriously, Miller and Trilling opposed crudely materialistic notions of reality, but they did so by swinging to the opposite extreme and defining the life of the mind as the very stuff of reality. Whereas Trilling's strategy would be to ridicule Parrington's 'peasant' conceptions of reality, Miller more subtly turned the tables on the genteel equations of reality with masculinity, ideas with femininity. For Miller, the life of the mind was as vigorous, risky, and real as the life of physical action and economic enterprise. Miller reacted against the old prejudice against alleged Puritan ideality, yet his reaction left this prejudice subtly intact. Puritan theological rigor came to represent the heroic spiritual adversary to the complacency and comfort of the commercial class and to the optimistic materialism of Progressive historians.

Miller mythologized Puritan ideas in such terms throughout his career, terms anticipating later critical glorifications of the 'tragic vision' of Hawthorne and Melville. The Puritan spirit, he wrote, undertook 'the perpetual judgment of all things by the loftiest conceivable standard and an unflagging intensity of purpose' (Miller 1939, 44–5). The Puritan was able to 'confront even horror without shrinking,' and if Puritanism failed to maintain this attitude it was only 'because the children were unable to face reality as unflinchingly as their forefathers. . . . The reason later generations ceased marching to the Puritan beat was simply that they could no longer stand the pace' (Miller 1939, 37, 59). For Miller, what unites Edwards with Emerson and later figures in American literature is the strength and courage 'to confront, face to face, the image of a blinding divinity in the physical universe, and to look upon that universe without the intermediary of ritual, or ceremony, of the Mass and the confessional' (Miller 1956, 185). Thus Miller's Puritan resembles the existentialist's isolated man, tragically alone in the world and responsible for facing reality without mediation.

Miller's reevaluation of the relationship between ideas and reality, thought and action, the individual and society, *was* necessitated by the shortcomings of vulgarized materialist historicism and literary criticism of the 1930s. Perhaps his greatest contribution was to reinvigorate an entire era with a new and compelling historical analysis capable of infusing the sixteenth and seventeenth centuries with a sense of urgency, rigor, and contemporaneity. Keeping any inquiry alive in the face of such concerted opposition as Miller faced is itself an undertaking of great worth. Miller's polemical opposition may have caused him, however, to tilt the scales too far in the other direction, keeping ideas and reality in nearly absolute opposition to one another. What emerges from much of Miller's work is a view of Puritanism as an idea rather than a total social and historical formation. His primary focus on the interaction between intellect and piety results in a searching and often profound analysis of Puritan theology, but only a schematic sense of the relationship between that theology and how it was actually translated into social practice. To be sure, Miller has had his critics. David D. Hall, for example, offers an alternative approach to Puritanism that includes the intellectual dimension but places it in its cultural context:

> An adequate definition of the Puritan movement must . . . seek to unite the experiential dimension with the formal structure of the Puritan intellect. It must locate the movement within a particular time period, and with reference to the Reformed tradition and Pietism. It must identify the bond between its rhetoric and its social consequences.
>
> (Hall 1971, 36)

Nina Baym criticizes Miller on much the same grounds: 'The great omission in Miller's splendid work was to have accepted the Puritans' written texts for the whole. Because of this he presented them as people who lived through words and almost entirely in the arena of doctrinal debate' (Baym 1979, 349). Puritan origins theorists of American literature since Miller have likewise not come close to identifying this bond between Puritan rhetoric and its social consequences, nor have they totally escaped the polarizing, idealizing tendencies common to many early theorists. Just as Miller modernized Edwards to find a 'usable past' – a lineage for his tragic view of isolated individuality – later theorists have similarly imposed any number of contemporary models on the Puritan past.

Puritanism as allegory: Yvor Winters, Richard Chase, and Leslie Fiedler

Actually a year *before* Miller's *The New England Mind* (1939), Yvor Winters's *Maule's Curse: Seven Studies in the History of American Obscurantism* (1938) was the first theory of American literature that attempted to integrate 'the formal structure of the Puritan intellect' into the history of American literature. Winters condemns the Puritan influence on American literature, but in contrast to early theorists, who demonstrated little understanding of Puritan thought, he bases his work in historical evidence rather than personal bias. *Maule's Curse* presents

Winters's view of American literature as an obscurantist tradition laboring under an 'allegorical' vision derived from New
England Puritanism. The major symptom of this burden is an
incapacity to distinguish subjective vision from either objective
fact or metaphysical reality. He then applies this characterization to American literature as a whole:

> The Puritan view of life was allegorical, and the allegorical
> vision seems to have been strongly impressed upon the New
> England literary mind. It is fairly obvious in much of the
> poetry of Emerson, Emily Dickinson, Bryant, Holmes, and
> even Very – Whittier, a Quaker and a peasant, alone of the
> more interesting poets escaping; Melville, relatively an out
> sider, shows the impact of New England upon his own genius
> as much through his use of allegory as through his use of the
> New England character.
>
> (Winters 1938, 4)

Though Winters refers only to the 'New England mind,' he, like
many theorists, equates this mind with the American tradition
as a whole. As we learn throughout *Maule's Curse*, this characteristically New England outlook encompasses a wide range of
faults: in Melville, the 'fusion of the physical with the spiritual,'
by which Winters means the confusion of the two realms which
prevents writers from distinguishing one from the other; in
Dickinson, a general stylistic character 'lacking in taste'; in
James, an intellectuality 'detached from social background' and
a 'moral sense . . . unsupported by any clear sense of ideas.'
Most importantly and most damagingly, the curse renders
American writers incapable of 'moral conviction and of moral
understanding' (pp. 165, 76, 175, 178, 11). Winters anatomizes
the works of Hawthorne, Cooper, Melville, Poe, Very,
Emerson, Dickinson, and James – primarily in light of these
charges. In 'The Anatomy of Nonsense' (1947), Winters
diagnoses similar faults in Henry Adams, Stevens, Eliot, and
Ransom, thus extending his theory of American literature well
into the twentieth century.

Winters attacks Puritanism on two closely related points: its
moral allegorization of experience, and its contradictory understanding of the human will:

The Puritan theology rested primarily upon the doctrine of predestination and the inefficaciousness of good works; it separated men sharply and certainly into two groups, the saved and the damned, and technically at least, was not concerned with any subtler shadings. This in itself represents a long step toward the allegorization of experience, for a very broad abstraction is substituted for the patient study of the minutiae of moral behavior long encouraged by the Catholic tradition.

(Winters 1938, 4–5)

In other words, since human conduct is predetermined by God as either all good or all evil, experience is reduced to an allegory in which moral choice is lacking. This allegory of saved versus damned souls, with no choice over their fate, literally demoralizes human experience. Such a simplistic dualism, Winters feels, denies the subtler shadings of human conduct and reflection.

Winters also finds a contradiction in the Puritan view of human will. American Puritanism, he contends, was a confused blend of orthodox Calvinism tempered but also diluted during the antinomian crisis. As a result, the sign of election became not the individual's inner assurance, which for Winters suggests a positive state of moral struggle, but merely 'the decision of the individual to enter the Church and lead a moral life' (p. 5). In American Puritanism the practical will was exalted both by the excitement of a new religious movement and by the challenge posed by the hostile physical surroundings, but denied from a doctrinal standpoint (i.e., in a predestined world, willfulness is not only futile, but sinful as well). This irreconcilable contradiction, Winters believes, rendered Puritanism a schizophrenic blend of antinomianism and Arminianism which undermined, if it did not totally destroy, Puritanism's trust in human reason. As Winters remarks in his chapter on James, 'It denied the importance of the whole subject of morality' (p. 172). This suspicion of reason and the will is, for Winters, the curse that Puritanism has placed on American writers.

There is one final effect of Puritanism, which, according to Winters, is a logical result of its contradictions. Cursed with their Puritan heritage of simultaneous exaltation and suspicion of reason, American writers have been deprived of a faculty with which to distinguish between the physical and metaphysical, between the human and the divine. This confusion results in an inordinate emotionalism in American letters, a lack of intellectual and moral integrity preventing American writers from achieving a coherent understanding, and thus a criticism, of human experience. The denial of freedom of the will, coupled with the intense, and yet abstract moral drama excited by Puritan Manicheanism, resulted in a moral sense which exerted itself with a vengeance, yet without a clear human or social focus. The Puritan legacy charged everything with a volatile moral significance, but denied the grounds for coherent moral understanding. To borrow T. S. Eliot's terms (which Winters rejects), Winters suggests that American writers have never found an objective correlative for their intense, unfocused emotionalism. They have 'symbols,' but those symbols are devoid of definite meaning. As Winters concludes his introductory chapter on Hawthorne,

> His dilemma, the choice between abstractions inadequate or irrelevant to experience on the one hand, and experience on the other as far as practicable unilluminated by understanding is tragically characteristic of the history of this country and of its literature; only a few scattered individuals . . . have achieved the permeation of human experience by a consistent moral understanding which results in wisdom and in great art.
>
> (p. 22)

Thus, according to Winters, the majority of American writers have, knowingly or not, drunk of the Puritans' blood. The picture Winters gives us of Puritanism and of American literature is of a desolate moral wasteland, a hodge-podge of symbols with inadequate referents (theological or otherwise) and unmotivated emotions – a literature of moral confusion and unreality. It is one of the most far-reaching indictments of American writing ever leveled.

In addition to bringing a more rigorous analysis to bear on Puritanism and American literature, *Maule's Curse* makes further contributions and stands as a milestone in critical studies of American literature. One needs to remember that in

1938 American literature was relatively unstudied and, for that matter, still anathema to many English departments. Winters was one of the first critics to subject American writing to the kind of theoretical rigor to which we have become accustomed. And, while his tone is often harsh (even insulting), his praise of American writers is generous. In his discussion of James's fiction, for instance, Winters not only formulates James's typical novelistic scenario clearly and accurately but also criticizes James's superficial grasp of society. Winters is particularly sharp on this matter, especially when comparing James with Edith Wharton, finding the former deficient precisely in so far as his New England heritage rendered him ignorant of American economics, classes, and manners. Another significant insight in *Maule's Curse* is Winters's anticipation of what Edmund Morgan was to term 'the Puritan dilemma' (Morgan 1958). Winters's analysis of the contradictions in Puritanism resembles Morgan's picture of the antithetical urges within Puritan society, specifically those of antinomianism and Arminianism and the 'problem of doing right in a world that does wrong.'

More generally, Winters identified tendencies in Puritanism which later critics have accepted as commonplaces. Whether they develop the implications of Puritanism's allegorical worldview, as does Richard Chase, the nature of Puritan symbolism, as does Charles Feidelson, or Puritanism's concept of the self, as does Sacvan Bercovitch, these later critics, among others, are working within the boundaries first defined by Winters. Despite their more thorough understanding of Puritanism, these studies nevertheless fail to place Puritan theology in its social context. One gets the impression from reading Winters, Chase, and Fiedler that the Puritans lived in a purely theoretical universe in which postulates were never tested or resolved in actual practice. They are all, in this respect, heirs to Perry Miller, or it might be claimed that Miller and others are heirs to Winters.

In *The American Novel and Its Tradition* (1957), Richard Chase acknowledges Winters as a pioneer in discovering the influence of the Puritan Manichean vision on American literature. For Chase, as for Winters, American literature is inherently dualistic and allegorical, both a logical and historical extension of the Puritan worldview. Both Chase and Winters maintain that American literature is tangential to the actuality of American experience, and they see the American writer as isolated from American society (a recurring theme in American studies). The difference is that whereas Winters repudiated romanticism and its legacy, Chase (and many theorists of American literature) works within a romantic tradition. For example, Winters *blamed* individual writers for their retreat from social and moral concerns, while Chase and many after him *sympathize* with the sensitive artist, alienated by the crass materialism of American society. Similarly, whereas Winters criticizes the allegorical mode of perception, Chase finds in it a new American romance genre peculiarly suited for exploring unresolved contradictions and discontinuities in American culture. The point is that Winters and Chase bring similar models to bear on the same writers and the same works, however opposed they may be in their evaluations.

Chase's distinction between the novel and the romance lies in 'the way in which they view reality.' American literature is defined by its free and loose rendering of reality, its 'abstract and ideal' conception of character, and its tendency to 'veer toward mythic, allegorical, and symbolistic forms' (p. 13). These definitive elements in American literature, Chase feels, result from three 'historical facts.' Two of these, man's solitary spiritual position in this country and 'the Manichean quality of New England Puritanism' (p. 11), explain American literature's tendency toward the romance rather than the novel. He argues that although American fiction 'is historically a branch of the European tradition of the novel, . . . it is the better part of valor in the critic to understand American romances as adaptations of traditional novelistic procedures to new cultural conditions and new aesthetic aspirations' (p. 14) that he identifies with American Puritanism. Chase uses his historical analysis to respond to Tocqueville, D. H. Lawrence, F. R. Leavis, and Winters, all of whom thought 'that the American novel [was] sick' and wanted to cure it (p. 9). Chase's project, in short, is an attempt to justify an American tradition founded by the Puritans. For Chase, the fact that American literature does not render social reality closely and critically is not only explained by its historical and cultural moment but represents its greatest contribution to the European novelistic tradition.

Both the negative and the positive views of Puritanism's

alleged abstract and allegorical reality have remained powerful constants in American literary criticism. When, in *The Power of Blackness* (1958), Harry Levin attributed what he saw as the nightmarish quality of American literature to the allegorical influence of Puritanism, the argument was already standard. Levin restates the familiar idea that Puritanism decisively subjectified religion: 'Revelation was no longer based upon dogma, but upon the mystical intuition or the poetic insight that could scrutinize the welter of appearances and discern the presence of hidden realities' (Levin 1958, 14). Levin also uses the familiar argument that 'American fiction sprang from religious allegory, a form which gave ample scope to the moralistic impetus' (p. 20). And Levin comes to the familiar, if vague, conclusion that 'a period of revolutionary storm and romantic stress' (p. 20) encouraged religious allegory and channeled it into dark, gothic romance. Limited as it is to Hawthorne, Poe, and Melville, Levin's study advances no exaggerated claims about American literature as a whole, but to describe even these three authors so exclusively in terms of their gothic and supernatural elements is perforce to exclude large masses of their work. Moreover, since he claims that a morbid fascination with blackness defines American literature more accurately than any social and material concerns could, Levin, like Miller and others, minimizes the importance of the social and realistic, as opposed to the psychic and internal, sides of Puritanism and American literature.

Though Leslie Fiedler's eroticized approach in *Love and Death in the American Novel* (1960) is in many ways strikingly original, it is characterized by the same use of allegorical dichotomies; gothic/sentimental, God/Devil, Fair Maiden/Dark Lady are some of his pivotal distinctions. According to Fiedler,

> The final form of Protestantism is Puritanism, whose basic mode of perception is allegorical and to which the sexes are therefore emblems of salvation and damnation. To the mid-eighteenth-century bourgeois, the male is *per se* the tempter, and the female *per se* the savior; it is as simple as that.
>
> (Fiedler 1960, 67–8)

Fiedler, of course, offers his own variations on the dominant theme, stressing, like Levin, the nightmarish quality of the

American mind, but also adding Freudian and Jungian sexual motifs to the picture: 'The original Puritan impulse had represented an extreme revulsion from Mariolatry, an absolute refusal to give the feminine principle its due' (p. 78). Elsewhere, Fiedler claims that American writers have polarized American women into 'Fair Maidens' or 'Dark Ladies,' or, more simply, into virgins or whores. In order to Americanize this cliché, Fiedler argues that 'the puritanical sense of conflict in the black and white melodrama of the *Sonnets* must surely have appealed to the Shakespeare-soaked Romantic writers of the nineteenth century' (p. 297). But Fiedler's basic view of the Puritan mind as allegorical and subjective is that which has characterized Puritan origins theories since the earliest practitioners first applied those inadequate labels.

Although their evaluations differ, Winters, Chase, and Fiedler agree closely in their descriptions of Puritanism. They all assume Puritanism was highly subjective and allegorical, even if they disagree on the value of these traits. Their Puritan world is a literary world, their history a literary history, and their American literature a relatively small group of writers. This overemphasis on ideas in defining and determining Puritan culture leads many critics to misconstrue major tenets of Puritanism. For instance, Winters, Chase, and Fiedler equate Puritanism with an allegorical worldview, stressing its subjective, antinomian strain as the basis of Puritanism's 'dreamlike' quality. Chase is representative when he allegorizes and simplifies not only Puritanism but all American culture, reducing complex cultural formulations to a group of mythic dualities:

> The American imagination, like the New England Puritan mind itself, seems less interested in redemption than in the melodrama of the eternal struggle of good and evil, less interested in incarnation and reconciliation than in alienation and disorder.
>
> (Chase 1957, 41)

Of these three critics, Winters alone substantiates his reading with references to specific Puritan ideas; all, however, treat theological abstractions as though they existed above Puritan society.

We can better understand how these recent critics' limited

vision of Puritanism influences their theories of American literature by studying their remarks on *The Scarlet Letter*. While
Winters grants that *The Scarlet Letter* 'is one of the chief masterpieces of English prose' (1938, 3), he spends the bulk of his
discussion on the flaws of Hawthorne's allegorical method
and his confused, characteristically romantic, moral stance.
According to Winters, *The Scarlet Letter* is a 'pure allegory' in
which Hawthorne, like the Puritans, reduces morality to dualistic categories. For Winters the novel is a study of sin in which
'Hester represents the repentant sinner, Dimmesdale the half-
repentant sinner, and Chillingworth the unrepentant sinner' (p.
16). Winters believes this to be an adequate description of
Hawthorne's plan for the story:

> Once Hawthorne had reduced the problem of sin to terms as
> general as these, and had brought his allegory to perfect
> literary form, he had, properly speaking, dealt with sin once
> and for all; there was nothing further to be said about it.
>
> (p. 16)

We have seen that Winters regarded Puritan notions of predestination and free will as cripplingly inconsistent, and since
he believed that Hawthorne's treatment of Hester is indicative of the Puritans assuming that 'any sin represented all sin'
(p. 20), we can see how Winters regarded Hawthorne's entire
conception of the novel as flawed. The drama is reduced to
melodrama, confused and excessive.

Winters also criticizes what he defines as another of
Hawthorne's novelistic procedures, 'the formula of alternative
possibilities,' which Hawthorne utilized to create an aura of
uncertainty around certain characters and events. This technique, illustrated by the townspeople's varying reactions to
what Dimmesdale reveals when he bares his chest in the final
scene, indicates, for Winters, how Hawthorne was prevented by
his Puritan heritage from developing a literary method of
determining the significance of an event or of rendering 'physical presence with intensity' (p. 20). This facet of Maule's curse
Winters associates with the Puritans 'looking for signals in
nature so long and so intently' that they became transfixed by
their own obsessions. Winters also argues that Hawthorne had
the capacity for dramatizing abstract conceptions, but not for

criticizing and organizing them, another flaw traceable to Maule's curse. Winters's main point through the discussion is that Hawthorne's Puritan heritage and his romantic intellectual environment deprived him of both the stable ethical and moral points of view from which to understand human experience. Winters's reading of *The Scarlet Letter*, then, centers on these four objections: it is too subjective; it presents characters or events without any specificity; Hawthorne is incapable of criticizing the conceptions he dramatizes; and, most important, it is 'pure allegory.' New England Puritanism is to blame for each of these flaws.

Though writing in a positive register, Chase and Fiedler describe *The Scarlet Letter* in much the same allegorical terms. For Chase, although the novel is 'not pure allegory,' it is 'a novel with (generally speaking) beautifully assimilated allegorical elements' (1957, 75). Whereas Winters had understood the novel as a study of the effects of sin, Chase views it as an externalization of Hawthorne's aesthetic sensibility:

> Chillingworth, Dimmesdale, and Pearl can be conceived as projections of different faculties of the novelist's mind – Chillingworth, the probing intellect; Dimmesdale, the moral sensibility; Pearl, the unconscious or demonic poetic faculty. Hester is the fallible human reality as the novelist sees it – plastic, various, inexhaustible, enduring, morally problematic.
>
> (p. 79)

While the characters are, for Chase, akin to archetypal figures, 'the symbols do not cohere until they have been made into projections of the faculties of the artistic mind and elements of a quasi-puritan allegory' (p. 79). Both Winters and Chase idealize the theme of *The Scarlet Letter*, interpreting the book as either moral or psychological/aesthetic allegory while missing Hawthorne's historical and social interests.

Like Winters's and Chase's, Fiedler's interpretation of Puritanism's influence on *The Scarlet Letter* emphasizes the allegorical and antinomian:

> Hawthorne's gestures at indicating the social backgrounds and historical contexts of his characters are half-hearted and unconvincing, a bow toward realism. And his book is finally

dream-like rather than documentary, not at all the historical
novel it has been often called – evoking the past as nightmare
rather than fact.

(1960, 51)

Fiedler regards passion as the central theme of *The Scarlet Letter*;
placing it in a Freudian context, he claims it is a 'book produced
out of the anguish of personal failure and the death of a mother'
(p. 237).

The allegorical perspective revealed by these critics' readings
of *The Scarlet Letter* has continued to dominate literary
approaches to Puritanism. Such unanimity should not, however, deter us from reevaluating the adequacy of this approach.
Recent historical and literary scholarship has been revising,
and often discarding, these assumptions by refocusing critical
attention on the material and social reality of Puritan culture.
In fact, the historical revision was well under way by the forties
and fifties with the early work of Edmund Morgan, Bernard
Bailyn, and other materially minded historians. In the course of
this shift, the long-standing scholarly search for a national
identity, characteristic of many theories of American literature,
has come under attack. To put it briefly, these approaches tend
to abandon holistic theories of cultural development and to
deny the primacy of ideas in determining history, revising them
with material, economic, and political analyses of smaller cultural units, minority groups, and towns. Much of the literary
work we have been discussing is superseded by these developments. I do not mean to suggest that literary critics need to
become rigorous historians. When literary interpretations
are predicated on unsound historical analysis, however, the
accuracy of a critic's historical theory becomes an important
consideration.

Historians have demonstrated that the social element in New
England was at least as important, if not more so, as strictly
religious thinking. Edmund Morgan's *The Puritan Dilemma*
(1958) deals with the social motivations for many seemingly
religious decisions during Winthrop's tenure as governor.[3] In
his earlier work, *The Puritan Family: Religion and Domestic Relations in Seventeenth-Century New England* (1944), Morgan demonstrated the pre-eminence of social, especially familial, relations

in Puritan thought. While discussing the domestic terminology in which Puritan religious rhetoric was often couched, Morgan goes so far as to suggest that 'the Puritans' religious experience in some way duplicated their domestic experience' (Morgan 1944, 166).[4] In *Wayward Puritans* (1966), Kai Erikson speculates about the social motivations and results of some major events in Puritan history, such as the antinomian crisis and the Pequot War, which have traditionally been cited as evidence for the allegorical mentality of the Puritans. And, more recently, in *American Puritanism* (1970), Darrett Rutman calls attention to the distortions caused by focusing primarily on Puritan theology. Rutman acknowledges that religious themes pervaded New England, but hastens to add that

> to pervade is not necessarily to dominate. There are economic, political, esthetic themes in the seventeenth century as well as religious, and if religion pervades these other themes, it does not follow that it dominates them.
>
> (Rutman 1970, 5)

The important point is that many Puritan origins theorists have not adequately understood just how Puritan ideas and rhetoric reflect specific social needs and produce certain results.

In Winters's case, this bias affects his understanding of specific tenets of Puritan theology as well. Winters repeatedly stresses the Puritan denial of freedom of the will and of the efficaciousness of good works; however, historical analysis suggests that the Puritans' social practice denied, or at least qualified, such theological dogma. For instance, Edmund Morgan, a student of Perry Miller, approaches Miller's concept of convenant theology in concrete terms, arguing that it emphasized voluntary and contractual participation in both religious and social matters.[5] Morgan also points out how the Puritans' educational philosophy disproves the view that the Puritans denied the importance of good works:

> For a people who believed in predestination and the absolute sovereignty of God the Puritans ascribed an extraordinary power to education. By the instruction of parents, they believed, a child could be led away from the evil to which he was naturally prone.
>
> (Morgan 1944, 94)

In *Their Solitary Way: The Puritan Social Ethic in the First Century of Settlement in New England,* Stephen Foster discusses Cotton Mather's Franklinesque program of good works, similarly reorienting our understanding of Puritanism:

> Mather's main labors for social regulation lay outside the church entirely, in the creation of a purely secular organization independent of either civil or ecclesiastical authorities though cooperating with both. The need to increase good works justified such a step in Mather's view. *For all their insistence on salvation by faith alone, Puritans had never slighted good works.*
>
> (Foster 1971, 62; italics added)

In asserting that the Puritans denied only that good works could suffice as determinants in an individual's salvation, these historians argue that the Puritans realized the dangers of relying exclusively on conduct, and that in this matter (as in their doctrine of 'weaned affections,' for example) they practiced caution and moderation, trying, through scrupulous examination, to determine the authenticity of any claim to justification. Thus, while Puritan doctrine is often radically otherworldly, and while Winters correctly points out some logical contradictions in Puritan thought, it is a mistake to assume either that these paralyzed rationality or that the Puritans inhabited an allegorical world. These common misconceptions simplify Puritanism, after the fashion of Miller, by separating ideas from reality. The Puritans, it seems, did separate this world from the next and did balance religious dogma with social necessity; most of Puritan life was lived this side of eternity. In so far as they make Puritan religious doctrine decisive or fail to locate it in a precise social context, Puritan origins theorists distort the actual reality of Puritanism. I draw on recent historical writing not to invoke a naive distinction between historical truth and literary (or critical) fabrication. Puritan history is, of course, still being written and debated, but these insights do help fill out a more realistic picture of Puritan culture by reminding us that the Puritans, too, lived in a complex social world and that their ideas are inseparable from their lives in that world.

As we have seen, these critical readings of *The Scarlet Letter* correspondingly attenuate its social significance by emphasizing its allegory and the isolated individuality of its characters. Chase, for example, defines 'character' in American literature in decidedly asocial terms: 'In a romance, "experience" has less to do with human beings as "social creatures" than as individuals. Heroes, villains, victims, legendary types confronting other individuals or confronting mysterious or otherwise dire forces – this is what we meet in romances' (1957, 22). Elsewhere, Chase adds,

> We are asked by [American] novelists to judge characters, not by measuring them against socially derived values, but by their adherence to an idea of conduct which is personal, intuitive, and stoic, and which, though it may come round to the universal values of Christianity and democracy, does so without much social mediation.

(p. 160)

Winters, Chase, and Fiedler each de-socialize *The Scarlet Letter*, analyzing it as an abstract study of the effects of sin on three individuals (Winters); as 'projections of different faculties of the novelist's mind' (Chase); or as a work 'produced out of the anguish of personal failure and the death of a mother' (Fiedler). *The Scarlet Letter* does, of course, examine the ravages of sin and guilt; it can be read in terms of psychological projections; and it may reflect Hawthorne's personal traumas. But defining the novel and its place in the history of American literature in terms of one theme simplifies not only the work as a whole, but the theme as well. For example, even if Hawthorne were not interested in the social context of sin (which, in *The Scarlet Letter*, he was), critics should none the less address the social and religious relationships which give sin its force. Moreover, by concentrating so narrowly on the individualistic implications they draw, these critics simplify the novel's social world (including the social pageants that frame it), the importance of political and religious power, and the way in which each of the main characters' identities is materially determined and maintained. For instance, Dimmesdale is prevented from confessing his sin as much by the community's view of him as by his own inherent weakness. In the case of a work such as *The Scarlet Letter*, which at first seems to spend an inordinate amount of narrative time in the minds of its protagonists, such an investigation of a social setting may be difficult, but it is no less necessary than it would be for so predominantly social a novel as Wharton's *The House of Mirth* or Chopin's *The Awakening*. By defining the work's social significance so simplistically, though, a critic like Chase seems to bring a social analysis to the novel while actually de-socializing it with mythic dualisms.

By subjectivizing *The Scarlet Letter*, these theorists also ignore or neutralize its commentary on a specific cultural era. In *Versions of the Past: The Historical Imagination in American Fiction*, Harry Henderson suggests that *The Scarlet Letter* derives much of its intensity through its dramatization of the moral and psychological implications of critical transitions in Puritan history, especially John Endicott's coming to power. Henderson feels that Hawthorne's strength was twofold: 'In addition to giving a new dimension to the characters of historical romance, *The Scarlet Letter* relates their tragedy to the inner history of New England's cultural disaster' (Henderson 1974, 125). Henderson examines the work as a historical meditation on competing Puritan views of history, arguing that 'the *dramatis personae* are . . . in large measure defined by their own attitudes toward history' (Henderson 1974, 124). Rather than diminishing the importance of individuality, a work such as Henderson's actually reconstitutes subjectivity on a higher plane by demonstrating that character is never simply subjective but is typical of specific social and cultural moments. These need not be the only areas of significance in *The Scarlet Letter*, but they do need to be incorporated into a theory of American literature which attempts to situate individual authors and texts in a historical and cultural configuration.

By defining Puritanism and *The Scarlet Letter* as pure, or semi-pure, allegory, Winters, Chase, and Fiedler miss the complexity of the relationship between Hawthorne's allegory and his realism. But, in fact, *The Scarlet Letter* and much of the Hawthorne canon, especially his short fiction and his realistic journals, subordinate allegory to the service of a criticism of American history. Intent on criticizing or praising the Puritan allegorical vision and its persistence in American literature, Winters, Chase, and Fiedler do not distinguish between pure allegory and the use of allegorical techniques for a broader purpose. In *Hawthorne's Historical Allegory* (1971), John Becker properly stresses the importance of distinguishing between the allegories within the narrative and Hawthorne's critique of them. *The Scarlet Letter* is to a large extent a study of characters imprisoned by their own, others', and society's allegorical definitions of their roles. According to Becker, 'Hester is allegorized by resistance to the Puritans. Chillingworth is reduced to an allegorical demon by his own moral choice. Pearl is allegorized by Hester' (Becker 1971, 106). Becker also includes Dimmesdale in this web of allegories, arguing that 'his deepest battle is very like [Hester's]: somehow to fight free of the allegorical vision which makes him a saint as it makes her a sinner' (Becker 1971, 117).

The Scarlet Letter, then, can be understood as a criticism, not an exemplification, of what Hawthorne regarded as a dehumanizing extreme in Puritanism. After all, throughout the work Hawthorne criticizes that alleged Puritan allegorization of experience which equates any sin with all Sin, and which denies what Winters calls the 'patient study of the minutiae of moral behavior.' The formula of alternative possibilities rejected by Winters because it deprives Hawthorne of a critical perspective on his materials, and praised by the others for its anticipation of modern perspectivism, actually serves a critical function. Hawthorne socializes the idea of knowledge through his use of this technique, and this is true in the case of the scarlet letter 'A,' the dominant example of Puritan signification which ostensibly allegorizes Hester's being. Hawthorne fills the novel with a plethora of interpretations of the 'A' which, far from degenerating into pointless perspectivism, unsettles the stable allegorical vehicle and tenor and subverts the Puritan autocracy's simple allegorical equation of 'A' with adultery, thus de-allegorizing and humanizing Hester's being and moral complexity. As the 'A' gradually accrues greater ranges of meaning and represents a variety of positive senses, so does our understanding of Hester and other characters in the novel. The same could be said of Melville's 'Doubloon' chapter in *Moby-Dick*, in which the different responses to the gold piece socialize and complicate, rather than undermine, the meaning of the doubloon, the chapter, and the novel.

Thus any approach to American literature which defines that

literature as essentially allegorical needs to transcend a strictly epistemological analysis of allegory and integrate a pursuit of what is allegorized, how, and why. For Hawthorne, allegory was a strategy for depicting social, religious, and moral reality, for reflecting psychological states, modes of perception, or systems of social relationships. As Becker says, Hawthorne

> saw allegorically, but he saw, as well, the damage that a naive allegory could do to the human person; and he used the allegorical mode to expose the distortion. He does not blur the distinction between allegorical and realistic characterization. He sees that allegorization is an actual phenomenon of human psychology, and that insight transforms his own allegory into a kind of superior realism.
>
> (Becker 1971, 109)

Along these same lines, Richard Brodhead goes so far as to compare *The Scarlet Letter* to major works of nineteenth-century realism:

> The central place that Hawthorne gives to the presentation of individual life as lived within the context of a particular social group and historical moment . . . links *The Scarlet Letter* to such far flung cousins as *The Red and the Black*, *The Mill on the Floss*, and *Anna Karenina*.
>
> (Brodhead 1976, 50)

The differences among these novels may well outweigh the similarities, but the notion of allegory as a 'superior realism' enables us to grasp the potential complexity of Hawthorne's meditations on American history.

In the 'Custom House' preface to *The Scarlet Letter*, Hawthorne himself balances the real and ideal in his theory of the romance. Comparing the tone of his romance to that of 'moonlight in a familiar room' with the familiar room representing the actual and moonlight the moral imagination, Hawthorne adds·

> Therefore, the floor of our familiar room has become a neutral territory, somewhere between the real world and fairy-land, where the Actual and the Imaginary may meet, and each imbue itself with the nature of the other.[6]

Hawthorne wants to maintain the balance between actual and ideal, history and imagination. Chase grants the balance implied in Hawthorne's theory, but he interprets the 'neutral territory' of Hawthorne's romance as 'a kind of "border" fiction; . . . the field of action is conceived not so much as a place as a state of mind – the borderland of the human mind where the actual and the imaginary intermingle' (p. 19). But Chase and others miss Hawthorne's deeper fusion of the actual and the ideal by projecting it outside of civilization ('between civilization and the wilderness'), and thus simplifying the complex interpenetration of actual and ideal, self and society, and fact and fabulation, not just in Hawthorne's work, but in many forms of fictional representation. One need not deny the allegorical or romance element in Hawthorne's work, or turn him into Zola in order to argue that any study of Hawthorne's achievement needs to account for his fusion of allegory, historical commentary, and realism. The readiness of critics to simplify or ignore the social significance of American literature reminds us of Norman Foerster's charge that American criticism, not American literature, is culpable for the apparent one-dimensionality of American writing.

Puritanism as rhetoric: Sacvan Bercovitch

The most provocative recent attempts to understand the impact of Puritanism on American thought are Sacvan Bercovitch's *The Puritan Origins of the American Self* (1975) and *The American Jeremiad* (1978). Bercovitch's project – these two works and the study he promises on the age of Emerson – is essentially a study of American ideologies. Critical of the American exceptionalist rhetoric he traces to its Puritan origins, Bercovitch attempts to expose the origins and the components – factual as well as fictional – of its hold on the 'American imagination.' An analysis of the origins of a distinctive American exceptionalist ideology, *The Puritan Origins of the American Self* casts new light on the question of Puritanism's influence on both the American Self and on American literature. Taking Mather's biography of John Winthrop as his focus, Bercovitch reconstructs the tradition of Puritan typology which Mather both accepts and inverts in the course of his *Magnalia Christi Americana*. According to

Bercovitch, Mather transformed the Puritan exegetical practice which interpreted secular history in light of the soteriological history of the New Testament. In order to define Winthrop as 'Nehemias Americanus,' however, Mather first had to interpret America itself as a sacred geography and to transform both America and American history hermeneutically, after the fashion of biblical figural exegesis. Bercovitch asserts that this hermeneutical inversion fused three entities – self, America, and American history – into one interchangeable complex that, in Mather, takes on the ultimate symbolic function of sacred prophecy and fulfillment of that prophecy.

The most important ramification of Mather's redemptive vision of New England is the corresponding invention of the American Self as an intermediate (between figure and fulfillment), corporate identity, fusing self with geography and history. The equation of the self with both America and the prophetic design of American history both universalizes and sanctifies (and thus inflates as well) the American Self, from which Bercovitch claims it is a logical step to later forms of American exceptionalism as diverse as Emerson's and Whitman's concepts of the representative American and the imperialistic rhetoric of manifest destiny. In other words, the self embodies America and American history, taking on the significance and scope of each. This constitutes what Bercovitch maintains is a 'distinctive symbolic mode,' and 'an emphatically American design,' a genre of auto-American biography, 'the celebration of the representative Self as America, and the American self as the embodiment of a prophetic universal design' (Bercovitch 1975, ix and 136). Bercovitch cites Hawthorne's Endicott, the hero of Franklin's *Autobiography*, and Natty Bumppo as representative examples of this American Self: 'These cases are very different from one another, but all three confirm American selfhood as an identity in progress, advancing from prophecies performed towards paradise to be regained' (p. 143). Bercovitch stresses the subjective, even solipsistic, implications of Mather's rhetoric, discovering therein the origins of America's fascination with both the meaning of America and the American Self.

Throughout his study Bercovitch attempts, as, he argues, did the Puritans, to balance the subjective with the social, the ideal with the real, and prophetic history with social history. Yet just as the particularities of space and time in Mather's work blur into an abstract 'composite ideal' and, in Mather's biography of Winthrop, 'the actual magistrate expands into an abstraction' (p. 5), so, in Bercovitch, does an interest in the social and political importance of the Puritan concept of self yield to a fascination with the decidedly atemporal, asocial, idealized rhetoric of Cotton Mather. At various times, Bercovitch refers to the Puritan Self as 'the invention of expatriate idealists who . . . proceeded, in an implicit denial of secular history, to impose prophecy upon experience,' as 'a giant effort at cohesion and control,' and he asserts that 'the palpable social effects' of this rhetorical strategy argue 'the importance of ideology (in the Marxist sense) in the shaping of the United States' (pp. 133, 186). But how are we to regard these 'expatriate idealists'? Did their effort at 'cohesion and control' survive? What is the importance of ideology? These questions are not pursued and their implications are left, for the most part, unstated.

Furthermore, while Bercovitch stresses both Mather's and his own attempt to do justice to the historical dimension of their subjects, his efforts in that direction serve strangely (even to one sympathetic to his work) to reinforce the subordinate status of actual, or literal, history, both for Mather and himself. Bercovitch claims that 'as *figura* Winthrop remains rooted in history,' that Mather's use of typology 'turns our attention to ordinary, temporal, geographical facts,' and that Mather's 'perspective on the supernatural future reveals the actual movement of history' (pp. 39, 58). But these claims lose their force as Bercovitch repeatedly recounts how even the most specific historical allusions in Mather 'blur the specific into a composite ideal,' how Mather's insistence on details 'forces them into the framework of the ideal,' and how 'history is invoked to displace historicism' (pp. 4, 5). Bercovitch might well have grappled with the apparent disjunction between Mather's rhetorical constructions and the historical facts they are intended to displace. Even if Mather blurs history into prophecy, however, Bercovitch's critical analysis of Mather's rhetorical method could better resist the centrifugal pull away from social history, perhaps replacing the historicism that Mather displaced.

Two more recent studies of Mather revise Bercovitch's reading on these grounds. In 'Cotton Mather and the Meaning of Suffering in the *Magnalia Christi Americana*' Karen Halttunen remarks that literary historians, Bercovitch included, 'have directed scholarly attention to Mather's literary techniques, and, in their efforts to place the *Magnalia* within broad historiographical and literary traditions, . . . have generally overlooked the immediate historical context of Mather's work' (Halttunen 1978, 312–13). Halttunen's reading posits a much closer (and less abstract) connection between Mather's subjects, his immediate historical context, and the *Magnalia* (Halttunen 1978, 315). David Levin's biography of Mather similarly reminds us that

> if *Magnalia Christi Americana* is epic, prophecy, 'auto-American-biography' [to use Bercovitch's phrase], jeremiad, hagiography, it is all these by virtue of being what Mather plainly intended it to be, a history. It is Mather's historical imagination and his fidelity to the historical record that justify the *Magnalia*'s continuing survival.
>
> (Levin 1978, 254)

Arguing that 'Mather was essentially a faithful historian, both in questions of fact and in interpretation' (Levin 1978, 255), Levin draws convincing connections between Mather's writings and their historical and social functions. If Levin is correct, Bercovitch exaggerates Mather's imaginative formulation of the symbolic American Self at the expense of the more literal significations of the *Magnalia*. What we should ask, it would seem, is *how* Mather's figures signify Puritan history, not how they escape it. For all their abstraction, Bradford's, Johnson's, Edwards's, and Mather's histories need to be read both literally and as metahistories, not just for their rhetoricity but for the signifying powers and mimetic strategies of that rhetoric. In other words, we should begin, not end, with Mather's rhetorical inversions.

Bercovitch's analysis deals primarily with American history and the American Self as symbols or myths. In his preface Bercovitch states that he believes 'the rhetoric of American identity' to be a 'central aspect of our Puritan legacy' (p. ix), and

throughout his book his interest in rhetoric and Puritan hermeneutics competes with his declared social interests. As the
title of his final chapter implies, it is 'The Myth of America'
which concerns Bercovitch, and he repeatedly resorts to figurative language in order to define both Mather's rhetorical
construction of America as well as the persistence of that
construction in the popular and literary mind as symbol, myth,
act of imagination, or mode. Bercovitch claims Mather asks us
'to consider American identity as a rhetorical (rather than a
historical) issue.' While Bercovitch labels this 'the furthest and
most audacious extension of colonial Puritan hermeneutics' (p.
132), he none the less defines subsequent American literature as
an extension of Mather's audacious rhetorical gymnastics. As
Alan Trachtenberg, among others, points out, Bercovitch's
study

> hoists Mather and the Puritans to the front ranks of American
> imaginative writers, as the inventors of a 'distinctive sym-
> bolic mode'; it hoists writing itself to a foremost position as a
> determining historical force; it lays claim to a Puritan basis
> for American romantic writing, which is as much as to say all
> subsequent writing of any significance; and it claims that the
> inner substance, the essential content of all significant Amer-
> ican writing is (virtually by definition) America itself – that
> is, America as an idea of selfhood, or the writer himself as
> America.

(Trachtenberg 1977, 461)

It is in his literary analysis of American history, his equation of
literary history with American history in its entirety, his virtual
textualizing of the American past and the American Self that
Bercovitch's study idealizes the very notion of America, after
what Bercovitch feels to be the fashion of Mather himself. It is
this, perhaps, that Nina Baym has in mind when she accuses
Bercovitch of 'writing an ahistorical form of literary history'
(Baym 1979, 352).

In this respect, Bercovitch extends Perry Miller's elevation of
mind over matter to a further extreme. Puritan ideas take on a
life of their own. That America or the American Self as Mather
developed it and Bercovitch explicates it may well be more an
imaginative construct than a literal fact seems likely, but defin-

ing America exclusively in symbolic terms and then granting those terms a primacy in literature and culture as a whole draw our attention away from the production and reproduction of the very ideology which mythicizes the meaning of America to begin with. For instance, how and why did such a conception of America gain such strength? Does it have 'radical' as well as 'conservative' implications? How have its various manifestations reflected different tensions in American culture? Who has projected and benefited most from such a mystification of American history and culture? And, most important for literary studies, how have writers treated the myth of America and American selfhood?

Bercovitch touches on some of these questions, but he does not really get beyond the myth to its origins or to its social ramifications. He so concentrates on the signifying form of Mather's vision that the content of that 'myth of America' seems less significant. To be sure, Bercovitch informs the reader that his subject 'is the development of a distinctive symbolic mode,' and that he has centered his analysis 'on the interaction of language, myth, and society, in an effort to trace the sources of our obsessive concern with the meaning of America' (p. ix). But even so narrow a definition of his project should not enable Bercovitch to define Puritanism and the massive power he attributes to its influence without more than passing reference to Puritan society as a whole. Bercovitch defines Puritanism, as did Miller and Winters, predominantly in terms of its religious and literary rhetoric without adequately relating that rhetoric to its social origins and functions. Since Puritan writers, especially the ministry, responded to their social settings in intricate and varied ways, a study of the persistence of an American 'symbolic mode' should analyze not only its setting in different periods but how the mode opposed or supported other elements in American society as well. Richard Lovelace stresses the necessity of grasping Mather's religious rhetoric in its social context:

> Considering, then, the pastoral origins of English Puritanism and the continuing freight of practical theology even in its systematizers, it is not surprising that Cotton Mather, who was by calling not a theologian but a pastor and evangelist,

would revert to the pure practicality of the original Puritanism, *subject as he was to an undeniable pull toward what was
pastorally marketable, what was useful for the edification of his people.*
(Lovelace 1979, 40; italics added)[7]

, To argue merely that the Puritans identified themselves with
America and justified their corporate identity and mission in
prophetic terms does not, in itself, do much to reveal the
dynamics of such rhetoric at any specific time. To study myth as
myth, without noting how it works, is a static procedure; it
overlooks the fact that the content coexists in time and space
with its expression. As Trachtenberg comments:

> We never see how the rhetoric works to enforce orthodoxy . . .
> nor do we see the content, the specific social vision embedded
> (perhaps disguised) in the rhetoric. . . . Any analysis of an
> idea or mode which functions ideologically must take the
> social reality into more than rhetorical account.
>
> (Trachtenberg 1977, 472–3)

Bercovitch's view of Cotton Mather as exemplary Puritan
casts further doubts on his claims. Levin's biography of Mather
stresses the degree to which both Increase and Cotton were in
fact part of a minority faction struggling against a rising tide of
change within New England society. Larzer Ziff remarks that
'Cotton Mather's peculiar unrelatedness to his society was
recognized by many in his time,' and he refers to the *Magnalia* as
'the greatest monument of clerical withdrawal from the political
scene,' as 'a work symbolic to the point of caricature,' and as 'a
monument to the alienation of the intellectual from a society
that no longer regards his interests as vital' (Ziff 1973, 216–17).
Bercovitch does acknowledge that Mather's 'myth is essentially
projective and elite, the invention of expatriate idealists' (p.
133). But then, by way of justifying both Mather's choice and
treatment of his subject, Bercovitch reminds us that

> mythographers tell us that the heroic 'super-individual'
> provides a model of tribal identity, and that mythic rituals,
> by reenacting the exploits of the patriarchs, transform bio-
> graphy (in Lévi-Strauss's phrase) into 'a form of history of a
> higher power than itself.'
>
> (p. 134)

Such remarks hardly justify defining the Puritan origins of the American Self in terms of Mather's hermeneutical inversion of Puritan typology. They rather evade the very questions Bercovitch asks. Mather's historical situation was the Puritan declension, when his image of America had already failed, primarily because it had lost both its religious and political potency in the face of insurgent economic interests.

What this points to is that Mather and many of the subsequent American literary spokesmen Bercovitch discusses have expressed their alienation from American society by means of a subjective, abstract, and nostalgic notion of America, immune to material changes and cultural contradictions. Many writers, including Mather, substitute imagination for experience and hardly reflect an informed awareness of American society as a whole or even their relationship to society. To be sure, in his remarks on the contradiction between private vision and public reality in Mather's and Emerson's thought, Bercovitch asserts that 'the most misleading commonplace of recent criticism is that our major literature through Emerson is Antinomian,' and he argues that the Puritan origins he has described are emphatically 'against "mere Antinomianism."' 'Emerson's hero, like Mather's Winthrop,' Bercovitch counters, 'derives his greatness from the enterprise he represents.' This claim, however, is undermined by the next sentence: 'Despite [Emerson's] distaste for, and fear of, the mass of actual Americans, he did not need to dissociate himself from America because he had already dissociated the mass from the American idea' (pp. 174–6). The crucial distinction here is between 'the actual America' and the 'American idea.' Bercovitch defines Mather's vision and its continued power over American expression in quintessentially antinomian terms, abstracting the individual from society and internalizing the American idea so thoroughly that it verges on solipsism. Although Bercovitch is himself sensitive to the subjectivism inherent in the American Self as he defines it, he does not offer a coherent and sustained criticism of it. And although he is right in maintaining that American literature has a tradition emphatically against antinomianism, his own attempt to demonstrate that element repeatedly calls attention to just the subjectivism he wishes to deny.

In fact, though Bercovitch would like to reject the equation of
New England with America, he actually reinforces it; his American tradition is the standard New England tradition *par excellence*: 'In retrospect, it seems clear that the Puritan myth
prepared for the re-vision of God's Country from the "New
England of the type" into the United States of America' (p. 136).
He explicitly asserts, 'the myth of America is the creation of the
New England Way' (p. 143). Besides Mather, the only American writers Bercovitch discusses in any detail as representatives of the American Self are Edwards, Franklin, Emerson,
Hawthorne, Melville, Thoreau, and Whitman, the suggestion
being that alternative American traditions have played little
part in forging American Selfhood. Those settlers in New
Sweden, New Amsterdam, Maryland, Virginia, and the Old
South as well as the Spanish settlers of the New World all exist
outside of and 'opposed to the hermeneutics of Puritan American identity' (p. 139), primarily because of their supposed
cultural adherence to the Old World. For example, the 'newness' of more mercantile colonies 'meant dependency or at most
imitation of the parent country' (p. 137). As a result, Bercovitch
claims Americans with African, Asian, Southern and Eastern
European origins and those of other religious origins fall outside
of representative American Selfhood. While such exclusions do,
perhaps, conform to the rhetoric of some major American
romantic writers, Bercovitch presses the implications of his
study into the twentieth century where their applicability to
modern American culture is dubious.

Bercovitch does address some of these ideological issues more
squarely in *The American Jeremiad*, at once an extension of his
typological reading in *The Puritan Origins of the American Self* and
a departure from it. *The American Jeremiad*, in fact, foregrounds
the political implications of jeremiad rhetoric, as well as the
complexity and resilience of that rhetoric's endurance. Whereas
The Puritan Origins of the American Self had left many such issues
implicit, *The American Jeremiad* addresses them head on. Bercovitch clarifies his focus on the practical, political impact of
Puritan rhetoric immediately: 'Myth may clothe history as
fiction, but it persuades in proportion to its capacity to help men
act in history' (Bercovitch 1978, xi). Bercovitch reveals the
ability of jeremiad rhetoric to help men act in history by creating

a myth that imaginatively conflates religious and political issues, transforming even the most despairing and critical energies into an essentially affirmative discourse. The American jeremiad, Bercovitch suggests, emerged as early as Winthrop's famous 'Model of Christian Charity' and was refined by both Mather and Edwards, and emerged in predominantly political guise as an effective political discourse during the American Revolution. Bercovitch claims that the rhetoric of the jeremiads – at once both despairing and affirmative – operates as a nearly impervious ideological vehicle assuring a powerful consensus within the confines of middle-class American political hegemony.

Bercovitch traces the endurance and ambidexterity of jeremiad rhetoric to its ability to allow for critics as diverse as Winthrop, Danforth, Mather, Edwards, the forgers of the American Constitution, Emerson, Thoreau, Melville, and even Hawthorne to mount criticisms, even condemnations, of American society while at the same time drawing on the ideals (largely mythic) of the American past and affirming the goals of the American future. These 'rituals of consensus,' as Bercovitch terms them, seem to deny (make unnecessary is, perhaps, more accurate) any perspective beyond one already inscribed within the fluid parameters of a nationalistic and patriotic discourse. Even our classic writers, many of whom wrote as cultural outcasts crying in the wilderness rather than as officially sanctioned apologists for America, 'labored against the myth as well as within it . . . [and] felt, privately at least, as oppressed by Americanism as liberated by it' (p. 179). The crucial move within the development of the jeremiad as a distinctive American ritual was performed in the eighteenth century by the 'Yankee Jeremiahs' who, as '"providence" itself was shaken loose from its religious framework to become part of the belief in human progress,' shifted the focus of figural authority by fusing biblical history with American experience, substituting a national and regional past for a biblical past, and translated typological fulfillment from sacred history into a 'metaphor for limitless secular improvement' (pp. 93–4). This complex maneuver closely resembles what Bercovitch early defines as the Puritan origin of American Selfhood and depends on an extension and adaptation of religious rhetoric to suit contemporary social pressures. It is this dynamism that Bercovitch attributes to jeremiad rhetoric that constitutes *The American Jeremiad*'s greatest contribution. What had appeared as a notion of the American Self that existed only in a relatively static, mythic realm is now more fully historicized, subjected to social pressures and scrutinized under changing forms. For instance, in a particularly trenchant passage, Bercovitch sums up the political advantages of the union between religious rhetoric and social strategy:

> Surely a major reason for the triumph of the republic was that the need for a social ideal was filled by the typology of America's mission. As this was translated into the language of the times, it provided what we might call the figural correlative to the theory of democratic capitalism. It gave the nation a past and future in sacred history, rendered its political and legal outlook a fulfillment of prophecy, elevated its 'true inhabitants,' the enterprising European Protestants who had immigrated within the past century or so, to the status of God's chosen, and declared the vast territories around them to be their chosen country. The rhetoric of trial provided moral support for the Federalists' emphasis on depravity. The concept of American revolution transformed self-reliance into a function not only of the common good but of the redemption of mankind. In virtually every area of life, the jeremiad became the official ritual form of continuing revolution. Mediating between religion and ideology, the jeremiad gave contract the sanctity of covenant, free enterprise the halo of grace, progress the assurance of the chiliad, and nationalism the grandeur of typology. In short, it wed self-interest to social perfection, and conferred on both the unique blessings of American destiny.
>
> (pp. 140–1)

Bercovitch traces the dynamism underwriting this American ritual into the writers of the American Renaissance, where his analysis illuminates some perplexing problems in new ways. Granting the same polarities that cultural theorists such as Richard Chase and Leo Marx identify as at the heart of American culture (see chapter 3 for my treatment of these critics), Bercovitch offers his own reading of the ambiguities of

American experience. For Emerson, America 'symbolized a state of soul, a mode of civic and moral identity, a progressive view of history, and a distinct but flexible concept of elect nationhood' (p. 183). Emerson was not, of course, a simple apologist for America's emerging middle class – 'he was often its severe critic. But his jeremiads were couched in terms that reaffirmed the basic tenets of the culture' (p. 184). Thoreau, too, existed in an ambivalent symbiosis with his neighbors: 'What makes *Walden* part of the tradition of the jeremiad is that the act of mimesis enables Thoreau simultaneously to berate his neighbors and to safeguard the values that undergird their way of life' (p. 186). For Melville, Ishmael embodies his quarrel with America, 'Ahab his quarrel with what America symbolically represents. The result is an irresolvable paradox which, pressed to its end, invalidates all terms of discourse' (p. 193). Henry Adams's *Education* fits in as it 'reverses all the effects of the jeremiad while retaining intact the jeremiad's figural-symbolic outlook' (p. 195). Summing up the pervasiveness of this paradoxical form, Bercovitch concludes:

> Whether the writer focused on the individual or on history, whether he sought to vindicate society or to ingest society into the self, the radical energies he celebrated served to sustain the culture, because the same ideal that released those energies transformed radicalism itself into a mode of cultural cohesion and continuity.
>
> (p. 205)

The American Jeremiad pushes Bercovitch's work to its furthest-reaching historical, social, and literary implications and is an achievement the subtlety, depth, and sensitivity of which signals a new direction in Puritan origins scholarship. Bercovitch is synthetic in his approach and committed to an ideological analysis of American literature. The importance of *The American Jeremiad* is clear – Bercovitch has identified 'the bond between [Puritan] rhetoric and its social consequences' that David D. Hall has called for and has focused his insights on the development of American literature, ostensibly through the early twentieth century, but with applicability to contemporary American culture as well.

The urgency and breadth of Bercovitch's contribution should

not, however, deter us from observing some of the limitations that qualify his work. Some assumptions and tendencies that informed *The Puritan Origins of the American Self* do, in fact, exert residual pressures on *The American Jeremiad*. For one, Bercovitch has again restricted his inquiry to a relatively élite circle of thinkers and writers – to 'our classic writers' (p. 179) – most of whom shared a homogeneous social perspective (Ann Douglas has dealt similarly with these writers in *The Feminization of American Culture*, where she traces their rhetoric and thematics to their eroding social base). In the case of 'our classic writers,' American criticism has demonstrated nothing if not the resonance of the writings of the American Renaissance, their ambiguities, their dualistic thematics, their ambivalence toward American popular culture. Bercovitch's claim that they represent an extension of the blend of despair and affirmation characteristic of early jeremiads seems, in this light, less original – more historical, to be sure, but similar to views expressed by D. H. Lawrence, Leslie Fiedler, Lionel Trilling, Richard Chase, and Leo Marx, all of whom stress the ambivalence of American literary language and the unresolved contradictions informing American culture. This is not to deny Bercovitch either his case or its importance, only to contextualize his work within the parameters of other theorists of American literature. It is Bercovitch's evaluation, not necessarily his description, of American literature that is different. But he, like most other theorists, has formulated a theory whose strength is mitigated by the small and homogeneous field of writers he accounts for.

A remark in Bercovitch's epilogue presents a different problem. 'To be American for our classic writers,' Bercovitch claims,

was by definition to be radical – to turn against the past, to defy the status quo and become an agent of change. And at the same time to be radical as an American was to transmute the revolutionary impulse in some basic sense: by spiritualizing it (as in *Walden*), by diffusing or deflecting it (as in *Leaves of Grass*), by translating it into a choice between blasphemy and regeneration (as in *Moby-Dick*), or most generally by accommodating it to society (as in 'The Fortune of the

Republic'). . . . In every case, the defiant act that might have
posed fundamental social alternatives became instead a
fundamental force against social change.

(pp. 203–4)

Bercovitch here outlines a perplexing conundrum, one capable
of effectively paralyzing critical thinking, but one which imputes a static political essence in American literary texts. To
argue that texts posing radical social and political alternatives
to the American status quo have been co-opted or diffused by
particular modes of consumption, by popular culture at large,
or by a critical community which itself deflects their radical
thrusts would cast these issues in a different light. What
Bercovitch grants, however, is an autonomous political essence
within the artifact itself, a political being that denatures its own
radical intent. Such an imposition actually de-socializes and
de-historicizes any given text's participation in a complex of
exchange (between, say, writers and readers of similar or
different historical epochs or different class perspectives) as well
as its referential status, which might be as complicated as
Hawthorne's 'Young Goodman Brown' or *The Scarlet Letter*,
both of which fuse cultural criticism of two specific eras – their
putative Puritan settings as well as Hawthorne's own social
milieu. Bercovitch denies literary works a multiplicity of recep-
tions by granting them a reified and impervious political message, which deconstructs itself. In this sense, Bercovitch too falls
into the same trap he claims American writers have been caught
in. His own approach, ostensibly oppositional toward the
pervasive 'rituals of consensus' he claims characterize American literary production, fails to mount an effective critique
because, while claiming to expose a dynamic and potent ideological brace for middle-class hegemony, he actually reinforces
that brace by lending credence to the idea of a one-dimensional
literary tradition that denies the possibility of a truly adversary
tradition within the American texts he discusses.

Both of these biases result in Bercovitch articulating a vision
of Puritanism and of the influence of jeremiad rhetoric as
seemingly stable, omnipotent, and impervious to contradictions. The vision may be accurate. But a number of variables
capable of weakening the hold of Puritan rhetoric over the

American imagination would have to be taken into account to verify its power. There have been, of course, scores of writers outside the canon of 'our classic writers' whose works cannot be domesticated by the jeremiad. While Ralph Ellison may fit, Richard Wright does not. Neither Theodore Dreiser nor Upton Sinclair seems caught in the web of paradoxes and ambiguities that Bercovitch claims denatures 'radical' American writers. In other words, writers of diverse ethnic, racial, and ideological perspectives may or may not fit Bercovitch's paradigm, but his canonical study doesn't account for their views. One would also like to see Bercovitch address the question of how and why the jeremiad rhetoric became so compatible with the interests of an American middle class. Were they always wed, as Max Weber might suggest, or did middle-class hegemony appropriate an existing rhetoric to fit its own interests? If so, could such an act of appropriation conceivably be conscious and intentional? If, as Perry Miller might claim, early American Jeremiahs cried out against a 'rising generation' of settlers more interested in catching cod than in worshiping God, how were they (and other elements of the American population – minorities, immigrants, women) seduced by a rhetorical complex originally formulated as a defense against their threats to theocratic hegemony?

The American Jeremiad breaks important ground for Puritan origins theorists. Bercovitch has situated Puritan rhetoric both historically and politically. What remains now is to free his inquiry from its narrowly canonical bias, its positivistic notion of literary politics, and to forge a critical method capable of elucidating the adversarial elements that may not be compromised by the ambiguities of jeremiad rhetoric.

Many of the problems of traditional Puritan origins theories of American literature stem from the tendency of theorists to interpret Puritanism as a monolithic entity. This idea of Puritanism makes several questionable assumptions: that American Puritanism is so different from the European Reformed tradition, especially in England, as to constitute an origin for a distinctive American mode; that American Puritanism is a unified body of thought and belief, and as such remains intact in later eras; and that the subsequent history of American culture and literature can be traced exclusively from the New England Puritans, at the expense of the literary production from different geographic, religious, and ethnic traditions. In *Puritanism in America*, Larzer Ziff casts doubts on the validity of such massive claims for Puritanism's influence:

> I would not want ... to be misunderstood as offering a modern version of the silly theory that the real history of America is the history of the spread on the continent of Anglo-Saxon habits and Anglo-Saxon ideals. The influence Puritanism exerts on modern life is great, but it is far from exclusive, and I here say so explicitly.
>
> (Ziff 1973, xi)

Most Puritan origins theorists, however, stray beyond Ziff's cautious assessment.

In order to substantiate their claims, Puritan origins theorists have to depict New England Puritans as revolutionaries who broke from the European tradition to invent America. Thus, Bercovitch, for example, ignores non-Puritan settlers on the ground that they were too derivative, too tied to the Old World way. At least two historians have questioned whether they were. Darrett Rutman offers extensive support that it was actually Virginia and the southern colonies that broke from English social forms, while New England was not only 'traditional within the English norm,' but, for a while, actually 'more traditional in character than English society itself' (Rutman 1970, 47, 73). Dealing more specifically with Puritan theology, David D. Hall argues that the differences between American Puritanism and European Reformed theology have been exaggerated by many scholars, especially Perry Miller; the two traditions 'were essentially congruent, if not identical' (Hall 1971, 41). Each of these claims should encourage us to look more skeptically at just how 'American' New England Puritanism actually was.

The assumption that Puritanism was a coherent and unified body of beliefs has similarly been called into question. Historians have recently stressed the difficulties and distortions in the general definitions of Puritanism we have seen Miller, Winters, Chase, Bercovitch, and others using. Both Rutman and Hall stress the limitations of narrow ideas of 'the New England mind' in light of more recent discoveries of differences within Puritanism arising from the variety of social sources and consequences of Puritan beliefs. T. H. Breen warns historians and critics against the tendency 'to homogenize early American culture, to stress common elements that prepared for later events' (Breen 1980, xvi, xi). He shows that Puritan cultural assumptions varied, often drastically, in relation both to settlers' geographic origins in England and to social positions. Emphasizing these differences within what is too loosely called 'Puritanism,' Breen states that 'the Puritanism of a person who left East Anglia in 1637 was different from the Puritanism of one who sailed in 1630 or 1642. The point is clearly that we should define as closely as possible the *specific context* of migration' (Breen 1980, xiii–xiv).

Finally, the many attempts to derive the whole history of American literature from New England Puritanism suggests the provinciality and narrowness of the American canon as defined by many theorists of American literature. By locating the roots of American literature in generalized notions of New England Puritanism, Winters, Chase, and Bercovitch restrict their studies for the most part to those writers and texts that can be read in the allegedly idealized terms of Puritan theology, its allegorical worldview, or its symbolic denial of actual American experience. This procedure simplifies and de-socializes both Puritanism as a specific cultural phenomenon and the subsequent history of American literature.

Marcus Klein's *Foreigners: The Making of American Literature, 1900–1940* (1981) offers a convincing alternative to the disturbing narrowness in Puritan origins theories. Drawing on research by John Higham, Oscar Handlin, and others, Klein points out that

> it was in the beginning of the last quarter of the nineteenth century, contemporary with the New Immigration, that American public spokesmen began to fashion ideology from the idea that America had an essential ethnic identity, namely Western-European and, more specifically, Anglo-Saxon or Nordic or English-speaking. The idea was romantic and fragile, but it came to have the force virtually of public policy.
>
> (Klein 1981, 20)

Klein's own theory of American literature inverts many Puritan origins ideas, arguing that a consolidated America did not emerge until the latter part of the nineteenth century. Klein also claims that the bold announcements of the 'new American' by such observers as Crèvecoeur, Emerson, and Whitman were little more than rhetorical posturings with little relevance to actual American society or selfhood. In fact, he argues, 'children of the Mayflower tended to invent Western culture, and children of the immigrants tended to invent America' (Klein 1981, x). Many critics, however, too readily take the rhetorical posturings for social truth without analyzing them in a social context. If, as Klein suggests, the entire search for Puritan origins is implicated in an ideologically charged defense of Anglo-Saxon, English-speaking American identity, we need a fuller cultural and social analysis of American literary criticism.

What is needed is a fresh approach to American Puritanism and its later influence, an approach capable of integrating religious, historical, political, and sociological research into literary investigation. Our Puritan origins theories are still paradigm-bound, reflecting the biases of different interpretive communities, but they can be corrected by appeals to 'real' history, however open to debate and problematic that history is.

3
'Nothing that is not there and the nothing that is': cultural theories of American literature

Whereas Puritan origins theorists posit a strong *presence* – the Puritan allegorical vision or a Puritan rhetorical construct – as the enduring core of American literature, cultural theorists tend to define the continuity of American writing as an *absence*. Different theorists trace different absences; Lionel Trilling and Richard Chase, for example, assume that American culture is too thin to generate a tradition of social observation, while Leo Marx argues that American politics has not resolved the social tensions caused by technology sufficiently to enable American literature to wrestle with the aesthetic problems of modernization and technology. Cultural theorists all, however, tend to invoke Cooper, Hawthorne, and James, who variously bemoaned the lack of substance – of tradition and institutions – that made the job of American fictionists especially difficult. James's famous catalogue from *Hawthorne*, though tinged with some irony, is typical:

> The negative side of the spectacle on which Hawthorne looked out, in his contemplative saunterings and reveries, might, indeed with a little ingenuity, be made almost ludicrous; one might enumerate the items of high civilisation, as it exists in other countries, which are absent from the texture of American life, until it should become a wonder to know what was left. No State, in the European sense of the word, and

indeed barely a specific national name. No sovereign, no court, no personal royalty, no aristocracy, no church, no clergy, no army, no diplomatic service, no country gentle-men, no names, no castles, nor manors, nor old country-houses, nor parsonages, nor thatched cottages, nor ivied ruins; no cathedrals, nor abbeys, nor little Norman churches; no great Universities nor public schools – no Oxford, nor Eton, nor Harrow; no literature, no novels, no museums, no pictures, no political society, no sporting class – no Epsom no Ascot! Some such list as that might be drawn up of the absent things in American life – especially in the American life of forty years ago . . . .

A dizzying list indeed. Cultural theorists do not enumerate the supposed gaps in American culture so exhaustively, but they do assume two things: that American writers have adopted a variety of literary strategies – the romance and the gothic, among others – to compensate for their impoverished social existence; and that the supposed absence of such traditional social forms means that there is no readily identifiable society to which American literature refers. These critics draw on history, psychology, theology, and, to some extent, politics – all in trying to define that elusive, absent cause of American literature.

Unreality in America: Lionel Trilling

In *The Liberal Imagination* (1950) Lionel Trilling begins by observing V. L. Parrington's dominance of 'our conception of American culture' and proceeds to correct various misconcep-tions representative of Parrington (and progressive, 'liberal criticism' in general), seriously calling into question the re-ceived idea of 'Reality in America,' and entering a semantic war to determine the very definition of 'reality' (Trilling 1950, 3).[1] Trilling's alternate 'reality' proved compelling, dealing a death blow to the Parrington school of social criticism, and emerging from the fracas as the dominant interpretation of American culture and literature. In fact, Trilling instituted so significant a rupture in critical approaches to American culture that one historian has, borrowing Thomas Kuhn's terminology, labeled it 'a paradigm revolution' (Wise 1973, 223). Indeed, Trilling's notion of reality and his strategies for discussing it have exerted

a tremendous influence on cultural theories of American literature. David Hirsch, for instance, while critical of Trilling,
argues that 'such books as Richard Chase's *The American Novel
and Its Tradition*, Marius Bewley's *The Eccentric Design*, and Leslie
Fiedler's *Love and Death in the American Novel* would hardly have
been possible had not Mr. Trilling pointed the way' (Hirsch
1966, 420). Agreeing with Hirsch, Nicolaus Mills believes
'Lionel Trilling is responsible for initiating a series of critical
misreadings of American fiction' (Mills 1973, 6). Leo Marx,
too, acknowledges Trilling's theory of culture as crucial to his
own and others' theories of American literature (Marx 1964,
341–2). In order to understand the power of Trilling's thesis, we
will look first at his place in the transformation of American
historiography and then at his analysis of American literature.

Trilling occupies pivotal positions in both American historiography and literary criticism; his work reveals the extent to
which the two disciplines can be mutually reinforcing. In
American historical writing, Trilling, along with Reinhold
Niebuhr, is frequently cited as an early proponent of the liberal
consensus school. Briefly stated, the consensus historians (including Louis Hartz, Daniel Boorstin, Richard Hofstadter, and
literary historians such as Henry Nash Smith, R. W. B. Lewis,
and Perry Miller) represent what Gene Wise calls the counter-
Progressive strain in American historiography dominant from
about 1950 to about 1965. Wise situates the consensus school as
a relatively conservative and subjective hiatus between the
socially, economically, and politically oriented Progressives
(Parrington included) and the New Left (e.g., Christopher
Lasch and William Appleman Williams). The relationship
among these schools is complex, but a brief examination of the
Progressive and counter-Progressive views of 'reality' reveals
some important differences.

'Progress' is a key term in the Progressive/counter-
Progressive debate (Wise 1973, 83ff.). The arrangement of
American experience and the historical figures each school
lined up to support their readings reflect their respective
interpretations of progress and of the 'American experience.'
Important tenets of Progressive historiography include a com-
mitment to progress, a lineage of historical heroes such as Roger
Williams, Thomas Paine, and Andrew Jackson, who struggled

against reactionary interests in support of a future of ever-increasing democracy, an interpretation of American history as a conflict between progressive and reactionary forces, and a desire to unmask the material roots of conflict in class struggle, politics, and economics. The counter-Progressive, or consensus, historians, on the other hand, shared a deep suspicion about progress, about how or, indeed, whether it came about. In the wake of World War II, and in the midst of the cold war and a reassessment of Soviet Marxism (what many saw as Stalin's betrayal of Marxism's humanitarian potential), consensus historians substituted a model of history characterized by ambiguity, paradox, and irony for the Progressive (they would say naive) model of steady, linear progress. Their insistence that noble motives might result in perverse ends and that Americans often stumbled into their futures rather than marching confidently forward convinced the consensus historians that the Progressive model was too simplistic to grasp the undercurrents of history. How else could the Hitler-Stalin pact and the horror of a 'civilized' world murdering millions be comprehended? The 'representative men' for the counter-Progressives included such kindred souls as Crèvecoeur, Melville, and Henry Adams, all of whom presumably perceived the human complexity and the ambiguities beneath the affirmative surface of American life. More important for our study, counter-Progressives shared the Progressive desire to unmask the underlying forces in history, but to do this they effected two major alterations: (1) they replaced the Progressive dualistic line-up of historical forces with a triadic (sometimes called dialectical) model that postulated some 'middle landscape' which synthesized various oppositions, and (2) they rejected the materialistic emphasis on economics and politics for an analysis of culture, focusing on human expression in psychology, art, and literature. Whereas Progressives wanted to understand what, *in fact*, was the reality of history, counter-Progressives stressed the primacy of how people *felt* about reality and how their myths, images, and symbols dramatized these feelings. In other words, the human mind and its responses (aesthetic and otherwise) came to constitute 'reality' for the counter-Progressives. They transferred the grounds of reality from economic and political *systems* to human *psyches*.

It is this change that Wise suggests ushered in a new paradigm in which ambiguities were perceived as the norm of experience, not mere exceptions to a march toward progress. Either side, of course, presents too simple and schematic a view of reality, but each in some ways exerts residual influence on historical and literary thinking. The two sides lined up against each other largely on the force of such static oppositions between external/internal; material/psychic; reality/ideology. The validity of either position is open to question, but the counter-Progressive revolt against Progressive historiography signaled a new set of priorities with regard to not only what constituted reality, but how to analyze that reality as well.[2] Also aiding this overall shift was the degeneration of Progressive criticism into the 'cult of the proletarian' (what Trilling seems actually to be rejecting) leading to a general denigration of all 'social' literature and criticism not conforming to the new set of standards.

Lionel Trilling reflects these counter-Progressive priorities, especially the triadic model and the internalization of 'reality.' In doing so, he established a tradition of cultural theories of American literature and popularized a view of society characteristic of them. In essence, Trilling's shift in historical perspective presaged a general shift in aesthetic evaluation, an elevation of works which tended to see reality as an ambiguous fabric and a denigration of those which dealt frankly with social, political, and economic matters. The new view of reality led to a new evaluation of 'realism.' Protest was out, equipoise in.

Though not a New Critic, Trilling privileged such New Critical catchwords as ambiguity, paradox, and irony in 'Reality in America' (1950). He attacked the Progressive critical standards which had regarded Theodore Dreiser as a writer of the first rank and had reduced Henry James to a finicky stylist of dubious quality and little sense of reality. Ostensibly a discussion of literary quality, Trilling's essay turns out not to be a consideration either of Dreiser's clumsiness or of James's excellence as a literary stylist, but rather of each writer's conception of reality. Trilling inverts the naturalist scheme of values, in each case turning literary and critical attention away from public, social issues toward private issues of individual con-

sciousness. He is concerned with 'culture' as a group phenomenon, but defines that concept in rather privatistic terms, as
in the sense of an individual's being cultured.

The influential notion of 'reality in America' emerges not
only from Trilling's essay of that name but from 'Art and
Fortune,' 'Manners, Morals, and the Novel,' and 'The Meaning of a Literary Idea.' From these essays, later theorists of
American literature have drawn key definitions of American
character, society, and the relationship between American
literature and American reality. According to Trilling,

> The great characters of American fiction, such, say, as Cap-
> tain Ahab and Natty Bumppo, tend to be mythic because of
> the rare fineness and abstractness of the ideas they represent;
> and their very freedom from class gives them a large and
> glowing generality; for what I have called *substantiality* is not
> the only quality that makes a character great. They are few
> in number and special in kind; and American fiction has
> nothing to show like the huge, swarming, substantial popu-
> lation of the European novel, the substantiality of which is
> precisely a product of a class existence. In fiction, as perhaps
> in life, the conscious realization of social class, which is an
> idea of great power and complexity, easily and quickly
> produces intention, passion, thought, and what I am calling
> substantiality. The diminution of the reality of class, however
> socially desirable in many respects, seems to have the practi-
> cal effect of diminishing our ability to see people in their
> difference and specialness.
>
> (Trilling 1950, 262)

While Trilling offers some astute comments on the differences
between European and American styles of representation, he
actually reduces the sense of literature's 'reality' in two ways.
First, he implies that 'great characters' are *an* if not *the* central
focus of critical attention and of social reflection. No one could
deny that great characters (Trilling would also add Huck Finn
to his catalogue) contribute greatly to a work's power. To grasp
those characters out of their contexts, however, can only simplify their status as centers of forces and as agents in historical
and social dramas. Ahab may violate maritime law and abstract
himself from his crew and from his economic responsibilities,

but his stature is incomprehensible outside of those contexts he denies with Promethean scorn. Natty Bumppo, too, may live on the borders between civilization and the wilderness, and he may be more conversant in Indian tongues than in the King's English, but his 'glowing generality,' if such a phrase even approximates his roles within Cooper's fiction, is due precisely to his relationships, complex as they may be, to two cultures of immense solidity. Second, by defining these characters' greatness *as* their abstractness, their freedom from class, Trilling validates a reified notion of subjectivity, one that can be imputed to American fictional characters or to an individual's social existence, but which fails to account for the extent to which any person's identity is a construct within a specific social and historical complex.

Just as American characters depart from the specificity and realism of European conventions, so the American novel and the very ability of Americans to understand society, according to Trilling, diverge from European counterparts. In a famous passage, Trilling comments on the strangeness of the American novel:

> Now the novel as I have described it has never really established itself in America. Not that we have not had very great novels but that the novel in America diverges from its classic intention, which ... is the investigation of the problem of reality beginning in the social field. The fact is that American writers of genius have not turned their minds to society. Poe and Melville were quite apart from it; the reality they sought was only tangential to society. Hawthorne was acute when he insisted that he did not write novels but romances – he thus expressed his awareness of the lack of social texture in his work.
>
> (p. 212)

Trilling's thoughts on character and society converge in his concept of 'manners,' defined as 'a dim mental region of intention of which it is very difficult to become aware,' as 'a culture's hum and buzz of implication, . . . the whole evanescent context in which its explicit statements are made,' and as 'that part of a culture which is made up of half-uttered or unuttered or unutterable expressions of value' (pp. 205–6). This reality of manners consists of the 'manners and the attitudes toward manners of the literate, reading, responsible middle class of people who are ourselves' (p. 207).

It is in 'Reality in America' that Trilling's idea of 'reality' most clearly informs his evaluations of Dreiser and James, as well as his rejection of Progressive historiographical assumptions. Various sets of oppositions pervade 'Reality in America,' most revolving around the public/private antithesis that separates Progressive from counter-Progressive historians. Trilling opposes 'public document' with 'art that [is] complex, personal and not literal'; a conception of reality as 'immutable,' 'wholly external,' and 'irreducible' (none of which accurately describe either Parrington's or Dreiser's visions) is set against Trilling's implicit conception of reality as relative, paradoxical, subjective, and mysterious; social and political commitment are antithetical to aesthetic quality (p. 4). Accusing Parrington of a 'limited and essentially arrogant conception of reality,' Trilling identifies his adversary with 'the chronic American belief that there exists an opposition between reality and mind and that one must enlist oneself in the party of reality' (p. 10). It is important to note that, while Trilling would like to abolish this simple dualism of reality versus mind, his solution, the 'literary idea,' actually reinstates the same opposition, though on a subtler level.

Trilling's main point of attack seems to be Parrington's alleged belief in a simple, fixed, and given material reality (pp. 4, 12). Moreover, Trilling attributes these same flaws to Dreiser, contrasting this 'peasant' mind with his own Jamesian-inspired conception of a 'complex and rapid imagination . . . with a kind of authoritative immediacy' (p. 14). All these oppositions crystallize in Trilling's final paragraph, his death-blow to both Parrington and Dreiser:

> Whether or not Dreiser was following the logic of his own life, he was certainly following the logic of the liberal criticism that accepted him so undiscriminatingly as one of the great, significant expressions of its spirit. This is the liberal criticism, in the direct line of Parrington, which establishes the social responsibility of the writer and then goes on to say that, apart from his duty of resembling reality as much as possible,

he is not really responsible for anything, not even for his ideas.
The scope of reality being what it is, ideas are held to be mere
'details,' and, what is more, to be details which if attended to
have the effect of diminishing reality.

(p. 21)

One thing clear in this passage is that Trilling is on the side of
ideas, attacking Dreiser's and Parrington's trivialization of
them while trying to forge a more synthetic understanding
of 'ideas' and 'reality.' Trilling also feels that liberal criticism's
denigration of 'ideas' is the result of its overemphasis on 'the
social responsibility of the writer' and 'his duty of resembling
reality as much as possible.'

In this sense, Trilling represents an important departure
from some of the primitive formulations and simplistic corre-
spondences of early Marxist criticism. Trilling realized, I would
argue, the errors of a crude base/superstructure model and
attempted to forge a more sophisticated strategy for transcending static, dualistic models of reality and of literary reflection.
One might go so far as to posit Trilling as a forerunner of some of
the Frankfurt School work of Theodor Adorno and Herbert
Marcuse, especially of Adorno's idea of negative dialectics and
of Marcuse's critique of instrumental reason and of the violation
of human life by technological systematization. By repeatedly
championing the integrity of individual consciousness and the
complexity of social reality, Trilling verged on a critique of
ideology far ahead of his time. What he offers in schematic form
seems to be nothing less than a critical method which, though
never explicitly or systematically formulated, is capable of
comprehending the various strategies humans use for processing reality, for unscrambling the chaotic barrage of media
impressions which saturate our existences. Not reducible to an
opposition of 'reality' versus 'consciousness,' Trilling's focus
could have been on the interrelationships between self and
society. There is, of course, no reason to view ideas and a
writer's social responsibility as mutually exclusive (it is also
questionable whether Dreiser, Parrington, or any writer could
actually divorce the two). Of course, what is at stake for Trilling
is more than Dreiser's or Parrington's literary production. As
Mark Krupnick remarks, 'Trilling was not just responding to

the texts but to Dreiser's involvement in Communist propaganda campaigns in the thirties and the use that was made of him in the forties by Stalinist literary criticism' (Krupnick 1986, 67). It is possible to argue, then, that literary criticism and literary texts served as pretexts for Trilling's anti-Marxism. As such, Trilling's work is valid and interesting. It does seem more than a little paradoxical, however, for Trilling, a proponent of the apolitical 'literary idea' and opponent of any ideological thinking, to use literary criticism not as a politically neutral exercise of negative capability, but as oblique political criticism. As Krupnick suggests, such slippage would not have been out of character. In his discussion of Trilling's reading of James's *The Princess Casimassima*, Krupnick notes: 'It is certainly a brilliant performance, but it tells more about Trilling's preoccupations in the forties than it does about the novel that Henry James wrote. James's story is a plausible pretext but, finally, only a pretext for Trilling' (Krupnick 1986, 69).

Trilling's description of reality in American literature, while enormously influential, has been criticized on many fronts, frequently where his ideas seem most promising. Both David Hirsch and Delmore Schwartz attack Trilling's definition of American reality. Comparing Trilling's reality to that which Eric Auerbach identifies with the Homeric epic's life 'enacted only among the ruling class,' Hirsch feels that Trilling can conceive reality only 'from the vantage point of *haute culture,*' that such a 'reality' is a tacit reaffirmation of the status quo, and 'that it must content itself with the limited truth available through empirical examination of "social facts"' (Hirsch 1966, 427, 431). Elsewhere, Hirsch expands on this idea, noting that Trilling's stress on the representation of manners 'induces him to denigrate the artistic legitimacy of any other kind of representation of reality' and fosters a critical disregard of the social and physical world and of the 'ordinary facts of human existence' (Hirsch 1971, 36). Mark Shechner, too, criticizes Trilling's 'suppression' of historical and political considerations when he notes that Trilling's

> sensitivity to ideology and its effects, based as it was upon a belief in the primacy of thought, was bought at a price; here, as elsewhere, Trilling suppressed those dimensions of social

reality that progressive realism played up: the depression, the unemployment, the vicious labor battles, the advances of Fascism in Europe – in short, the general desperation.

(Shechner 1978, 12)[3]

Nicolaus Mills argues that Trilling 'laid the groundwork for seeing American fiction as romantic [and] its concerns as overwhelmingly idealistic,' and mounts an exhaustive critique of Trilling's genre criticism and its flaws, especially its exaggeration of the actual differences between English and American fiction and its distortion of American literature's relationship to reality.[4] These criticisms all underscore the relationship between Trilling's cultural and literary thought, especially by stressing the degree to which Trilling's cultural analysis concentrates on the buzz and hum of the middle class to the exclusion of a material analysis of social relations and of the relationships among economics, history, and consciousness. Trilling, like other consensus thinkers, is more concerned with what people say than with what might underlie that buzz and hum of implication, and he has defined the essence of reality in accord with that preference, a strategy particularly damaging for his arguably social project.

A more subtle bias in Trilling's thesis lies in his concept of a 'literary idea' and its implications for a theory of literary representation. Trilling's idea of the 'literary idea,' in addition to his explicit remarks on American culture and American literature's 'tangential' relationship to that culture, not only aligns him clearly with consensus historiography but also constitutes his position as a founder of the cultural theory of American literature to which Lewis, Chase, Fiedler, and Marx adhere.

Much of Trilling's polemic in 'The Meaning of a Literary Idea' is directed against New Criticism's glorification of literary autonomy, its attempt to purge literature of ideas. To the contrary, Trilling argues that 'the most elementary thing to observe is that literature is of its nature involved with ideas because it deals with man in society, which is to say that it deals with formulations, valuations, and decisions, some of them implicit, others explicit' (p. 282). In fact, in much of the essay's first part, Trilling refutes the autonomy theories of T. S. Eliot,

René Wellek, and Austin Warren, who, in their zealous defense of the autonomy of poetry, Trilling feels, in a Burkean moment, 'presume ideas to be only the product of formal systems of philosophy' and who, in their insistence on the 'indirection and the symbolism of the language of poetry,' forget that 'poetry is closer to rhetoric than we today are willing to admit' (pp. 287, 290). Trilling's defense of literature as a vehicle of rational thought and ideas, then, does mark an important departure from New Critical orthodoxy and attempts to forge a more coherent synthesis between text and world, between individual and society. However, as we noted in chapter 1, while Trilling (with many other theorists of American literature) does signal a break from formalist aesthetics, that break is far from complete. In the second part of 'The Meaning of a Literary Idea,' an essay in which Trilling tries to restore literature as a socially significant, cognitive form of expression, he inadvertently reinstates some crippling New Critical assumptions about what literature is and how it works.

Trilling's main thrust in the second part of this essay, dealing with 'the relation of contemporary American literature to ideas' (pp. 291–2), is to distinguish between 'ideas' and 'ideology' (by which he means dogmatic or programmatic writing), by way of privileging the former while condemning the latter. The essay's criticism of ideology takes much the same form as it did in 'Reality in America,' an attack on writers like O'Neill, Dos Passos, and Wolfe, whose intellects, Trilling argues, were not adequate to the difficulty of literary work. Their minds had been 'violated by ideas' (p. 299); they had succumbed to the cardinal sin of writing programmatic or ideologically committed literature, which falls beyond Trilling's definition of what literature should be. Trilling's 'literary idea' is a notion derived from Keats and Eliot and is similar to some New Critical tenets derived from their works.[5] According to Trilling, 'whenever we put two emotions into juxtaposition we have what we can properly call an idea.' And, in a similar vein, 'what comes into being when two contradictory emotions are made to confront each other and are required to have a realtionship with each other is . . . quite properly called an idea' (pp. 283, 298). Ideas in a literary work grant it an 'autonomous' quality which exceeds 'our powers of explanation' and enables us to have a 'living, reciprocal relation' (p. 294) with it. Writers whose works embody ideas 'have wisdom and humility about themselves' since 'they seldom make the attempt at formulated solution, they rest content with the "negative capability,"' and 'are not under any illusion that they have conquered the material upon which they direct their activity' (pp. 298–9, 297). 'Ideology,' on the other hand, is 'not the product of thought; it is the habit or the ritual showing of respect for certain formulas to which, for various reasons having to do with emotional safety, we have very strong ties of whose meaning and consequences in actuality we have no clear understanding' (p. 286). 'Intellectual passivity' invites violation by an ideology; intellectual strength rests in 'negative capability.'

The definition of the literary idea as the juxtaposition of antithetical emotions echoes I. A. Richards's and Cleanth Brooks's definitions of poetry in general, all stressing the paradox, tension, and ambiguity of the idea's linking of opposed terms. Also, like Eliot and some New Critics, notably John Crowe Ransom, Trilling fears 'that the intellect will dry up the blood in our veins and wholly check the emotional and creative part of the mind' (p. 286). Trilling, like Ransom in his defense of 'the world's body,' wants to protect the existential freshness of both life and literature from what he perceives as a world veering toward a new, mechanical reduction of human potential. Since ideology presumably threatens the living spontaneity and integrity of an individual or of a literary text, the work of a writer with an 'idea' to communicate (a writer whose mind has been violated by an idea) violates Trilling's literary standards by making a statement rather than exploring two opposed emotions held in poetic balance. The proper work of literature, then, transcends such criteria as right or wrong – Trilling's standards are, finally, formal rather than ethical:

> Intellectual assent in literature is not quite the same as agreement. We can take pleasure in literature where we do not agree, responding to the power or grace of a mind without admitting the rightness of its intention or conclusion – we can take our pleasure from an intellect's cogency, without making a final judgment on the correctness or adaptability of what it says.
>
> (p. 291)

We can, of course, recognize 'the power or grace' of a mind without being seduced by its morality or politics (however similar or different they may be from our own). Trilling's separation of intellectual assent from ideological consent or 'final judgment' is, however, too neat. Trilling's distinction of pleasure and either agreement or final judgment simply creates another strategy for fragmenting critical activity around arguably invalid poles.

This paradoxical balance of opposites which Trilling defines as the idea proper raises problems. It is clear that Trilling means to criticize simplistic ideas (ideology) just as he criticized Parrington's and Dreiser's simplistic conception of reality, and it would be difficult to fault him for those aims. But Trilling's literary idea not only fails to offer a coherent grasp of the relationship between literature and society, but treats the inquiry into – and possible resolutions of – social problems as nonliterary by definition. To offer solutions would imply some commitment, some belief that one knew some answers (or at least had some suggestions) to social or political questions; and that, to Trilling, is arrogant and ideological (liberal and literal), not literary. Literature's role is the balancing, not the resolving, of tensions. To balance opposing emotions, ideas, or what have you, is to place them beyond any resolution other than the static 'synthesis' of both A and B.

In *Lionel Trilling: Criticism and Politics* (1980), William M. Chace suggests that such a conflation of literary with social values is central to Trilling's work in general. Chace points out how Trilling subordinated material conceptions of society and history to events of the mind and the critical imagination: 'things of specific density fell away from [Trilling's] mind just as brute matter fell away from the minds of the symbolist poets who transmuted the everyday into the imperishable' (Chace 1980, 11). According to Chace, 'one feels always in reading Trilling that the political history to which he was responsive was one that had become abstract, coagulated, and general' (Chace 1980, 13). Furthermore, Chace places Trilling in his historical context in terms suggestive of the development of consensus historiography:

Trilling's disengagement from the 'particularism' and 'everydayness' of history issued also from another characteristic of

American intellectual life as conditioned by the 1930's. Though that life had experienced political optimism followed by political disillusionment, it had also made an alliance of sorts with the literary modernism exemplified by such ... figures as Proust, Eliot, Joyce, Kafka, and Mann.

(Chace 1980, 15–16)

Trilling's position is complex in its attempt to fuse literary and social thought and to correct simplistic definitions of right and wrong or of true and false by suggesting that, in reality, these oppositions partake of each other. Also, as I have mentioned, given Trilling's historical moment, the valorization of complexity, irony, and other values associated with modern literature were probably viewed as a possible counterforce for an emerging society in which technology, positivism, and media hype seemed to predominate.

But Trilling, at least in his early work, simplifies this realization by stopping at mere juxtaposition and satisfying himself with an intellectual stalemate, which he would have us believe is a type of dialectical literary resolution. Mark Krupnick provides a pertinent reading of Trilling's brand of dialectical thinking. 'It's important to see that Trilling makes no claim to be offering either a worked-out doctrine or a new position,' Krupnick offers;

> He stands coolly aloof from the enthusiasms of the intellectuals in order to recall them to what he takes to be old, timeless truths. His mind works dialectically, not as the Marxists understand the dialectic – to bring about historical change – but to keep the culture on a steady course and maintain an always threatened equilibrium.

(Krupnick 1986, 58)

Krupnick suggests that Trilling tactically redefined the term 'dialectic' to combat Marxist, especially Stalinist, appropriations of this crucial concept. However, a fundamental semantic problem remains. One might add that Trilling's dialectic is also not Hegelian, not a dialectic in any sense, if we take dialectic to imply tension and dynamism heading, because of inherent instability (philosophical or political), toward a new form of resolution or synthesis. The fact is that Trilling's dialectic is antithetical to such notions, functioning almost counter-dialectically as a tool for a kind of stasis – 'maintaining an always threatened equilibrium.' Trilling's simple rejection of the Parrington/Dreiser school in favor of Jamesian subtlety is a case in point. Rather than working through to a vision of reality (or strategy for representing it) that might accommodate both a Dreiserian and a Jamesian mode, Trilling opts for an easier and more contradictory polemic. He values negation for the sake of negation and contradiction for the sake of contradiction. He pursues neither the negative capacity of ideas to demystify ideals, nor the dynamism of a dialectical resolution to contradictions. He abstracts the notions of negation and of contradiction from the social and literary contexts from which they derive and then offers them as absolute values for literary production and evaluation. Literary ideas, then, are abstracted ideas whose beings are considered only in intratextual, formal terms, not in relation to the specific social and historical worlds of their genesis.

While Trilling's critical project, as Krupnick reveals, did have an implicit political program, it is offered in a manner consistent with Wise's outline of counter-Progressive historiography. Trilling transforms ideas into symbols and myths, freeing them from society and history and divorcing literary from social value. Summarizing the New Left's rejection of a Trillingesque juxtaposition of opposites, Gene Wise notes: 'Ambiguity in a novel – in, say, *Moby-Dick* or *The Great Gatsby* – might be a fascinating thing to watch and analyze. But ambiguity in social order usually works to someone's unmerited benefit, and someone else's undeserved injustice' (Wise 1973, 107). If Trilling's dialectic functions to maintain 'an always threatened equilibrium,' one must realize that such an equilibrium is itself a great paradox, resulting as it does in inequality and oppression. Such a dilemma may well have troubled Trilling deeply, may, for that matter, have inspired much of his work, but his literary theory does not adequately integrate social reality with literary value, and his literary evaluations reflect this discord.

Parties of one: R. W. B. Lewis

In *The American Adam: Innocence, Tragedy, and Tradition in the Nineteenth Century* (1955), R. W. B. Lewis focuses his cultural analysis on the issues of 'innocence, novelty, experience, sin, time, evil, hope, the present, memory, the past, tradition,' most of which, he claims, permeated the dialogue of American culture in the years subsequent to 1820, a dialogue that represents the 'contentious effort to define the American character and the life worth living' (Lewis 1955, 2, 3). Lewis is careful to admit that 'there may be no such thing as "American experience,"' but he also maintains that 'there has been experience in America, and the account of it has had its own specific form' (p. 8). Lewis's study is a sustained and coherent analysis of how the years following the War of 1812 looked to some American thinkers who grappled with the promise, the possibilities, and the hopes of a new culture in a new environment of seemingly boundless and relatively untouched nature. Appropriately, 'the major (if not the only) "matter" by which [American writers] have sought to advance their craft' is, for Lewis, 'the matter of Adam':

> a radically new personality, the hero of a new adventure: an individual emancipated from history, happily bereft of ancestry, untouched and undefiled by the usual inheritances of family and race; an individual standing alone, self-reliant and self-propelling, ready to confront whatever awaited him with the aid of his own unique and inherent resources.
>
> (Lewis 1955, 127, 5)

Lewis claims that three distinct groups participated in the cultural dialogue concerning this American Adam and labels them the parties of Memory, Hope, and Irony. However, the cultural 'dialogue,' Lewis demonstrates, was often not a dialogue at all, but two opposing monologues. He characterizes these extreme sides (the parties of Hope and Memory) as either 'the arrested development of infantile innocence' or 'the premature old age of a paralyzing absorption with sin,' poles elsewhere characterized as 'the hopeful and the nostalgic' and 'the idealists and the orthodox Calvinists' (pp. 60, 63). We don't learn much about the party of Memory in *The American Adam*. Jonathan Edwards's 'intolerably bleak conclusion' that any assertion of human oneness or unity 'must account for guilt and an evil taint on any individual soul, in consequence of a crime committed twenty or forty years ago, remaining still, and even to the end of the world and for ever' (p. 66), represents, however, something like a major plank in that party's platform. But, for the most part, this so-called party of Memory remains a largely unanalyzed and statically conceived counter to the party of Hope throughout Lewis's study.

The party of Hope, on the other hand, has numerous lucid campaigners, all of whom affirm the promise of the autonomous individual once freed from traditional constraints. Lewis's attitude toward the party of Hope is, perhaps, best captured in Henry James, Sr's descriptions of Emerson as 'his fair, unfallen friend,' and of Thoreau as 'literally the most childlike, unconscious and unblushing egoist it has ever been my fortune to encounter in the ranks of manhood' (p. 55). Lewis's critique of the party of Hope takes two forms. First, in Oliver Wendell Holmes, Lewis criticizes the naive faith in science. Dubbed 'the medicine man' by Lewis, Holmes believed that 'the realm of spirit could be overhauled by going about it in a scientific manner,' and asserted that 'science would provide the new religion and the new prophets and mediators; science would write the new testament and invent the new metaphors' (p. 37). Lewis rejects Holmes's displacement of religion with science, the rational, scientific optimism that enables Holmes to elide the moral complexity inherent in a religious perspective on life. Rather like Hawthorne's Aylmer in 'The Birthmark,' and much like Benjamin Rush, who in 'The Influence of Physical Causes upon the Moral Faculty' celebrated the promise of science to remake humans in the likeness of God, Holmes felt that science offers a panacea for issues that Lewis believes are more than skin deep.

While Walt Whitman voices comparable faith in the new science as well, Lewis argues that the poet's belief in infinite newness and an originary poetics capable of creating new worlds immune to those evils transmitted through history from the old is the second major weakness of the party of Hope. Terming Whitman's *Leaves of Grass* 'a Yankee Genesis: a new account of the creation of the world . . . with a happy ending for Adam its hero; or better yet, with no ending at all,' Lewis believes Whitman endows the creature with the role and powers of the Creator and propagates a 'new species of human' (pp. 45–6). The major problem in this newest testament, Lewis argues, is Whitman's simplistic reduction of human experience. As in Emerson's early assertion, evil, for Whitman, was privative, not a metaphysical force beyond human correction. His sea, unlike Melville's, had 'no sharks in it – no ancient, lurking, indestructible evil powers' (pp. 44–5). Even Whitman's catalogues of the violent, the grotesque, and the sordid are rendered one-dimensional affirmations of 'a particular beauty of a different coloration,' not of an evil that resists imaginative transfiguration (p. 48). In addition to his hope and his too-simple transcendence of evil, Whitman's poetry, Lewis feels, too quickly creates, like the poet's 'noiseless, patient spider,' new worlds 'out of itself,' rather than discovering the world out of which it emerges. Whitman stands alone (and this sense of solitude troubles Lewis), projecting a world that diminishes the forces of history and evil as well as the stature they lend to individual existence.

Despite charging both Holmes and Whitman with moral shortcomings, Lewis was also charmed by the optimism and force of their assertions, largely because he perceived them as necessary (and powerfully engaging) adversaries for his third party division, the party of Irony. Both the parties of Hope and Memory miss the essential drama of life. The party of Irony alone perceives the complexity of the issues and argues that hope and memory can't so simply be abstracted. Lewis notes that Henry James, Sr, for one, 'escaped the sterilities of both sides . . . by seeing the moral problem in unvaryingly dramatic terms: as a process, a story, with several grand climacterics' (p. 60). Lewis defines many of these complex thinkers primarily through their negations of the party of Hope's idealism. For example, whereas the hopeful believed that denying the Fall could render life more cheerful, Horace Bushnell 'was sure it succeeded in making it duller' by rendering life 'flat, colorless, undramatic, and boring' (p. 71). Similarly, Hawthorne

> was neither Emersonian nor Edwardsean; or rather he was both. The characteristic situation in his fiction is that of the Emersonian figure, the man of hope, who by some frightful mischance has stumbled into the time-burdened world of Jonathan Edwards.
>
> (p. 113)

Lewis puts the matter succinctly when he suggests that 'the party of Irony consisted of those men who wanted both to undermine and to bolster the image of the American as a new Adam. . . . Their aim was to enlarge. The shared purpose of the party of Irony was not to destroy the hopes of the hopeful, but to perfect them' (p. 193).

Throughout *The American Adam*, Lewis depicts the party of Irony as giving prose form to this dialogue that Lewis posits is definitive in mid-nineteenth-century America. What is impressive about Bushnell, Lewis suggests, 'is the dialectical power he brought to bear upon the contemporary discussion, a power which in fact helped to disclose the actual existence *of* a discussion' (p. 67). In similar terms, Melville's deep understanding of the nature of plot (the particular example Lewis cites is the several paragraphs culminating in the 'Catskill eagle' passage near the end of 'The Try-Works') stems from his 'poetic' (read: dialectical or triadic) grasp of narrative:

> Indeed, one way to grasp this passage and Melville's achievement in general is to notice that Melville is *not* posing static alternatives but tracing a rhythmic progression in experience and matching the rhythm as best he can in language. This is the way of a Platonist, and not of a polemicist; much more, it is the way of a poet. The best kind of poem is a process of generation – in which one attitude or metaphor, subjected to intense pressure, gives symbolic birth to the next, which reveals the color of its origin even as it gives way in turn by 'dying into' its successor. Such a poem does not deal in dichotomies but in live sequences.
>
> (p. 133)

Melville understands the nature of truth 'poetically' as well: 'Melville was increasingly sure that truth was double – that it was dialectical and contained, so far as any poet could utter it, in a tension' (p. 143). The historian Francis Parkman belongs to Lewis's party of Irony because he brought to his craft the dialectical skills of complex analysis: 'What interested him was the struggle, not its resolution; the quality and power of the assaults, not their conclusion. What interested him was struggle in general – as the condition of life' (p. 170).

Finally, whereas the excitement of this struggle had enlivened

the writing of the nineteenth century, Lewis concludes his study
by revealing the absence of any such dialectical vitality in the
American writing of his own time:

> The contemporary picture is not a dishonest one. It contains
> many remarkable and even irreversible psychological,
> sociological, and political insights. It seems to be the picture
> most clearly warranted by public and private experience in
> our time. But it remains curiously frozen in outline; it is
> anything but dialectical and contains within it no opposite
> possibilities on which to feed and fatten. In it irony has
> withered into mere mordant skepticism. Irony is fertile and
> alive; the chilling skepticism of the mid-twentieth century
> represents one of the modes of death. The new hopelessness
> is, paradoxically, as simple-minded as innocence; and it is
> opposed only by that parody of hope which consists in an
> appeal for 'positive thinking' – a willful return to innocence
> based upon a willful ignorance, momentarily popular in the
> market place of culture but with no hold at all upon the
> known truth of experience.
>
> (p. 197)

By virtue of its own dynamism, then, the nineteenth century,
even with its more naive assertions of either hope or despair, is
preferable to the twentieth century, where no ideas clash.
'Ours,' he mourns, 'is an age of containment' (p. 190), in which
we settle too quickly and simply for one-dimensional answers to
complex moral and cultural dilemmas. Thus, twentieth-
century literature's failure to sustain the irony/dialectic that
had provided nineteenth-century writers with 'opposite possibilities' that Lewis celebrates as 'fertile and alive,' and its
degeneration into the 'chilling skepticism' represents a crisis not
so much isolable in literary production, but of religious faith.
The simple-minded posture of 'positive thinking' (what Trilling
might define as 'ideological thinking') is, for Lewis, a 'substitute
for morality' (p. 197).

The religious bias of Lewis's study situates *The American Adam*
within the tradition of 'tragic vision' readings of American
literature, of which Roy R. Male's *Hawthorne's Tragic Vision*
is probably the greatest example. A 'fortunate fall' renders
Lewis's Adam as the essential type for American fiction.

Clustered around this notion are some of Lewis's central concerns:

> As a metaphor in the area of human psychology, the notion of the fortunate fall has an immense potential. It points to the necessary transforming shocks and sufferings, the experiments and errors – in short, the experience – through which maturity and identity may be arrived at.

(p. 61)

Lewis returns to these terms at crucial junctures in his discussion. As Horace Bushnell believed,

> Fortunately, . . . there had been a fall. Happily, there had been a sin. And consequently, there had followed the long story of educational experience. All of that experience was at the disposal of each new member of the race. The new member inherited the corruption, but he likewise shared in the wisdom. If he could never regain Adam's radical innocence, he need never regress to Adam's ignorance. Conscience was, after all, higher than innocence.

(p. 73)

Lewis appreciates Hawthorne's achievement in similar terms. The major action in *The Marble Faun*, for instance, is

> the transformation of the soul in its journey from innocence to conscience: the soul's realization of itself under the impact of and by engagement with evil – the tragic rise born of the fortunate fall. It is a New World action – my supposition is that it is *the* New World action, the tragic remainder of what Lawrence called the myth of America.

(p. 122)

Likewise, in *Billy Budd*, Melville introduces his vision of Christ-like innocence with a hopeful dawn (a 'glorious, glad, golden sun') and, at Billy's hanging, 'returns again to the dawn – but a dawn transfigured, "seen in mystical vision." Melville salvaged the legend of hope both for life and for literature by repudiating it in order to restore it in an apotheosis of its hero' (p. 152). Finally, at the conclusion of his discussion of Orestes Brownson and his stress on communion (in both the religious and the social sense), Lewis states his position most clearly. Communion, he claims, 'was the concern which, more than any other, linked together the varied members of [the party of Irony] in the dialogue of the day' (p. 192).

Several concerns link these statements with a host of others throughout *The American Adam*. Lewis focuses on the necessity and benefits of recognizing sin, on the experience through which sin is central to human culture, on the paradoxical perspective that such recognition throws on such notions as hope, the past, and the future, and, finally, on the 'maturity' (read: ironic detachment) of wisdom to which the fortunate fall gives birth. Lewis also affirms the necessity of maintaining a living tradition, reminiscent of Eliot's, which functions as a positive force for social coherence, even as it qualifies any hopes for radical human improvement. Crucial, too, for Lewis is believing that these are not *merely* literary matters, although he addresses only articulate, literary statements of this tragic vision of life. As in Melville, hope is salvaged 'both for life and for literature.' Like Trilling's readings of the American literary past, Lewis's also respond to the cultural currents of his own times.

What, then, are the implications of Lewis's study? It might appear that he works beyond the narrowly conceived canon and the relatively asocial tendencies of other theorists by insisting on the *cultural* dialogue concerning 'the matter of Adam.' This cultural context can also be seen as a strategy for socializing the idea of literary production, apprehending each voice in the complex and varied dialogue which Lewis documents so thoroughly. We can also be grateful to Lewis for illuminating a particular debate which clarifies not only the texts he cites, but other major works such as Melville's *The Confidence-Man* and Hawthorne's *The Blithedale Romance*, two texts which, to some extent, combat the affirmations of transcendental optimism. We need, however, to address a few ways in which Lewis's study *also* qualifies and limits its own claims, partially, I would argue, in spite of his own plans for *The American Adam*.

Lewis does address writers no other theorist of American literature accounts for, including Orestes Brownson, Henry James, Sr, Francis Parkman, and Robert Montgomery Bird, and he includes not only literary texts but scientific writing and religious theory as well. And he situates the dialogue he examines in a cultural context. However, as we shall see is the case for Leslie Fiedler, Lewis's stress on the mythic 'matter of Adam,' while provoking him outside traditional canonical parameters, still defines the territory of his study in rather limiting terms. I would not suggest that the omission of writers such as John Winthrop, Cotton Mather, Benjamin Franklin, or Benjamin Rush (all of whom fall outside of Lewis's chronological frame), or of writers like Edgar Allan Poe, Washington Irving, Harriet Beecher Stowe, or Frederick Douglass (all of whom fall squarely within that focus *and* who have significance for the themes Lewis pursues) necessarily undermines his thesis. However, given the fairly large claims for his study (Lewis *does* posit 'the matter of Adam' as the definitive American theme), it does seem a puzzlingly narrow range of writing. Perhaps, though, we should look more to 'the matter of Adam' itself with some suspicion. During a historical period characterized by such events as war with Mexico, two major bank failures (1837 and 1857), and a nation on the verge of splitting over the issue of slavery, one might suppose that any dialogue, even over 'the matter of Adam,' would necessarily engage such issues of national identity and international politics. And yet, nowhere in *The American Adam* does Lewis suggest that the cultural dialogue he isolates exists in any such cultural context. In fact, there is little, if any, mention of a world existing beyond the texts Lewis analyzes.

More important than the mere absence of diverse writers and of historical pressures that probably encroached upon even the most abstract considerations is the effect such absences have on Lewis's study. Take for instance his valorization of ironic balancing of opposed tendencies and of 'maturity' as definitive of the mental state common to the party of Irony. Lewis can offer maturity and ironic balancing as valued modes of thinking only by separating literary and critical production from the political and social turbulence that characterized both the mid-nineteenth and mid-twentieth centuries. Certainly Michael C. Colacurcio's recent study of Hawthorne (1984) and the Melville studies by T. Walter Herbert (1980), Carolyn Karcher (1980), and others offer eloquent and brilliant refutations of such assumptions. For all its stress on cultural dialogue, Lewis's work remains basically within the boundaries of literary themes and textual structures conceived apart from other areas of cultural practice and social significance. One needs to ask, finally, in what way Lewis means us to read his stress on dialogue and to what extent that notion of dialogue is capable of enlightening American culture, broadly speaking. Furthermore, Lewis presents each writer as more or less alone, not involved with other writers or thinkers, and certainly not members of a 'party' in the sense suggesting common affiliations or enabling any one writer's work to represent the others. For all the political implications of his terminology, Lewis distances his themes and the writers he studies from engagement with issues beyond their private thematics in so far as they relate to 'the matter of Adam.'

The authors Lewis privileges as ironists end up validating a common array of New Critical notions of irony, balance, tension, and ambiguity. It is finally the ironic perspectives of writers like Hawthorne, Melville, Parkman, and others rather than the affirmative thematic content of their work that Lewis regards as central. They exist, as, say, I. A. Richards would argue the language of poetry exists, to counter the scientific optimism of a Holmes or a Whitman by qualifying their scientific certainty and hope with a strong sense of skepticism based largely on religious assumptions of innate human depravity. Lewis's sense of cultural dialogue informs literary production in general. In essence, the party of Irony can be defined as those who still know the meaning of a literary idea in Trilling's sense, those who refuse to think ideologically or one-dimensionally and who resist having their minds violated by *an* idea, whether hopeful or nostalgic. In fact, Trilling's sense of dialectical thinking permeates Lewis's study, usually by being attributed to writers of the party of Irony as the complexity which separates them from their more limited contemporaries. The party of Irony, one might say, 'nothing affirmeth.'

The affinity between Lewis's and Trilling's ideas of dialogue and its centrality to literary thinking is strong in Lewis's description of his own method:

> The debate, indeed, may be said to *be* the culture, at least on its loftiest levels; for a culture achieves identity not so much through the ascendancy of one particular set of convictions as through the emergence of its peculiar and distinctive dialogue. (Similarly, a culture is on the decline when it submits to intellectual martial law, and fresh understanding is denied

in a denial of further controversy.) Intellectual history, properly conducted, exposes not only the dominant ideas of a period, or of a nation, but more important, the dominant clashes over ideas. Or to put it more austerely: the historian looks not only for the major terms of discourse, but also for major pairs of opposed terms which, by their very opposition, carry discourse forward.

(p. 2)

Like Trilling, Lewis envisions an ongoing, perhaps permanent, dialogue in which the ascendancy of any one set of terms or convictions signals trouble. He regards debate as cultural health. Again like Trilling, he resorts to fairly severe terms, 'intellectual martial law,' when speaking of any triumph within the debate-model he prefers. He does, however, imagine this dialectic moving *forward*, a stance that may distinguish him from Trilling, who regarded the function of his dialectic as, in Mark Krupnick's terms, protecting a delicate equilibrium, though this possible difference is, I suspect, more a rhetorical than an ideological matter. Whereas Trilling's dialogue operates *primarily* on the level of literary thinking, Lewis embeds his own dialectic within a habit of mind more precisely suggestive of religious thinking. The crucial similarity, however, is that for both Trilling and Lewis, a dialectical model is abstracted from the social sphere into the more private realm of individual consciousness and, thus, privatized as a mode of individual survival in a hostile world rather than culturalized in the broader sense.

Lewis comes close to making this explicit himself in *The Picaresque Saint* (1959). In that later work, while not nationalistic as he is in *The American Adam*, Lewis none the less suggests that the modern writer, like the modern literary character, 'tries to hold in balance . . . , by the very contradictions of his character, both the observed truths of contemporary experience and the vital aspiration to transcend them' (Lewis 1959, 31). Lewis's definition of the picaresque saint also echoes a statement by F. Scott Fitzgerald that Trilling quotes and that Mark Krupnick suggests could well stand as the epigraph for *The Liberal Imagination*. According to Fitzgerald, 'the test of a first-rate intelligence is the ability to hold two opposed ideas in the mind, at the same time, and still retain the ability to function' (Krupnick 1986, 68; Trilling 1950, pp. 245–6). Lewis's picaresque saint and Fitzgerald's/Trilling's 'first-rate intelligence' both resonate with the qualities Lewis had earlier attributed to his party of Irony as well as with various New Critical aesthetic preferences. Lewis, like Trilling, attempts to maintain a vision of 'the doubleness of things' (p. 24) by valorizing an ironic perspective that resists resolution. It hardly seems possible, however, that cultural critics writing after two world wars, two market crashes, and the Korean conflict could offer ironic balance, maturity, or personal survival as plausible responses to cultural conflicts without such a stance having important ramifications for their 'cultural' approach to American literature.

Lewis's place in American literary studies and some of the paradoxes of his work can, in part, be understood as manifestations of a so-called religious revival among intellectuals following World War II. *Partisan Review* considered the revitalization of religiosity significant enough to devote a year-long symposium to the issue of 'Religion and the Intellectuals' (1950). Many of the concerns voiced by the editors and the participants shed suggestive light on Lewis's work, not only on some of his major propositions but on the direction of his thought and its relationship to other cultural activity during the cold war.

'There is no doubt,' the *Partisan Review* editors claim in their introduction, 'that the number of intellectuals professing religious sympathies, beliefs, or doctrines is greater now than it was ten or twenty years ago, and that this number is continually increasing or becoming more articulate' (*Partisan Review* 1950, 103). To explore this phenomenon, the editors posed five areas in which they felt this religious revival was apparent and important, including questions concerning historical causes, the strength of religious convictions, religion and culture, religion and literature, and religious consciousness. Two topics the editors asked their contributors to address are of specific relevance for our study of Lewis:

1. From a naturalistic point of view, all events (including those of history) have their causes, and the present revival of religion would not be an exception. What do you think are the causes of the present trend? Is it due to the worldwide failure

and defeat of a real radical movement in politics? To a renunciation of hopes for any fundamental social improvement? Or to some kind of breakdown in the organization of modern society, to which religion would seem to supply a remedy? . . .

4. Religion and literature. The revival of religion has perhaps been most noticeable in the literary world. Does this imply some special dependence of the literary imagination upon religious feeling and ideas? Is the present emphasis upon myth among literary theorists connected with the renewed interest in religion?

(*Partisan Review* 1950, 104–5)

The suggestions that a return to religion may signal a retreat from social engagement or that myth criticism has a religious foundation are not, by any means, shocking. I do, however, feel that these topics and the contributors' responses to them (even in terms of provocative verbal echoes) illuminate some of Lewis's concerns and help account for his accomplishment in *The American Adam*, not simply as a retreat from social and political turbulence or from the failure of political programs, but also as a principled attempt to discover a 'usable past' at a time when the future itself was threatened. The editors' mention of 'a renunciation of hopes for any fundamental social improvement' *does*, I would add, place us squarely within Lewis's thematics.

James Agee, one of the participants in the *Partisan Review* symposium, cites the loss of confidence in science, in materialistic optimism, and in reason as three disenchantments that might 'ripen for conversion [to religion] intellectuals of various levels and temperaments' (p. 107). Agee's remarks on 'science' are especially pertinent. Science appeals to

those who have outgrown the still popular delusion that 'science' is potentially omnipotent – i.e., is God. Those who, more pathetically, have outlived the millennial glow of hope or certainty that ultimately, indeed pretty soon, Science would settle all the imponderables and solve all the problems of living.

(p. 107)

Without insisting on the matter, I would like to suggest that Agee's concerns, even his language, anticipate Lewis's critique of the scientific optimism characteristic of Holmes, Whitman, and other representatives of the party of Hope. According to Lewis, Holmes *had* attempted to replace God with science and *did* believe in science as a panacea for all the 'imponderables.' Lewis's own hope, it might be argued, is to protect those imponderables from being flattened by definitive answers. Agee's suggestion that religion is for those who have 'outgrown' their delusions about science is also later articulated by Lewis as the 'maturity' of the party of Irony. Even Agee's reference to 'the millennial glow of hope' is nearly synonymous with Lewis's depiction of the party of Hope and its various members' millennial exhortations. William Phillips, who attacks the new religious movement, does so in similar terms.

> I would be more impressed by the new religiosity if it did not preen itself on its imagination and profundity. It looks down on the secular mind, and is quite ready to dismiss scientific and naturalist thinking as arid, schematic, and generally insensitive to the mysteries of literary and human existence.
>
> (*Partisan Review* 1950, 482)

Interestingly, Phillips's depiction of the religious revival as regarding scientific thinking as arid and alien to the complex mysteries of literary thinking resembles rather closely some of Lewis's remarks affirming just those notions, though for Phillips they represent much of what is *wrong* with the religious revival.

William Barrett, another symposium participant, responds in equally relevant, though slightly broader, terms:

> The greatest shift in the intellectual climate from the nineteenth to the twentieth century is probably the slow and gradual loss of the once passionate hope in human possibilities. Where the nineteenth century was exalted and tormented by that absorbing question, What might man become? – we today are willing to settle for simply hanging on. The question everywhere in the background today . . . is one of survival.
>
> (p. 459)

What Barrett traces here could almost stand as an outline for *The American Adam*. Like Lewis, Barrett reproaches the intellectual climate of the twentieth century for its skepticism, though he accounts for that milieu of 'simply hanging on' as a strategy for survival in a nuclear age rather than simply, as Lewis suggests, as a habit of mind. Also like Lewis, Barrett characterizes the nineteenth century's 'passionate hope' and its ambivalence toward the question 'what might man become?' (for Lewis, 'the matter of Adam') in complex terms (it exalted *and* tormented the nineteenth century) similar to those Lewis attributes to the party of Irony. While Lewis might reveal still greater complexity and deeper ambivalence, Barrett's depiction of the era and its contrast to his own times resonates throughout *The American Adam.*

More generally, many of the symposium's contributors remark on the threatening social and political dilemmas looming over the nation and world as powerful motivations for a return to religion among intellectuals. Philip Rahv depicts an intelligentsia 'possessed by the spirit of consolation and . . . lured by the promise of metaphysical certainty and social stability' (p. 241). Other participants are more specific in their terms. John Dewey, for example, remarks that

> the two Wars . . . render it unnecessary to argue that the belief, previously current among all intellectuals of the liberal type, that we were entering upon an epoch in which there would be steady, even if slow, advance toward a peaceful world order, has undergone a tragic shock.
>
> (p. 129)

Like Lewis, Dewey registers a 'tragic shock' at the collapse of hopes based on gradual social and scientific advances. William Barrett sounds a similar note when he argues that world communism, the A-bomb, and the H-bomb are the issues generating a new religiosity:

> For the first time [Americans] are beginning to doubt seriously that man is sufficient to himself and can solve his own problems. But, again, the reaction seems typically American: religion is clutched at like another tool or instrument, as if it might solve the international problem of the atom when all else failed.
>
> (p. 458)

Such remarks appear in many of the responses, including those from James T. Farrell, Jacques Maritain, and Paul Kecskemeti, most of whom situate the postwar religious revival in the context of political instability. Whereas some praise it and others attack it, the respondents are basically in agreement over its function in the intellectual climate of cold war American culture.

This is obviously not the place to judge the merits of either side of this complicated issue. What I would like to suggest, however, is that whereas the *Partisan Review* forum tends to approach the issue of 'Religion and the Intellectuals' in its social and historical context, Lewis manifests many similar perspectives and even discovers many similar problematics in the texts he studies without, however, pursuing the likelihood of those cultural texts being firmly rooted in social and political contexts. I would not argue that Lewis's religious perspective is itself at the root of this problem. He seems intent on viewing American culture from a religious point of view (and on elevating writers and texts which confirm his vision) in a positive search for meaning within the social world. In this respect, Lewis resembles Yvor Winters, in that both propose a moral scheme as a counter to a malaise they detect at the heart of American culture. Lewis proceeds, however, to cast his diagnosis in terms which deny not only the specificity and solidarity of social experience, but also the possibility, even the desirability, of scientific or social approaches to the problems he addresses. In so doing, he also devalues writers and texts that remain committed to social and cultural representations and that offer descriptions and posit solutions this side of Melville's 'mystical vision' in *Billy Budd*. It would have been conceivable, even provocative, for Lewis to argue that 'the matter of Adam' was, itself, a discourse embedded in the more explicitly social and political debates of the era, but his remarks on questions of 'American identity' remain too abstract to carry such weight.

Robert Weimann argues that the stance of 'ironic balance' amidst social turmoil which, he feels, characterizes both Lewis's and Ihab Hassan's studies of American literature is 'at bottom a quietist (not to say an apologetic) mode of reaction to a world and to activities in this world that were neither ironic nor balanced. . . . The irony and paradox were not in the making of history but in the mode of historiography' (Weimann 1976, 138). Weimann's charge may well be just. What concerns me more, however, are the consequences Lewis's historiographical assumptions have for his theory of American literature. I believe Lewis's priorities, his theory of dialogue, and their impact on his study need to be understood, along with Trilling's related terms, as critical strategies that, intentional or not and quietist or not, define as out of consideration writers and texts whose modes of apprehending the social world are not characterized by ironic balance and ambiguity, such texts as could test, qualify, or demolish the coherence of their theories of American culture and literature. Lewis defines the American tradition in terms that, despite his stress on cultural dialogue, reinforce Trilling's notions of 'the literary idea' and cultural dialectics as well as his assumption that American literature has only a tangential relationship to American society. Lewis reconstitutes these critical insights in explicitly religious terms that further, if the *Partisan Review* critics are correct, remove literary analysis from areas of social significance. Oddly, Lewis resists placing the two areas of inquiry, religious and social, in the kind of dialectical fusion he believes constitutes the party of Irony's major literary virtue. Like the party of Memory, the realm of social and historical issues remains unanalyzed, perhaps suppressed, in Lewis's study.

The romance of America: Richard Chase

In *The American Novel and Its Tradition* (1957), Richard Chase synthesizes Trilling's observations into a coherent cultural theory of American literature. Drawing on Trilling's remarks about American literature's 'tangential' relationship to American society as well as his 'dialectical' theory of culture, Chase rechristens the American novel as the American romance, a generic definition of substantial influence. Joel Porte, another romance theorist, has acknowledged Chase as the founder of cultural/romance theories, remarking

> Students of American literature – notably Richard Chase – have provided a solid theoretical basis for establishing that the rise and growth of fiction in this country is dominated by

our authors' conscious adherence to a tradition of nonrealistic romance sharply at variance with the broadly novelistic mainstream of English writing.

(Porte 1969, ix)

That Porte attributes the origin of this view to Chase rather than
to Trilling is an oversight; the critical perspective he mentions
originates, though in less systematic form, in Trilling's work.
Chase's affinities with Trilling are, at any rate, most evident in
his transformation of Trilling's insights into a new definition of
American fiction which elevates its supposed radical alienation
from society into a generic norm. Like Trilling, Chase describes
American literature's estrangement from American society, but
he does not attempt to analyze what the status of such a
supposedly anti-mimetic literature may be. Whereas Trilling at
least worked *toward* a socially informed apprehension of literature (a corollary of his politics), Chase abandons the quest to
situate American literature in a mimetic tradition.

Chase's thesis answers those, like Lawrence and, presumably, even Trilling, who think 'that the American novel is sick'
and want to cure it. Chase intends to correct this misconception
by defining American fiction for what, 'right or wrong, it *is*'
(Chase 1957, 9). What distinguishes American from English
prose fiction, according to Chase, is that 'since the earliest days
the American novel, in its most original and characteristic form,
has worked out its destiny and defined itself by incorporating an
element of romance' (p. viii). In itself, this assertion of a
romance *element* in American fiction poses few problems. Chase,
however, actually posits the romance as the definitive American
genre and denies it a referential function.

Chase echoes Trilling's view of reality in defining the romance's distinctive qualities. Like Trilling, for example, Chase
suggests that 'doubtless the main difference between the novel
and the romance is in the way they view reality,' the novel
rendering reality 'closely and in comprehensive detail,' the
romance feeling 'free to render reality in less volume and detail.'
This relative freedom incorporates a wide range of qualities:
'potential virtues of mind, which may be suggested by such
words as rapidity, irony, abstraction, profundity'; the power to
express 'dark and complex truths unavailable to realism'; and

the freedom 'to render reality in less volume and detail, . . . [to] more freely veer toward mythic, allegorical, and symbolistic forms' (pp. x, xi, 13). Like Trilling, who contrasts the 'glowing generality' of American fiction with the substantiality of European writing, Chase argues that the 'abstractness and profundity of romance allow it to formulate moral truths of universal validity' and that characters in American romances are similarly abstract and ideal (one might infer they have nothing 'American' about them). They will not be 'complexly related to each other or to society or to the past,' but are beyond class distinctions, with origins enveloped in mystery (pp. xi, 13).[6] Chase is in essential agreement with William Gilmore Simms, who states, 'The Romance is of loftier origin that the Novel. It approximates the poem.' But Chase differs from Simms in suggesting that 'American fiction has approximated the poetry of idyl and of melodrama more often than of epic,' to which Simms had compared it (pp. 16, 17). Throughout his discussion, Chase contrasts American romance with the English novel, which, he asserts, 'renders reality closely and in comprehensive detail' and which presents characters in class-specific solidity (p. 12). Again echoing some of Trilling's ideas, Chase says that the romance signifies

> an assumed freedom from the ordinary novelistic require-
> ments of verisimilitude, development, and continuity; a
> tendency toward melodrama and idyl; a more or less formal
> abstractness and, on the other hand, a tendency to plunge
> into the underside of consciousness; a willingness to abandon
> moral questions or to ignore the spectacle of man in society, or
> to consider these things only indirectly or abstractly.
>
> (p. ix)

Chase offers a historical analysis for 'the contradictions which have vivified and excited the American imagination' (p. 11). Citing earlier theorists such as Tocqueville, Lawrence, and Van Wyck Brooks, who placed such contradictions as ideals versus practice, mental versus passional, and highbrow versus low-brow at the heart of the American experience, Chase traces these contradictions to three 'historical facts': 'the solitary position man has been placed in in this country'; 'the Manichaean quality of New England Puritanism . . . [which]

seems less interested in redemption than in the melodrama of
the eternal struggle of good and evil, less interested in incarnation and reconciliation than in alienation and disorder'; and
'the dual allegiance of the American, who in his intellectual
culture belongs both to the Old World and the New' (p. 11).
Such a historical orientation, however vague, also seems incon-
gruous in light of Chase's otherwise ahistorical readings.

Chase's readings of individual works tend to pivot around his
perception of these contradictions in the American experience.
Of Charles Brockden Brown, Chase notes,

> The world of *Wieland* is melodramatically conceived. It is an
> abruptly dualistic, Manichaean world, there being a whiff of
> brimstone about the villain and of divinity in the titular hero.
> It is clear . . . that the radical dichotomy of things will never
> be resolved by the merely formal belief of the characters in
> their deism and rationalism but can be escaped only by
> transcendent experiences of horror, heroism, love, or death.
>   (p. 38)

Chase later makes the more sweeping remark that 'the imagination that created *Moby-Dick*, and other great American works
from *The Scarlet Letter* to *Light in August* . . . does not settle
ultimate questions; it leaves them open' (p. 114). *Billy Budd* is a
case in point. Although its opening pages insist on a political
significance lurking in the narrative, Chase argues, 'still the
final impression we get from Melville's story is less the mystery
of incarnation than the mystery entailed in the eternal contradiction of good and evil, the kingdom of light and the kingdom of
darkness. The political structure of society cannot countenance
this extreme polarity. But this polarity may, nevertheless, be the
very substance of the aesthetic imagination' (p. 115). Likewise,
Huck Finn's life 'simply continues its pattern of unresolved
contradictions; he will go on as the impassive observer and
participant in abruptly alternating experiences of contentment
and horror' (p. 148). Chase also prefaces his discussion of
'Three Novels of Manners' by admitting that 'the American
literary mind is not necessarily *fated* to move always toward high
tensions, extreme situations, and unresolved contradictions,'
but quickly adds that 'it usually has done so when it has been at
its best' (p. 161). In this final remark, we detect another

suggestion that Chase's argument is as much prescriptive as descriptive.

Chase concretizes this oblique connection between American romance and American society in his various readings. These interpretations offer variations on Chase's main theme, but they are united by his argument against the social referentiality of American literature. Concluding his discussion of Charles Brockden Brown's melodramas, Chase suggests that melodrama 'is suitable to writers who do not have a firm sense of living in a culture. The American novelists . . . do not have a firm sense of a social arena where ideology and psychology find a concrete representation and are seen in their fullest human significance' (p. 41). Elsewhere Chase simply denies that social or political readings of American literature are relevant. While he agrees that *The Scarlet Letter* does have a feminist theme as well as other social and political meanings, he believes 'one makes a mistake to treat Hawthorne, either in *The Scarlet Letter* or *The Blithedale Romance*, as if he were a political or social writer. He is a very canny observer of political fact. . . . But no coherent politics is to be derived from Hawthorne' (pp. 73–4). Chase does not explain how he concludes there is no coherent politics in Hawthorne or why the absence of such a systematic political position precludes Hawthorne's works from having an important social or political meaning. A bit like Trilling here, Chase would define politics as dogma or propaganda, not as a complex set of relations between characters and their society. It is on points like this that Fredric Jameson's injunction about politics as the ultimate horizon of all literature is most informative (Jameson 1981, 17).

Less problematically, Chase notes that 'like the romancer,' Isabel Archer 'refuses to impute significance to human actions unless they are conceived as being exempt from the ordinary circumstances of life' (p. 134), although even this view seems to exaggerate Isabel's grounds for marriage and her philosophy of clothing into definitions of her character as a whole. Chase argues that 'the comparative social dullness of America' cripples the fictional careers of novelists of manners, whom he somewhat tautologically regards, by definition, as 'writers of second or third rank.' 'Whenever it turns out to be a brilliant and memorable book, the American novel of manners will also be a romance; more than likely the observation of manners and the painting of the social scene will be a by-product of the romance that really engages the author's mind' (p. 160).

Chase thus anchors his claim for the primacy of romance by devaluing the non-romance elements in major authors. For instance, while 'the great writers, such as Melville, Hawthorne, or Faulkner, sometimes approach the novel of manners, . . . it is not their natural style, they seldom sustain the tone, and there is always something else in these books more arresting than the observation of manners' (p. 158). Such a remark does seem true – once we have already defined romance as more arresting than the social significance of American fiction, and once we have reified the possibilities of an 'observation of manners.' In a different strategy, Chase also explicitly denies the importance of what social significance major texts seem to possess:

> On the whole our novelists have not been interested in social manners but in 'personalities of transcendent value,' . . . personalities who transcend among other things the amenities and discipline of social intercourse. It does not matter very much on board the Pequod that Ahab is a bourgeois entrepreneur, Starbuck a petty bourgeois, and Ishmael an aristocrat. Such social differences matter scarcely more at a table in a Paris café described by Hemingway in *The Sun Also Rises*. We understand characters in Melville and Hemingway as we do in most American writers, by what they are at heart. . . . We are asked by these novelists to judge characters, not by measuring them against socially derived values, but by their adherence to an idea of conduct which is personal, intuitive, and stoic, and which, though it may come round to the universal values of Christianity and democracy, does so without much social mediation.
>
> (pp. 159–60)

Again, the line between description and prescription seems fine. Although Chase does not acknowledge Trilling in such remarks, his argument that American characters are mythic, free from class definition and significance, and that they represent abstract ideas indicates a continuity between the two critics. Chase also derives from Trilling the notion that the 'American novel tends to rest in contradictions and among extreme ranges of experience,' that it attempts to resolve contradictions only in 'oblique, morally equivocal ways,' if at all, and that it is content to discover and explore (not to 'colonize') 'a new place and new state of mind' (pp. 1, 5). According to Chase, the American imagination has been stirred not by tragic or Christian modes of resolution but rather 'by the aesthetic possibilities of radical forms of alienation, contradiction, and disorder' (p. 2). In fact, it is on such grounds that Chase distinguishes 'romance' from 'myth,' which he equates with the archetypal fall from innocence into experience. Romance, he counters, 'pictures human life in a context of unresolved contradictions – contradictions which, for better or for worse, are not absorbed, reconciled, or transcended' (p. 244).

What I would like to propose is that Chase has superimposed Trilling's definition of American literature's tangential relationship to American reality upon Trilling's concept of the literary idea. Whereas Trilling argues that juxtaposing antithetical emotions is how *good* literature expresses 'ideas,' Chase defines American literature 'at its best' as tangential, and argues that that tangentiality most often is manifested in terms of various antithetical (i.e., juxtaposed) forces, myths, or ideas. This paradoxical array of unresolved extremes has thus been transformed from a model for historical analysis to an aesthetic virtue to, in Chase's usage, a theory of American culture, all focusing on the question of reality in America.[7]

The apolitical unconscious: Leslie Fiedler

Leslie Fiedler's place among cultural theorists of American literature owes less to any explicit debt to Trilling or Chase than to his similar assault on socially oriented interpretations of reality in American literature. *Love and Death in the American Novel* (1960) is, in some ways, a rarity among works expounding theories of American literature, as Fiedler not only anchors his discussion of American fiction in a detailed reading of English prototypes but ranges widely beyond orthodoxy to include a host of noncanonical writers. In fact, to this day Fiedler remains an advocate of 'opening up the canon' of American literature.[8] Such a comparatist and anti-canonical point of view, Fiedler feels, is essential to trace 'the major meaning of our literature and culture,' and 'to define what is peculiarly American in our books,' namely 'the themes of love and death as treated by our major writers – and especially ... the duplicity with which those themes are handled in the United States' (Fiedler 1960, 11–13).

The psychosexual thesis of *Love and Death in the American Novel* has, of course, outlived the scandal which surrounded its publication. 'The failure of the American fictionist to deal with adult heterosexual love and his consequent obsession with death, incest, and innocent homosexuality,' Fiedler argues, has produced a national literature which, paradoxically, in its 'innocent' and 'almost juvenile' way is 'notoriously at home in the children's [preadolescent] section of the library' (pp. 12, 24), primarily because it evades, or defends against, its own disruptive tendencies so well. Fiedler expands D. H. Lawrence's famous argument about the childish surface of classic American literature into a massive theory of the American novel. According to Fiedler, 'it is maturity above all things that the American writer fears, and marriage seems to him its essential sign' (p. 338), suggesting as it does a variety of tedious compromises with the drudgery, dullness, and responsibility of a social existence and of a mature vision of women, as well as of one's own parents. Since there 'is finally no heterosexual solution which the American psyche finds completely satisfactory,' American writers have set out on an alternative odyssey:

> The quest which has distinguished our fiction from Brockden Brown and Cooper, through Poe and Melville and Twain, to Faulkner and Hemingway is the search for an innocent substitute for adulterous passion and marriage alike. Is there not, our writers ask over and over, a sentimental relationship at once erotic and immaculate, a union which commits its participants neither to society nor sin – and yet one which is able to symbolize the union of the ego with the id, the thinking self with its rejected impulses?

> (p. 339)

The answer, Fiedler suggests, has been no. In place of love (seduction and marriage), which, according to Fiedler, 'in one form or another has remained the novel's central theme,'

American writers have substituted the gothic mode, turning
'from society to nature or nightmare out of a desperate need
to avoid the facts of wooing, marriage, and childbearing'
(p. 25).

The result: a 'novel of terror,' characterized by the American
writer's 'obsession with violence and his embarrassment before
love,' two sides of the same coin. Our writers have always felt
that a 'bargain with the Devil' is 'the essence of American
experience' and have resorted to the gothic for the 'cheapjack
machinery . . . to represent the hidden blackness of the human
soul and human society' and for its metaphor of 'a terror
psychological, social, and metaphysical.' Suggesting that
Hawthorne's 'Young Goodman Brown' would seem to be *the*
quintessential American tale, Fiedler notes the diversity of this
American theme:

> In Hawthorne, the scientist and the social reformer, in
> Melville, the ruthless exploiter of nature and the magnetic
> leader of men; in Twain, the refugee from culture, the young
> man who goes West; in Faulkner, the self-made man fighting
> for status and security – in each, some standard and respected
> American type is identified with the black magician who
> bartered away his soul.

(p. 433)

Selling their souls to the Devil and escaping from society and the
adult responsibility which it demands, American writers have
taken refuge in a world of sadomasochistic dreams in which
women can appear only as the mythic types of Dark Lady, Good
Good Girl, or Good Bad Girl. Even the dark-skinned com-
panions such as Queequeg, Chingachgook, or Jim, whom the
American hero generically takes in homoerotic 'marriage,' is an
ambiguous Janus-like figure, 'a dream and a nightmare at
once.' Fiedler is careful to point out that these 'are not merely
matters of historical interest or literary relevance.' He 'closes
the gap' between literature and society by suggesting that this
revulsion from adult love and the subsequent refuge in a
nightmare of neurotic evasions 'affect the lives we lead from day
to day.' This is 'a pattern imposed both by the writers of our past
and the very conditions of life in the United States from which
no American novelist can escape, no matter what philosophy

he consciously adopts or what theme he thinks he pursues' (pp. 1–30, passim).

Fiedler argues that the evasion of heterosexual love and the flight from conventional society has resulted in a series of homoerotic relationships between a white male (Natty Bumppo, Ishmael, Huck, Henderson) and a dark-skinned male companion (Chingachgook, Queequeg, Jim, King Dahfu). This homoeroticism and the American writer's inability to portray women in any but the most mythic terms are only one side of Fiedler's work. Equally pervasive is Fiedler's devaluation of literature as social document, a peculiar stance for a critic so self-professedly 'cultural' as Fiedler. In fact, his position on literature's social significance reveals a contradictory view of reality in America at the heart of his method. On the one hand, Fiedler suggests that a 'balance between psychological and sociological insights' is essential to his approach and declares that all the contexts of a work are critical, 'its lexical or verbal one, no more or less important than the sociological, psychological, historical, anthropological, or generic' (pp. 8, 10). Some of Fiedler's readings reflect such a balanced perspective. He can, for instance, approve of George Lippard as a 'pre-Marxian socialist' who thought 'of his novels, stories, and pamphlets . . . as weapons in the holy war of labor.' Lippard's horror pornography fuses social and sexual radicalism by capitalizing on the darkest erotic and sadistic fantasies of a repressed upper-class reader (pp. 244–5).

The major thrust of *Love and Death in the American Novel*, however, dilutes such a social perspective. Not that Fiedler does not lay claim to elucidating socially significant themes; he does. He recognizes society and history, however, only as projections of individual psychology or of collective myth – a framework antithetical to social and historical specificity. Fiedler's definition of reality is, like all theorists', example bound. While he has for years advocated 'opening up the canon,' his own selectivity in *Love and Death in the American Novel* has led Irving Howe, among others, to accuse Fiedler of 'simply ignoring those writers and books that might call the thesis into question' and to remark that 'what Fiedler disregards . . . is awesome' (Howe 1960, 17). Fiedler's exclusions are characteristic of many theories of American literature, but the terms on which he declares certain writers unimportant link him with Trilling and Chase, and thus with the counter-Progressive revolt against Progressive historiography.

Fiedler's thesis, like Trilling's, is an anti-thesis, formulated in opposition to critics such as Parrington, who apparently was mistaken in his decision to regard Charles Brockden Brown from a realist perspective and to view his Godwinian politics as his most admirable feature (pp. 153–4). Fiedler redefines literature's significance as not simply different from but opposed to such explicit social and political criteria. In other words, Fiedler discards writers such as Dos Passos, Steinbeck, and Dreiser by conscious design. As Robert Gorham Davis remarks, 'Fiedler is quite consciously reacting against the social criticism of the '20s and '30s. . . . Whereas [Granville] Hicks had found American writers wanting in relation to the class struggle, Fiedler does the same with ideal genital sexuality' (Davis 1960, 11). While he may endorse Lippard's works as 'a prime example of art as social action,' Fiedler's thesis is against the idea of literature as a reflection of external social reality.

This bias takes two forms – mythic, psychosexual interpretations unconcerned with non-mythic significance, and polemic against irretrievably social writers. Fiedler defines American literature in explicit terms:

> Such a mode can, of course, not be subsumed among any of those called 'realism.' Our fiction is essentially and at its best nonrealistic, even anti-realistic; long before *symbolisme* had been invented in France and exported to America, there was a full-fledged native tradition of symbolism.
>
> (p. 28)

Fiedler adds a more polemical note when he rejects Chase's thesis:

> To speak of a counter-tradition to the novel, of the tradition of 'the romance' as a force in our literature, is merely to repeat the rationalizations of our writers themselves; it is certainly to fail to be *specific* enough for real understanding. Our fiction is not merely in flight from the physical data of the actual world, in search of a (sexless and dim) Ideal; from Charles Brockden Brown to William Faulkner or Eudora Welty, Paul Bowles or

John Hawkes, it is bewilderingly and embarrassingly, a gothic fiction, nonrealistic and negative, sadistic and melodramatic – a literature of darkness and the grotesque in a land of light and affirmation.

(p. 29)

Whereas Chase had accepted Trilling's thesis that American literature had only a tangential relationship with social reality, Fiedler rejects them both, arguing instead that American literature is by definition written against the social form of American life.

He is astute in remarking that Chase merely repeats 'the rationalizations of our writers' and is not specific enough, but Fiedler's own study hardly balances the scales. For one thing, Fiedler's description of the United States as 'a land of light and affirmation' is patently inadequate to sustain any social inquiry. Here Fiedler resembles the hazy radicalism and nay-saying virulence which Henry May argues characterized early (and shoddy) versions of American cultural dissent. But for one who grants the complexity of psychic reality, Fiedler unnecessarily truncates his own possibilities for an analysis of literature's function as social behavior. In Freudian terminology, if Trilling defines literature in terms of 'manifest' content, what people express in symbolic or mythic language, Fiedler's reversal locates *all* meaning in the 'latent' level. As in D. H. Lawrence's studies, the literal level of American literature is reduced to mere evasion, significant only in so far as it alerts the perceptive critic to the deeper level which it distorts. It is also difficult to understand how Fiedler can accuse Chase of lacking in specificity, when Fiedler himself uses only the most abstract and mythic terms (innocence/experience, Good Bad Boy, Good Good Girl, etc.) to explicate the 'reality' of American literature. In fact, Fiedler elsewhere acknowledges his kinship with Chase in a review of contemporary scholarship in American literature:

Richard Chase and Leslie Fiedler each reflects in his own way a similar preoccupation with myth: a sense that the deepest meanings, meanings which extend beyond the single work to a whole body of books, are to be sought in the archetypal symbols to which succeeding writers compulsively turn.

(Fiedler 1958, 170)

We should not forget, however, that Fiedler is redefining literary significance. American literature's inwardness is meant to verify the presence of 'a place in men's lives where pictures do in fact bleed, ghosts gibber and shriek, maidens run forever through mysterious landscapes from nameless foes; that place is . . . the world of dreams and of the repressed guilts and fears that motivate them' (Fiedler 1960, 140). The turning of the modern novel from 'mythology to psychology, from a body of communal story to the mind of the individual is an enterprise typical of our times' (p. 40), Fiedler asserts, and Trilling would likely agree. But Fiedler's version shifts to the sexual unconscious, and his artist is defined as 'the questing lover,' not just the detached questers for the origins of symbolism and language itself, as we shall see in Charles Feidelson and John Irwin.

The American reality Fiedler traces has its origins, not surprisingly, in Charles Brockden Brown. According to Fiedler,

> Brown established . . . a tradition dealing with the exaggerated and the grotesque, not as they are verifiable in any external landscape or sociological observation of manners and men, but as they correspond in quality to our deepest fears and guilts as projected in our dreams or lived through in 'extreme situations.' Realistic milieu and consistent character alike are dissolved in such projective fictions, giving way to the symbolic landscape and the symbolic action, which are the hallmarks of the mythopoeic novel.
>
> (pp. 155–6)

In this vein Fiedler defines Brown's social and historical contexts as 'half-hearted and unconvincing' bows to realism; Fiedler corrects readers who would grant them significance by asserting '[*Wieland*] is finally dream-like rather than documentary, not at all the historical novel it has been often called – evoking the past as nightmare rather than fact' (p. 231).

Another strain in Fiedler's work which removes literature from the realm of social significance is his abstracting of characters into mythic or repressed symbols. We have already remarked on Fiedler's tenuous rationale for criticizing Chase's lack of specificity – Fiedler's own approach is equally schematic. In addition to denaturing all Jamesian women into either Dark Ladies or Fair Girls, Fiedler views many other characters only as dream images. *Tom Sawyer* and *Huckleberry Finn*, for instance, 'are seen as the same dream dreamed twice over, the second time as nightmare,' and, more specifically, 'Miss Watson's Jim is the Becky Thatcher of *Huckleberry Finn*. They cannot be present in the same book' (pp. 280–2). Twain's dreams, moreover, are not related to any social context other than the nostalgia for a lost childhood innocence. Fiedler's mythicizing is even more objectionable in his readings of minority figures in American literature. On the one hand, he can level an implicit charge of racism against critics like D. H. Lawrence, who, by ignoring texts such as 'Benito Cereno' and *The Narrative of Arthur Gordon Pym*, write 'a history of our fiction with No Negroes Allowed' (p. 398). But Fiedler is, if anything, even less sensitive to racial and ethnic characters or authors, interpreting them as projections of trans-historical archetypes, 'for in the dreams of Caucasians forbidden impulses are typically projected in dark-skinned figures' (p. 179). In Cooper and Brockden Brown 'the dark-skinned savage is used to represent the unconscious mind,' and, in *Moby-Dick*, minority characters represent 'a single author arguing with himself, one impulse of his own mind evoking the counter impulse. . . . The sinister natural figure of Fedallah is set against the virtuous natural figure of Queequeg' (p. 196). In Mark Twain, 'Nigger Jim confronts Injun Joe, the dark-skinned protector contrasted with the dark-skinned aggressor' (p. 196). In a footnote Fiedler justifies such a reading:

> Recently, we have grown more and more aware of how in the Civil Rights Movement the aspirations of Negroes for full freedom and the struggle of homosexuals to be accepted are oddly intermingled. And it is no use protesting (as Ralph Ellison has done, for instance) that they should be kept separate and pure. For better or for worse, they are mythically one in our deepest imagination.

(p. 366)

It is difficult to conceive how 'aware' Fiedler could have been to the reality either of blacks or of homosexuals. He expresses in a passage like this the inability to perceive the Other as anything but a deviation from the white, heterosexual norm. In remarks like these, Fiedler can perceive human representations only in

the most abstract mythic categories, not in socially or historically specific terms; but, of course, this is a problem endemic to
myth criticism. Fiedler, in fact, anticipates Northrop Frye's
mythicization and de-politicization of reality. In *The Critical
Path* Frye recounts an incident in People's Park (Berkeley) in
which demonstrators were being dragged away by police. Frye
perceives not a historically specific event, but the reenactment
of a timeless myth – 'demonic symbolism, the pastoral mode,
the myth of expulsion from Eden, and the murder of Abel
archetype.'[9] For both Fiedler and Frye, mythic abstractions
function to deflect attention from literature (and from reality) as
a critical account of social or political struggle, defining textual
mediation of reality in the psychoanalytic or mythic terms of
evasion, condensation, and the like. Like many counter-
Progressive historians, they see American literature and history
as the tireless repetition of the Same.

Fiedler's polemic against social and political writing and
criticism stems from his rejection of their themes and of their
political commitment. In fact, socially and politically explicit
literature, not to mention criticism, is, itself, merely another
evasion of the primary psychodrama, though on a less interesting level. In *An End to Innocence: Essays on Culture and Politics*
(1948), Fiedler anticipates his argument in *Love and Death in the
American Novel*. In one essay in particular, 'Adolescence and
Maturity in the American Novel,' Fiedler, like Trilling before
him, attacks the innocence and the inadequate vision of reality
of an entire literary movement, the proletarian novelists of the
thirties: 'The record of the so-called "proletarian" novel in the
United States is one of the most absurd episodes in our literary
history' (Fiedler 1948, 198), primarily because proletarian
writers fell prey to an innocent faith in leftist idealism. Thus
Fiedler rejects Anderson, Steinbeck, Dos Passos, Farrell, Wolfe,
and Dreiser (essentially the same writers Trilling attacked)
because of their 'moral obtuseness, political sentimentality, and
naive faith in documentation' (Fiedler 1948, 196). All this is
done, as Trilling did it, without any significant consideration of
their writing other than Fiedler's assertions that they do not live
up to his standards.

In place of such social writers, Fiedler posits Faulkner,
Melville, and James as the American novelists who function as

living influences, as they were pioneers in their 'boldness of images, subtlety of insight, and especially the willingness to plunge deep below the lintel of consciousness' (Fiedler 1948, 199). They possess 'an overall moral maturity' and, though not religious, 'enjoy playing poetically with the counters of orthodoxy: Original Sin and Salvation and the Dark Night of the Soul' (Fiedler 1948, 197). Fiedler defines Melville as the very core of the American tradition:

> There is a Melville whom one scarcely knows whether to call the discovery or invention of our time, our truest contemporary, who has revealed to us the traditional theme of the deepest American mind, the ambiguity of innocence, the 'mystery of iniquity,' which he had traded for the progressive melodrama of a good outcast (artist, rebel, whore, proletarian) against an evil bourgeoisie.
>
> (Fiedler 1948, 197)

Of course Melville can only be 'our truest contemporary' and can only reveal to us 'the traditional theme of the deepest American mind' by conforming to literary and cultural criteria which Fiedler and his contemporaries had defined as truly 'American.'

In *Love and Death in the American Novel*, Fiedler renews his campaign against explicitly social writers, linking them with naive sentimentality, his catch-all term of contempt. Most generally, Fiedler lumps any variety of 'social protest' with trans-historical myths in order to discredit all social writing that is not sophisticated enough to camouflage its themes with gothic trappings:

> To this very day ... the sentimental novel of social protest survives, dedicating itself to such latter-day issues as anti-Semitism, racial discrimination, the atom bomb, McCarthyism, etc., etc., eternally searching for new examples among the abused 'little people' to set in the position of the Persecuted Maiden.
>
> (Fiedler 1960, 262–3)

Fiedler associates these evasions with such issues as anti-tobacco and alcohol campaigns as well as wife-beating on the grounds that 'the child has bent under the swinging [tavern]

door to cry "Is my father in there?" from the beginning of time.'
Fiedler projects a sense of futility and cynicism upon any
reformist impulses.

Elsewhere, Fiedler deflects the political impetus behind
World War I and II novels and the proletarian novels of the
thirties away from politics as such into 'apocalyptics: a commitment to revolution which is essentially a dedication to horror,'
arguing that 'we have lived [Nazism] in our viscera and our
nerves as a bad dream, in which, though we die for it, we cannot
really believe' (p. 481). Finally, Fiedler argues for the superiority of Ralph Ellison's *Invisible Man* over the 'passionate, incoherent books of Richard Wright' because 'Ellison has bypassed all
formulas of protest and self-pity [Fiedler often equates the two]
and cast off the restrictions of mere realism' and has taken on 'a
special quality of grotesqueness.' According to Fiedler, 'to
discuss . . . in the light of pure reason the Negro problem in the
United States is to falsify its essential mystery and unreality; it is
a gothic horror of our daily lives' (p. 493).

Fiedler's campaign against social and political writing and
criticism fits into the larger, cultural context of his work. Fiedler
projects American artists into the cultural role of professional
nay-sayers to the superficial optimism of a culture addicted to
affirmation. Borrowing Melville's insight into Hawthorne's
work, Fiedler defines the task of the American writer: 'To
express this "blackness ten times black" and to live by it in a
society in which, since the decline of orthodox Puritanism,
optimism has become the chief effective religion is a complex
and difficult task' (p. 27). Therefore, Fiedler concludes that
expressing 'what he fears is true' about life is the obligation of
the American gothic writer, his 'obligation to negativism, which
the sentimental genres cannot fulfill and which realism converts
to mere pamphleteering' (p. 503). Fiedler elsewhere refers to
'the writer's duty' as saying '"Nay!" . . . to deny the easy
affirmations by which most men live, . . . not to console or
sustain, much less to entertain, but to *disturb* by telling a truth
which is always unwelcome' (p. 432). In less apocalyptic
moments, Fiedler expresses the same adversary function of
gothic art as shaking 'the philistines out of their self-satisfied
torpor' and as mocking 'the squares' (p. 135).

Fiedler's definition of the artist as the alienated adversary of

bourgeois culture, as 'obligated to deny the self-serving affirmations' and 'to shock the bourgeoisie into an awareness of what
a chamber of horrors its own smugly regarded world really
was' (p. 135), recalls Trilling's reification of nay-saying into
a cultural and critical imperative. The important difference,
however, is that while Trilling's notions of how the 'opposing
self' opposed or of how an 'adversary culture' was adversary
were capable of changing to suit changing cultural moods,
Fiedler's sense of negation is static and mythic. Culture, at
least the philistine culture, is shallow and affirmative, and the
American artist is the 'professional revolutionary' who reveals
the psychosexual charnel house underlying and undermining
the self-satisfied bourgeoisie. Fiedler's brand of sexual radicalism, is, however, ineffectual on its own terms. On the one hand,
Fiedler's 'shocking' pronouncements on American culture are
trivialized by his voyeuristic sensationalism; on the other, his
refusal to approach literature's adversary aspects in social or
political terms has rendered his critique impotent and safe. In a
commodified culture capable of appropriating many forms of
'radical chic' as just so many more self-consuming trends,
Fiedler is, to use his own terms, just another Good Bad Boy, 'the
Tom Sawyer of the current generation, crying at all the
windows, "Come on out and play!"' (p. 289).

An American fable: Leo Marx

In *The Machine in the Garden* (1964) Leo Marx recapitulates the
major themes of earlier cultural theories of American literature,
though in subtler, more explicitly historical terms. Consciously
drawing on Trilling, Chase, Lewis, and Smith, Marx reconstitutes their 'dialectical' theory of culture, complete with
Trilling's notions of contradiction, negation, manners, and the
literary idea. Marx is more overtly concerned with the social
and concretely historical implications of literature, especially in
his critique of Eliot's and Trilling's interpretations of *Huckleberry
Finn*, though his adherence to the psychologized implications of
Trilling's approach in *The Machine in the Garden* qualifies his
formulation of a coherent 'social theory' of American literature
and, in fact, may not, as he intends, bridge the gap between

literature and literary criticism and the world of society and politics.

Marx states that his study 'is not, strictly speaking, a book about literature,' but rather 'about the region of culture where literature, general ideas, and certain products of the collective imagination – we may call them "cultural symbols" – meet.' He is more concerned with demonstrating how the pastoral ideal has, in American history, science, and literature, exerted a lasting and powerful 'metaphor of contradiction' which has ordered the notions of meaning and value in the American past as well as in the present (Marx 1964, 4). Marx's claims for his thesis are actually larger though. As is the case for most theorists, Marx's reading of American literature pivots on an implictly prescriptive definition of literature and on the exclusion or homogenizing of the many American texts and traditions which are not easily accommodated in his theory. For instance, while the popular mind has used pastoralism as a vehicle of escapism, Marx deals primarily with 'high literary culture,' 'the classical canon of our literature,' and he argues that 'our best writers' have transcended the simple pastoral mode for the 'larger, more complicated order of experience' known as 'complex pastoralism' (pp. 10, 11, 25). Furthermore, complex pastoralism, Marx argues, exemplifies 'a view of life which dominates much of our literature. It is a complex, distinctively American form of romantic pastoralism' and 'the most final of all generalizations about America' (pp. 229, 353). There is more at stake in Marx's book than the humble 'some versions of American pastoral' which he early defines as his purpose.

Marx's thesis draws on Trilling and Chase for its model of culture, but Marx significantly revises their approaches to account for the impact of industrialization on the American literary imagination. Marx in fact criticizes Chase for ignoring the rapid industrialization of America as one of the major causes of the contradictions in American society and fiction. According to Marx, the most 'profound contradiction of value or meaning' in American life stems from the fact that 'within the lifetime of a single generation, a rustic and in large part wild landscape was transformed into the site of the world's most productive industrial machine' (p. 343). Marx's concentration on 'our best writers' for examples of how complex minds responded to this root contradiction echoes another of Trilling's beliefs, that a culture's 'great artists are likely to be those who contain a large part of the dialectic within themselves' (p. 342). Not a 'Marxist' in the political sense, Marx none the less attempts to address the impingement of capitalism and industrialization on human life, though he does so more in sentimental and aesthetic than in political terms.

Before examining major literary statements embodying the contradictory 'Two Kingdoms of Force,' however, Marx traces prototypes of American pastoralism in Virgil's *Eclogues* and Shakespeare's *The Tempest*. More importantly, he also examines the roots of either side of the American dialectic in a variety of subliterary American sources such as Robert Beverly's *The History and Present State of Virginia* and Thomas Jefferson's *Notes on Virginia* (two major prototypes of the 'garden' thesis) as well as articulations of the 'machine' antithesis by Tench Coxe in *Report on Manufactures* (1791), Timothy Walker in 'Defense of Mechanical Philosophy' (1831), and an 1847 speech by Daniel Webster, all of whom had used the language of the 'technological sublime' to associate technology and industrialization with progress, democracy, and the general liberation of human potential. Though there are complexities in each of these works, Marx argues that they schematically oppose the terms pastoralism and technology in too simplistic and affirmative a fashion; they overlook the naive primitivism of the pastoral just as they overlook the darker implications (such as those doubts expressed by Carlyle) of industrialization. For the truly representative American mode Marx turns to Hawthorne, Thoreau, Melville, and Mark Twain, who synthesize these opposed 'forces' in the 'complex pastoral' mode. Whereas the celebrations of either machine or garden were too simple, the complex pastoral incorporates a 'counterforce' which 'brings a world which is more "real" into juxtaposition with an idyllic vision' (p. 25). It brings the machine into the garden and forces us to grasp them in their contradictory interpenetration. What Marx suggests then is a dialectical synthesis capable of grasping the static opposition of machine versus garden in a more dynamic interpenetration. In fact, such a recognition of a multivalent, complex reality is Marx's nearest affinity with other cultural theorists – they all reject simplistic interpretations of American culture. Like Trilling, Marx balances opposites in aesthetic equipoise.

Marx's model for this American mode is Hawthorne's 'Sleepy Hollow' note of 1844. While reposing in a harmonious natural bower that unifies 'society, landscape, and mind,' Hawthorne has his reverie shattered by the sudden, harsh shriek of a locomotive whistle, 'forcing him to acknowledge the existence of a reality alien to the pastoral dream.' According to Marx, 'what begins as a conventional tribute to the pleasures of withdrawal from the world – a simple pleasure fantasy – is transformed by the interruption of the machine into a far more complex state of mind' (pp. 11–15). This complex state of mind is what constitutes our best writers' responses to the basic contradiction between the machine and the garden; 'indeed it is difficult to think of a major American writer upon whom the image of the machine's sudden appearance in the landscape has not exercised its fascination' (p. 16).

In each case, American writers can cope with this complex state only through what Marx calls a 'virtual resolution.' That is, incapable of formulating a practical solution to so profound a contradiction and unwilling to simplify it in sentimental fashion, they achieve aesthetic unity without suggesting how the problems posed by technology could be solved. The conflict which the counterforce to the pastoral idyll arouses is mitigated in the aesthetic consciousness, a way, Marx suggests, 'of saying that the episode belongs to a timeless, recurrent pattern of human affairs' (p. 31). However, in its American manifestation the virtual resolution is precarious, the machine representing a new force which cannot be accommodated by traditional pastoral models of 'the middle landscape.'

Marx's readings demonstrate three varieties of this 'strong urge to believe in the rural myth along with an awareness of industrialization as counterforce to the myth' (p. 229). His 'versions of pastoral' include the transcendental (*Walden*); the tragic ('Ethan Brand' and *Moby-Dick*); and the vernacular (*Huckleberry Finn*). At the heart of each version Marx discovers a conflict between pastoral impulses and industrial reality that ends in a virtual but not a real resolution. Thus, Thoreau's description of the design formed by a melting railroad bank is 'a pageant evoking the birth of life out of inorganic matter' and 'a figurative restoration of the form and unity [of nature] severed by the mechanized forces of history' (pp. 261–2). This virtual resolution has 'nothing to do with the environment, with social institutions, or material reality,' but is 'a product of imaginative perception, of the . . . mythopoeic power of the human mind, . . . a matter of private and, in fact, literary experience' (p. 264). Hawthorne's Ethan Brand represents the Faustian desire in modern man, the industrialization of the New England land-scape, and 'a maimed, alienated man.' 'Ethan Brand' can, with its transparently idyllic ending, offer only an ironic restoration of the middle landscape, one that

> conveys Hawthorne's inchoate sense of doom awaiting the self-contained village culture, not the institutions alone, but the whole quasi-religious ideology that rests, finally, upon the hope that Americans will subordinate their burning desire for knowledge, wealth, and power to the pursuit of rural happiness.
>
> (p. 277)

In *Moby-Dick* Melville's juxtaposition of Ahab's destruction (Marx regards him as 'the perverted, monomaniac incarnation of the Age of Machinery') and Ishmael's salvation is a tacit endorsement of 'the Ishmaelean view of life: a complex pastoral-ism in which the ideal is inseparably yoked to its opposite' (p. 318). But Melville's truth, his virtual resolution, is a 'symbol-maker's truth,' unconcerned with society or politics. In *Huckleberry Finn*, the steamboat's smashing of the raft signifies not only the machine/garden conflict, but, prophetically, Mark Twain's setting the novel aside for three years. By making Huck light out for the territories at the book's conclusion, Mark Twain 'seizes an elusive truth.' This virtual resolution admits that 'the ten-sion at the center of [the] book . . . is the very pulse of reality; it may be suppressed, and it may, for a time, be relieved, but eventually it is bound to reappear in a new form' (p. 340). *Huckleberry Finn*, then, pays paradoxically historical homage to the timeless contradiction between pastoral idyll (personal freedom) and encroaching technology.

In these, his major readings, as well as in his remarks on *The Octopus*, *The Education of Henry Adams*, and *The Great Gatsby*, Marx admits that 'American writers seldom, if ever have designed satisfactory resolutions for their pastoral fables' (p. 364). But Marx looks beyond American literature for a possible explanation for 'this recurrent metaphor of contradiction' and concludes that the metaphor

> makes vivid, as no other figure does, the bearing of public events upon private lives. It discloses that our inherited symbols of order and beauty have been divested of meaning. It compels us to recognize that the aspirations once represented by the symbol of an ideal landscape have not, and probably cannot, be embodied in our traditional institutions. It means that an inspiring vision of a humane community has been reduced to a token of individual survival.
>
> (p. 364)

Marx is quick to add that this 'inability of our writers to create a surrogate for the ideal of the middle landscape can hardly be accounted as an artistic failure.' These writers have only internalized and dramatized 'the root conflict of our culture,' the actual resolution of which is primarily the responsibility of society, not of artists. It is a 'problem that ultimately belongs not to art but to politics' (p. 365).

This is a stirring conclusion to an important study. Marx's elucidation of the social and political implications latent in the theme of the machine in the garden is important, as is his insistence on placing the study of literature in a political perspective. But his thesis that the works themselves do not present explicit critiques or offer any but 'virtual resolutions' rests on some inadequately developed literary assumptions. His method, too – indebted as it is to Trilling's ideas as well as to those of consensus historiography in general, and bound, as it is, to largely conventional readings of canonical texts – prevents him from advancing a more trenchant analysis. In order to offer some directions in which the Marx thesis may be revised, I shall examine his internalization of literary significance and his 'dialectical' analysis of cultural contradictions.

Following Trilling's example for cultural theories, Marx approaches American literature primarily in psychological terms. Like both Trilling and Henry Nash Smith, Marx grants a primacy to 'myths' and to the symbols and images with which

Americans have responded to historical change, but he places these 'cultural symbols' in contrast to history, rather than envisioning them as part of history. The *primary* subject of all American literature, Marx argues, is 'the contrast between two conditions of consciousness.' This dialectic may provide a valuable working approach to the way in which literature mediates social reality and historical change, but it should not be conceived in the anti-mimetic terms in which Marx couches his argument. Hawthorne, he posits (echoing both Fiedler and Chase), 'is not interested in directing attention from himself to what is happening "out there" in the great world of political and institutional change, . . . his chief concern is the landscape of the psyche' (p. 28). Hawthorne's private notes may not intentionally direct attention to what is happening 'out there' in material reality. But to suggest that such an introverted intention characterizes all of American literature's treatment of the interrupted idyll misses the point, not just of such explicitly polemical works as *Walden*, but of other interrupted idylls throughout the American tradition.

While Marx is concerned with the connections between literature and politics, he seems reluctant to specify the category of 'consciousness' and to argue that the politics are actually in the literature. He may privilege complex pastoralism because it grasps the machine *in* the garden, but, while he pushes in this direction, Marx does not allow the 'machine' of politics into the 'garden' of the literary text. His separation of them is evident in his relegating the solution of the conflict he traces 'not to art but to politics,' as though the twain did not actually meet, or as though the literature he discusses never offered explicit critiques or actual resolutions. In order to synthesize machine and garden, Marx polarizes politics and literature, granting the latter a status apart from the crudeness of dehumanizing partisanship. Similarly, Marx's habit of defining 'virtual resolutions' primarily in aesthetic and psychological terms – which are opposed, as in the case of *Walden*, to 'social institutions or anything "out there"' – denies the likelihood that Thoreau intended his experiment to be grasped both as an actual alternative to existing political institutions *and* as a matter of individual consciousness. In fact, the mutual dependence of Concord's social norms and Thoreau's individual rebellion against them in *Walden* as well as in 'Resistance to Civil Government' points to a dialectical grasp and definition of each term. Thoreau could not formulate a new ethic in a social or political vacuum; his own analysis grows dialectically out of the old order. This is not simply a matter of consciousness, but of political consciousness. But Marx, like Trilling, defines great artists as those who do not propose solutions (which is variously denigrated as 'sentimental,' or 'simple pastoralism'). From their detached perspectives, artists dramatize without taking sides.

Equally important are Marx's notions of dialectics and contradiction and their similarity not only to Trilling's 'literary idea' but also to Lewis's and Chase's practices of 'cultural criticism.' Trilling's literary idea, by definition, keeps two conflicting ideas or emotions in a balance, preventing a resolution that would affirm one or the other. Such, too, is Trilling's notion of cultural conflict, or contradiction, as the mutual cohabitation of two ideologies, neither one triumphing. Marx's dialectical theory of culture is, despite his distancing himself from Trilling, remarkably similar both in theory and practice to Trilling's. Marx accepts Trilling's thesis that the '"very essence" of a culture ... resides in its central conflicts, or contradictions' (p. 342). Regarding culture as a battlefield of various conflicts is, of course, an essential premise of dialectics. We should remember, however, that for Trilling the conflicts (contradictions) existed for their own sake, not as a thesis and antithesis capable of giving birth, through synthesis, to a new thesis. As we saw Gene Wise remark, Trilling structures a debate and 'doesn't want either side to win'; instead, he valorizes debate for debate's sake. Marx may not intentionally hypostatize the terms of his dialectic, but the mythic aura surrounding the machine, the garden, and their timeless conflict abstracts them from any dynamic, dialectical context, freezing them instead in static opposition. This, in short, is the difference between coexistence and contradiction.

Robert Heilbroner's cautionary remarks against reductive notions of dialectics are pertinent here. Aligning himself with both Hegelian and Marxian dialectical thought, Heilbroner points out that 'the ultimate and irreducible nature of all reality is motion, not rest, and that to depict things as static or changeless is to disregard or violate the essence of their being.'

Heilbroner also warns that 'the presence of conflicts within social processes does not in itself suffice to establish these conflicts as contradictions. . . . Thus the task of dialectical inquiry is not to make sweeping statements about the omnipresence of contradictions, but to identify the particular contradictory tendencies . . . within a given social process' (Heilbroner 1980, 32, 39).

While Marx situates complex pastoralism in a specific American context – nineteenth-century industrialization – the 'Sleepy Hollow' motif, he suggests, is more significant as recurrent myth:

> When we strip away the topical surface, particularly the imagery of industrialism and certain special attitudes toward visible nature, it becomes apparent that the underlying pattern is much older and more universal . . . a modern version of an ancient literary device . . . which has been used by writers working in the pastoral mode since the time of Virgil.
>
> (p. 19)

This underlying timeless model attenuates the historical thrust of Marx's argument by defining the conflict between industrialization and pastoralism in America as merely one more manifestation of a trans-historical psychic tension.

Marx's alignment of machine versus garden and the 'synthesis' of the machine in the garden, that 'larger, more complicated order of experience' called complex pastoralism, falls short of a dynamic dialectical inquiry in another respect. Marx's putative synthesis is merely another cohabitation of opposites, like Trilling's literary idea and R. W. B. Lewis's 'party of Irony' and 'tragic optimism.' But cohabitation of opposites is not necessarily contradiction in the dialectical sense. By lining up machines in gardens in a static manner, Marx sets up a mythic tableau that defies synthesis or resolution. Marx's notion of contradiction, then, abstracts the conflict between machine and garden (history and myth) as a self-evident reality, rather than regarding them as a symptom or vehicle for social change, the signs of which are inherent in the texts themselves, not just as 'virtual resolutions,' but as implicit critiques of industrial capitalism.

This is not simply a theoretical difference between conflict and contradiction, but a question for Marx's mythic approach. By concentrating on the conflict between pastoral myths and technological reality, Marx is deflected into a discussion of industrialism rather than of the human significance of the social relations inherent in capitalism. Industrial capitalism, as Alan Trachtenberg notes, 'had other effects beyond its scars upon the landscape and its mechanization of values. It transformed an entire social structure, the relations among people' (Trachtenberg 1965, 44–5). By privileging the opposition of two modes of consciousness, however, Marx ignores the revolution in social relations which the opposition reveals.

Marx's insistence on the single conflict between technology and pastoralism dominates his readings of 'Ethan Brand' and *The Octopus*, obscuring their authors' respective social commentaries. Marx describes the decaying and alienated 'jolly fellows' who come to witness Ethan Brand's return as 'broken, unfulfilled men' and 'victims of change,' but limits the causes of these problems to mechanization. In the same vein, Marx states that 'Ethan is at once an agent and a victim of scientific empiricism or "mechanism"' and links his unpardonable sin with the 'Faustian drive of mankind' and 'the great sin of the Enlightenment – the idea of knowledge as an end in itself' (pp. 272, 273, 277). Marx interprets the tale's conclusion as an ironic restoration of the ideal middle landscape, since, after the elimination of the evil represented by Brand, Hawthorne adopted a patently idyllic jargon that too simply reinstates the hollow bliss of simple pastoralism. Admittedly, Hawthorne would not have endorsed so naive a reversal of American history. Marx's reading, however, ignores the final exchange between Bartram, the lime burner, and his son. When Bartram notices the shape of a human heart in the ribs of Brand's burned skeleton, he comments, 'Was the fellow's heart made of marble? . . . At any rate, it is burnt into what looks like special good lime; and, taking all the bones together, my kiln is half a bushel the richer for him.' Bartram then smashes Brand's skeleton into fragments, thus ending the story. The tale concludes, then, not on a note of shallow pastoral affirmation, but on Hawthorne's dramatizing of the human reduction of other humans into commodities, an indictment of capitalism's perversion of social relations, not simply of mechanization or of Faustian egotism. Marx's insistence on the machine/garden opposition, however provocative a reading of one scene in 'Ethan Brand,' fails to account for the likelihood of Hawthorne's placing degraded human relations, not the pastoral myth or technological modernization, at the center of the tale. In 'Ethan Brand,' I would suggest, the Faustian and mechanical imagery associated with Brand are secondary indicators of the primary economization of social values.

In his brief comments on *The Octopus*, Marx similarly misses the underlying critique of social relations. He refers to the locomotive's mangling of the herd of sheep as so obvious an example of the 'rapid industrialization of an "underdeveloped" society' (p. 343) that he calls it a 'cliché' of American writing. But, as Donald Pizer points out, this is simply not Norris's theme. According to Pizer, the novel's theme 'is not the conflict between technology and nature or between the kingdom of power and the kingdom of love, as Mr. Marx suggests,' it is rather 'that technology and the landscape are allied rather than opposed in the forward thrust toward human betterment,' nearly a complete refutation of the Marx thesis (Pizer 1963, 537–8). Pizer counters Marx by taking the machine/garden dualism a bit deeper:

> Individual engines, such as that which destroys the flock of sheep, do not symbolize the machine as a power antithetical to that of nature. Rather, they symbolize a particular railroad company whose monopolistic practices are antithetical to a particular natural law.

> (Pizer 1963, 537)

W. F. Taylor, on whom Pizer draws, adds further clarification of Norris's place in the context of the American economic novel. Taylor suggests that

> the struggle between the ranchers and the railway monopoly typifies the most far-reaching and important class conflict of that age in America, the conflict between the middle classes and the plutocracy; and the main issue between ranchers and railroad – the disposal of the public lands – has been from the very beginnings of America one of those half dozen absolutely primary factors that have shaped the entire course of our economic history.

> (Taylor 1942, 296)

More generally on Marx's theme, Taylor suggests,

> What our novelists put on *un*favorable record, what they subjected to telling exposure and criticism, was not the Machine itself but the misuse of the Machine by Society; not industrialism *per se* but the workings of an industrial order administered by a *laissez-faire* capitalism.
>
> (Taylor 1942, 325)

Marx might agree with both Pizer and Taylor, but he does not take his own analysis much beyond the mythic confrontation of technology and nature. By reifying the contradiction between them, Marx misses the specific use Norris makes of the clash in *The Octopus*, that of signaling the political and economic abuse of technology. This might resemble a timeless clash of values, but the particular form such a clash takes in an era of expanding capital cannot adequately be grasped by labeling it mythic, just as human behavior under consolidated capital cannot be simplified as 'human nature.' Masking the dynamic of a specific economic system as a timeless constant beyond human intervention can only further mystify a social construct Marx would like to clarify. Marx's interpretation comes precariously close, in fact, to endorsing Shelgrim's amoral and deterministic advice to Presley, 'Blame conditions, not men' – advice which Taylor correctly states 'has rather the disconcerting effect of a verdict given against the evidence' (Taylor 1942, 299). It is possible to accept Marx's readings on the more abstract level of recurring imagery in American texts, but the image of the machine in the garden is not the most significant reality. While Marx is concerned with consciousness, the social element in American literature is not the mythic clash of static opposites; it is a human problem.

The Phelps farm revisited: cultural theorists on *Huckleberry Finn*

Cultural theorists' readings of *Huckleberry Finn* present an interesting example of how a particular romance or mythic (the two aren't necessarily identical) paradigm can not only denature its object of study, but can accumulate an interpretive inertia that infuses even readings meant to challenge it. I am not arguing that the readings of *Huckleberry Finn* popularized by T. S. Eliot and Lionel Trilling are the only readings brought to Mark Twain's work, but rather that they *have* demonstrated a remarkable resilience in cultural theories of American literature.

Like Eliot before him, Trilling uses formal grounds to explain and defend the problematic final episode of *Huckleberry Finn*. Trilling admits that there is a certain 'falling off' to the conclusion, but argues that 'it has a certain formal aptness' and that it permits 'Huck to return to his anonymity' while reinstating Tom Sawyer's absurd literary romanticism in a way that returns us to the beginning of the novel, a cyclical patterning Trilling tacitly values. It is true that he places the novel in a social context and argues against a universalizing interpretation of Mark Twain's 'moral meaning' by insisting on its 'particular moral reference to the United States in the period after the Civil War' (Trilling 1950, 115, 113). For Trilling, however, *Huckleberry Finn*'s moral truth refers primarily to the mythic morality of 'some simplicity, some innocence, some peace' that had gone out of American life following the war. It is more the privatistic importance of this tragic fall from innocence that concerns Trilling, not Mark Twain's human drama of humans enslaving and exploiting other human beings under a system of economic degradation.

Richard Chase similarly limits the scope of Mark Twain's social criticism by collapsing the novel's concerns into questions of style and myth, implicitly suggesting that those matters are separable from social and political questions. 'Apart from any and all of its meanings *The Adventures of Huckleberry Finn* (1885) delights the reader first and last by its language' (Chase 1957, 139), Chase contends, and few would disagree with the delight he registers in Huck's language. To separate that language from 'any and all meanings,' however, can only fragment what ideological thrust that language possesses. Chase does relate the novel's language to what he considers 'the greatness of *Huckleberry Finn*,' that is, 'the simple clairvoyance of the truth it tells' (p. 142). Throughout the discussion, Chase refers to the brutality and exploitation the novel depicts in antebellum society, but he does so only vaguely, and finally, like Trilling, he reduces the range of the novel's criticism to that of 'a pastoral fiction that looks back nostalgically to an earlier and simpler America,' an assertion that Chase believes 'does not need arguing' (Chase 1957, 148).

Leslie Fiedler's is, of course, one of the most notorious statements on the novel. But his remarks on *Huckleberry Finn* are broader than the specifics of the putative homoeroticism he finds in American fiction. Despite Fiedler's insights into Mark Twain's social satire, he regards Huck Finn not as a typical embodiment of nineteenth-century America's social contradictions nor as an unwitting demystifier of social and political violence, but rather as 'the first Existentialist hero,' a product of 'a terrible breakthrough of the undermind of America itself,' as 'a myth,' and as the 'anti-American American dream' (Fiedler 1960, 286–7). In all these remarks, Fiedler stresses Huck's proto-modernist alienation and impotence as a historical agent.

Far more complex are Leo Marx's ambivalent assessments of *Huckleberry Finn*'s significance. Marx's 1953 review of Eliot and Trilling's readings of the novel attacks on ethical grounds their formalist denaturing of Mark Twain's social text. He argues that, 'like many questions of form in literature, . . . this one is not finally separable from a question of "content," of value, or, if you will, of moral [read: social] insight' (Marx 1953, 425). According to Marx, 'to take seriously what happens at the Phelps farm is to take lightly the entire downstream journey' (Marx 1953, 425). Thus Trilling's rationalization of the conclusion, while couched in moral terms, actually returns us to the brutality of Jim's enslavement and Huck's subordination to Tom's literary schematization of life. Mark Twain's conclusion trivializes not only Jim's humanity but Huck's ethical growth as well. In essence, Marx rejects Trilling's moral standards, replacing them with a larger, more public morality:

> Perhaps the kind of moral issue raised by *Huckleberry Finn* is not the kind of moral issue to which today's criticism readily addresses itself. Today our critics, no less than our novelists and poets, are most sensitively attuned to moral problems which arise in the sphere of individual behavior. They are deeply aware of sin, of individual infractions of our culture's Christian ethic. But my impression is that they are, possibly because of the strength of the reaction against the mechanical

sociological criticism of the thirties, less sensitive to questions of what might be called social or political morality.

(Marx 1953, 435)

Here Marx touches on the general shift from a social (Progressive) to an individualistic (counter-Progressive) perspective in American criticism, the reaction against all social criticism, and Trilling's reflection of both these trends.

Whereas this earlier essay argues for a frankly *social*, vigorously *public* reading – one in which the distinction between a personal and a social or political morality is crucial – Marx's rereading in *The Machine in the Garden* ten years later complicates these matters. Consistent with his thesis on the dialectic of machine (industry and technology) and garden (pastoralism and aesthetics), Marx casts *Huckleberry Finn* as a 'deliberate effort to reclaim the past' in the midst of a society increasingly committed to technology. Hence Huck's withdrawal from a repressive civilization, a movement Marx associates with similar beginnings in *Walden* and *Moby-Dick*. Unlike earlier readers, Marx does not simply polarize the freedom and 'caring' of the raft with the oppressiveness, brutality, or hypocrisy ('carelessness') of the various elements on the shore. Rather he argues that the two worlds were interrelated in Mark Twain's imagination, that they resisted any simplistic reduction and generated instead a new (dialectical) vision capable of accommodating their interpenetration. By the middle of the book, Mark Twain establishes a 'rhythmic alternation between idyllic moments on the river and perilous escapades on shore,' but as the raft floats southward, Mark Twain's complex fusion, Marx suggests, seems to be unraveling: 'The contrast between the two worlds becomes more nearly absolute, and the possibility of imagining a comic resolution virtually disappears' (Marx 1964, 336). But it is with his pressing the trial of his hero to a final choice (Huck's decision to tear up the letter exposing Jim and to 'go to hell' for it) 'that Clemens relinquishes the possibility, once and for all, of a satisfactory comic resolution' (p. 338). Marx endorses this fusion of the 'pastoral ideal with the revolutionary doctrine of fraternity,' but argues that it is 'achieved at the cost of literary consistency and order' (Marx 1964, 338).

This nearly formalist stress on literary consistency and order echoes the remarks of both Eliot and Trilling, whom Marx had attacked for their formalism. The difference is that Marx feels no compunction to justify the novel's final quarter to support his view of its coherence. In fact, he agrees with Hemingway's influential dictum that the book's conclusion is 'just cheating.' '"Cheating" may not be the correct word,' he qualifies, 'but the "real end" does coincide with the crisis of Chapter 31' (Marx 1964, 340). Marx's position here repeats his earlier insistence that 'to take seriously what happens at the Phelps farm is to take lightly the entire downstream journey.' His tone and his description of how the novel reflects social and political concerns, however, have changed. While Marx may not have completely abandoned his earlier, overtly political morality, his mythic and personalistic biases in the *Machine in the Garden* reading certainly attenuate whatever political thrust he attempts to advance. Whereas he had criticized the limitations of Trilling's focus on 'moral problems that arise in the sphere of individual behavior' and on 'individual infractions of our culture's Christian ethic,' he later seems to reinforce those concerns precisely by reducing the novel's dialectic to a relatively static (it is, after all, a timeless pattern) opposition of machine/garden *and* by situating the novel's moral and political world in the experiences and crucial decision of one individual character. Although he gets closer to the text's social essence than do others before him, Marx finally participates with Eliot, Trilling, Chase, and Fiedler in narrowing the possible ranges of meaning *Huckleberry Finn* can have for theorists of American literature. He poses slightly different answers, but they are to essentially the same questions.

These cultural theorists share a number of important assumptions about *Huckleberry Finn*. For one, they agree that the final one-fourth of the novel is problematic – 'flat,' 'cheating,' a 'falling off' – though they evaluate those problems variously. Second, nearly every theorist situates the river, the brilliant colloquial language, and the growth of Huck Finn as a reflective and human protagonist at the center of the novel. Finally, Trilling, Chase, and Marx agree that the novel partakes of a nostalgic longing for a lost simplicity, that its wistful retrospective is a tribute of sorts to a more unified moment in American culture. Further, this nostalgia underpins whatever mythic symmetry or circularity that these critics see in the text. Various readings refer in passing to the brutality Huck witnesses during this drift downriver, to the moribund and hypocritical Christianity of the South – to Pap's degeneration, to Colonel Sherburn's pompous machismo, and so forth – and they posit, albeit erratically, such characterizations as the major thrust of Mark Twain's fragmented and picaresque social criticism. These theorists advance such descriptions and evaluations of the novel in large part because of two of their several shared assumptions: their insistence that the end of the novel is an artistic problem and their belief in the centrality of Huck Finn in the novel. Each of these assumptions is supported and reproduced by an inadequately social view of the work.

Even at the thematic level the assertion of a 'falling off' at the end is questionable. In fact, far from a 'falling off,' the final section of the novel, it could be argued, *unifies* and *intensifies* the novel's main themes. Similar things happen, but the stakes are higher – matters of life and death, freedom and slavery. For instance, the Phelpses are 'kind and good' people who embody the various positive traits of the Widow and Miss Watson, Judge Thatcher, the Grangerfords, and the Wilkes sisters – they care for their own kind. However, like those who capitulate more actively to a slave system, the Phelps family, too, represents the subtle and covert racism that takes the death of a 'nigger' lightly and locks a runaway slave up in a tiny shed. No less than their predecessors in the novel, they foreground the contradictions of an economic and political complex predicated on propriety, religiosity, family unity, and racial violence. Whereas one or two of these characteristics had been stressed in earlier episodes, the Phelps episode integrates them into their ideological totality.

Other constituents of the final chapters similarly crystallize themes from the rest of the narrative. The textual bias of southern society, which had been manifested in the authority of the Bible (or of Shakespeare), the legal code of Judge Thatcher, the maudlin poetry of Emmeline Grangerford, the looming presence of Sir Walter Scott, and the Wilkes will, takes its final duplicitous form in Tom Sawyer's suppression of the document (a legal will) that attests to Jim's freedom and in his imposition of his reading of the romance tradition onto Jim's life. Tom forces Jim to accept the slogans, sentiments, and conventions of a lineage of white prisoners just as he forces Huck and the gang members to go 'by the books' throughout the novel. The basic opposition of truth either mystified or destroyed by textual mutilation is different only in degree from Tom's Arabian Nights fantasies, the King and the Duke's butchery of Shakespeare, or the complicity of the Bible and the legal code with an economic system of exploitation and murder.

The necessity for disguise, too, reaches its culmination in the final scenes. Huck, Jim, the King and the Duke (on several occasions) all had to don disguises for a variety of reasons ranging from relatively innocent (as in Huck's dressing as a girl to gather information from Mrs Judith Loftus) to arguably necessary (dressing up Jim to protect him from slave hunters) to unmitigated duplicity (the King and the Duke posing as the Wilkes brothers from England). More coincidental and less obviously motivated is Huck and Tom's exchange of identities during the entire stay at the Phelps farm. Of course the illusion of Huck as Tom and Tom as Sid *does* underline the instability of Huck's character (it also reinforces Huck's obvious reverence for Tom's style) as well as Tom's doubleness – he is both the rebellious boy *and* the goody two shoes. So, while disguising Huck as Tom and Tom as Sid seems less necessitated by external contingencies, it none the less partakes of the duplicity and self-serving motives of the earlier disguises and strengthens Mark Twain's critique of a society predicated on lying and illusion.

Most importantly, Jim's imprisonment and the very real danger he faces as well as the cruelty of Tom's strategies and his desire to keep the game going 'for the rest of our lives and leave Jim to our children to get out' can be defined as 'a falling off' only if one mythicizes, marginalizes, or disregards the question of slavery and freedom in the novel. Jim's dilemma – being legally free but not knowing it *and* being locked up and tormented as though he were still a slave – synthesizes the various dilemmas he has been in throughout the novel, whether as the chattel property of the Widow, disguised as a mad Arab, or tied down to present the image of his being a captured slave. As with the other images, Jim's literal and figurative imprisonments (in the shed *and* in Tom Sawyer's imagination) reconstitutes subtly and critically the entire world of the novel.

The same mode of intensification informs Mark Twain's system of doubling events around a false/genuine, play/serious axis. Early such doublings include the actual circus Huck sees versus the Royal Nonesuch, Tom's gang robbing the Sunday-school picnic versus both the actual robbers on the Sir Walter Scott and the Duke and the King's attempt to steal from the Wilke's girls, Colonel Sherburn's murder of Old Boggs versus the play version performed for drinks immediately afterward. In the final section of the novel two such moments fulfill these earlier scenes. Huck's remarking 'it was like being born again. I was so glad to find out who I was' when he is mistaken for Tom Sawyer can be read as a false rebirth and reversal compared to his earlier development in relation to Jim – his 'rebirth' into a more humane and egalitarian consciousness. More importantly, Jim's actual quest for freedom is absolutely trivialized by the gaming version Tom Sawyer imposes on him and Huck.

It is also possible that this scheme of fake/authentic doubling is a key to the complexity of Mark Twain's social commentary. Set before the Civil War but written during Reconstruction, the novel may well articulate a complex scheme of mimetic strategies aimed at both eras. If this is a plausible approach, the antebellum slave system could represent the serious or authentic institutional version of slavery while the era of Reconstruction, ostensibly signaling emancipation but actually the scene of equally brutal racism and exploitation, represents a false version of slavery, though a serious one at that. It is also conceivable, given Mark Twain's own cynicism, that these poles could be reversed and that Reconstruction is cast as the period of actual slavery, more genuine and profound because less officially and legally sanctioned.

Such a suggestion poses one possible reason why critics haven't been able adequately to account for the conclusion. If the text is contradictory (and this is not to say flawed), its own doubleness and the relation between its components is more a political than an aesthetic problem. The shared view that the novel harks back to a simpler time suggests two notions. Theorists of American literature have not grasped the complexity of Mark Twain's historical meditation, one at once retrospective *and* contemporary. They have not yet worked out a cultural theory of literature capable of accounting for the multivalence of literature's mediation of social and historical reality. Eric J. Sundquist argues that 'Benito Cereno,' like other notable works of nineteenth-century American fiction – he includes *Huckleberry Finn* – continues powerfully to engage us and

> tends to live as vividly in our memories as in actual encounter and seems to haunt us so in retrospect . . . because it fully exploits, by reflected narrative action and by the formal suspension of moments of crisis, impending problems at once relegated to the historical past but nonetheless alive in the fictional present.

> (Sundquist 1981, 107)

I would like to extend Sundquist's apt reading to include the critical present still vexed by the historical crises so frequently at the center of American texts. Cultural theorists, however, persist in projecting Mark Twain's account back to its ostensible historical context, protecting their own eras from its critical vision. Second, cultural theorists of American literature haven't necessarily avoided the facts of racial violence and political oppression, but they have projected them into a remote historical era and diffused them with a nostalgic gloss. In other words, American criticism may not be able to grasp the contemporaneity of Mark Twain's account precisely because accepting the continuation of racism and political violence after the Civil War into the present poses the threat of having to accept its pervasive existence in contemporary America *and* of having either frankly to deny the relevance of such criticism of literature or to avoid such issues altogether. This is speculative, to be sure, but consistent with the firm injunctions against social criticism common to most theories of American literature. The scenario would look something like this: the avoidance or denial of overtly political and economic issues in literary texts (this can be done in any number of ways) functions as a strategy which frees contemporary criticism from integrating social and political issues into academic literary criticism. Reading *Huckleberry Finn*, then, or any text for that matter, becomes a slightly antiquarian procedure, peripheral, at best, to one's immediate social and political existence. This is not to suggest that individual critics consciously plan to operate on such assumptions, only that the history of American criticism might well have built into it the conventions and rhetorical strategies that result in such a truncation of social significance.

The second major critical bias which I feel denatures the enterprise of cultural theorists of American literature supports the above reading that contemporary American ideology has obscured the social and political implications of *Huckleberry Finn* in particular and the entire field of American literature in general. It is reasonable to assume, given the usual stress on the character of Huck Finn, that one, perhaps the most, decisive reason that the final section of the text is so problematic is due to Tom Sawyer's reappearance and displacement of Huck as the narrative's dominant figure. Critical emphasis on the individual character of Huck rather than on Mark Twain's broader representation of an entire social, political, and economic construct provides one explanation for such an emphasis. As Trilling announces and others practice, 'The great characters of American fiction . . . tend to be mythic because of the rare fineness and abstractness of the ideas they represent; and their very freedom from class gives them a large and glowing generality' (Trilling 1950, 262). In other words, theorists of American literature have tended to abstract character from social milieu and 'have not turned their minds to society,' a quotation from Trilling originally meant to describe American fictionists, not critics. Thus, there has been an emphasis away from viewing characters as 'typical' (to borrow Lukács's term) historical agents in a specifically, though complexly and variously, determined milieu. When Tom Sawyer reappears, the presence, the lucid vision, and the colloquial genius of Huck Finn get submerged and Tom, as a childish version of all the absurdity of adult culture, reasserts his dominance in the world of the novel. If Huck is seen as the center of the novel, then, his displacement and the corresponding domination of Tom Sawyer is regarded as an artistic failure, if not a moral lapse on Mark Twain's part. It is a critical commonplace to assume that Mark Twain lost control over his materials. It seems equally valid to suggest that the hiatus between that scene and his finishing the novel could have provided the time and reflection for a refinement of the novel's concerns. I wouldn't push this point, as it is clear that Mark Twain's texts often are confused, and, as Hershel Parker lucidly demonstrates in *Flawed Texts and Verbal Icons* (1985), sometimes incoherent. I am not attempting to impose order on the text, only to suggest that the final section does not back off or cheat on the issues Mark Twain introduces into his narrative.

Huck's displacement poses the problems it does for yet another reason. Cultural theorists agree that the novel falls off, perhaps because the idyllic image of Huck's finely rendered individuality, his eccentric yet usually penetrating vision, and sometimes (though not always) his forging, with Jim, of a proto-utopian relationship so starkly contrasted to the social miasma beyond that self-contained world of the raft, has seduced many critics into believing that it could be actualized. In other words, Mark Twain's image is so compelling that many theorists of American literature have projected it beyond the social panorama that not only denies its foundations but also poses so potent an opposition to it that Huck's and Jim's moments on the raft and the insights each of them gains cannot ever actually be mistaken as possibilities within the social and historical moment that generates them as antitheses. Theorists deny or forget the fact that Huck and Jim can only represent a precarious and simplistic negation of their milieu, a negation incapable of reentering society and of reconstituting the social order on a higher plane. Once Mark Twain draws his tale to its inevitable historical and political conclusions, theorists of American literature retreat from confronting that darkness, compared to which the banality of the Duke and the King's evil, the religious hypocrisy, and absurd violence all pale. Huck's craft – a raft powerless to combat the general drift and fated to be borne by it – is an appropriate metaphor for the political status of his life. The privatistic bias of cultural theorists – best expressed by Trilling but endorsed by others – results in their abstracting the individuals from the larger social context which defines their individuality, whether positively by reproducing and fostering humane ideals, or negatively by being the generating context for oppositional thinking. As long as 'society' or 'politics' are perceived in vague and positivistic terms as threateningly 'out there,' a force or complex of forces limiting individual development, cultural theorists won't be adequate to the task of formulating the complex fusion of social context and individual existence in literary works.

There is one other possible inference to be drawn from cultural readings of *Huckleberry Finn*. It is possible that Tom's displacement of Huck challenges not only the aesthetic and political preferences of cultural theorists, but the very basis of a liberal education as well. We might all *want* to believe in the possibility of the autonomous individual capable, once liberated from the crushing conventions of social forms, of refining and humanizing human consciousness. Painless *evolution* seems infinitely more desirable than social *revolution*. Huck's failure to maintain his hard-won moral and ethical conscience once he returns to society poses the likelihood that individual liberation without a corresponding social revolution is as powerless and erratic, as vulnerable to being smashed, as is the raft that bears Huck and Jim downstream. Such a realization, it would seem, demolishes liberalism's basic premises about individuality and about educational ideals. Such a political reading of critical readings may shed light on why cultural theorists of American literature, many of whom are committed to these liberal ideals, haven't granted the coherence, seriousness, or centrality of *Huckleberry Finn*'s conclusion. Huck's lighting out for the territories may be simple escapism, or it may signal a negation of his original negation – an important affirmation of a new mode of existence, but it must be viewed as the culmination of the entire narrative, not only of its delightful first half.

4
American literature should not mean but be: self-reflexive theories of American literature

The search for a distinctive American 'style' has been a recurring theme in American writers' and critics' struggle for literary independence. From the seemingly anti-aesthetic 'plain style' of the Puritans to Franklin's homely maxims for ethical uplift to famous nineteenth-century statements such as Emerson's notes on language in *Nature* (1836) and in 'The Poet' (1844), A. B. Johnson's *A Treatise on Language; or, The Relation Which Words Bear to Things* (1836), Horace Bushnell's 'Preliminary Dissertation on the Nature of Language, as Related to Thought and Spirit' (1849), and C. S. Peirce's semantic investigations, American writers and philologists have been preoccupied with the possibilities of an 'American' language. As R. W. B. Lewis notes, after the War of 1812 'more vehement patriots even regretted that Americans were forced to communicate with one another in an old, inherited language' (Lewis 1955, 13). Theorists of American literature before Matthiessen largely subordinated the stylistic study of American literature to a consideration of American themes, to *what* American writers said rather than *how* they wrote. Beginning with the New Criticism's interest in 'how' poems work, however, and continuing through theories of symbolic form, structuralism, and, presently, post-structuralist semiotics and deconstruction, style and how a style can be peculiarly American have emerged as primary considerations in theorizing about American literature.

Such 'stylistic' or 'self-reflexive' theories of American literature include works by Charles Feidelson, Jr, and Richard
Poirier, to cite two major representatives, as well as others
by Edwin Fussell, Jerome Klinkowitz, and John Irwin. The
specific interests of these critics vary from symbolism to stylistic
'worlds elsewhere' to wars for independence from English
'style' to the image of hieroglyphic writing. The common
denominator is their belief that the 'Americanness' of American
literature lies in its language or 'style.' Some argue that style
protects individuality against the constraints of convention,
while others see language only in relation to itself. Two seminal
statements of literary modernism underwrite each of these
critics' aesthetics: Wallace Stevens's definition of modern
poetry as 'the poem of the mind in the act of finding / What
will suffice,' and Archibald MacLeish's maxim, 'a poem should
not mean but be.' For all their interest and originality, however,
the 'worlds elsewhere' discovered by 'self-reflexive' theories of
American literature are very familiar territory.

D. H. Lawrence and American art-speech

While primarily a psychological critic, D. H. Lawrence established some recurring themes of self-reflexive theories of American literature in *Studies in Classic American Literature*. Well before
the institutionalization of aesthetic autonomy, the 'language of
paradox,' and the organicism associated with New Criticism,
Lawrence formulated his own self-reflexive theory by positing a
theory of 'literary' language that is only obliquely intentional
and antirational. In fact, Lawrence's dialectic between mental
and blood consciousness, between reason and experience,
serves both his psychological and his stylistic analyses.

Lawrence distinguishes 'art-speech' from ordinary discourse
and the author's intentions from the work's realized meaning,
both concerns anticipating two major tenets of New Criticism —
their distinction between logical or propositional language and
poetic or dramatic language; and the intentional fallacy. On the
first issue, Lawrence notes, 'the curious thing about art-speech
is that it prevaricates so terribly, I mean it tells such lies . . . and
out of a pattern of lies art weaves the truth. . . . Truly art is a sort
of subterfuge' (Lawrence 1961, viii). The duplicity of art-speech

may be common to all literature, but Lawrence suggests that it takes peculiar form in American literature. 'Americans,' according to Lawrence, 'refuse everything explicit and always put up a sort of double meaning. They revel in subterfuge' (Lawrence 1961, viii). While Lawrence seems to apply this love of subterfuge to Americans as a whole, it is intensified in American literature: 'The old American art-speech contains an alien quality, which belongs to the American continent and to nowhere else.' There is a 'new voice' and a 'new feeling' in American literature (p. 1).

On the question of the artist's relationship to his words, Lawrence advises: 'Never trust the artist. Trust the tale.' While an artist consciously sets out to 'point a moral and adorn a tale,' the tale as a rule 'points the other way,' producing 'two blankly opposing morals, the artist's and the tale's.' Therefore, when we read *The Scarlet Letter* we can 'accept what that sugary, blue-eyed little darling of a Hawthorne has to say for himself, false as all darlings are,' or we can read 'the impeccable truth of his art-speech.' Lawrence's concept of an American character, already prone to prevarication and further complicated by the subterfuge of art-speech, leads Lawrence to define the critic's proper function as 'saving the American tale from the American artist' (p. 2).

Lawrence's application of this theory of language to American literature and history suggests a slippage bordering on cultural schizophrenia in our 'classic American literature.' The American Puritans 'never came here for freedom of worship. . . . They came largely to get *away*' (p. 3). 'Crèvecoeur the idealist puts over us a lot of stuff about nature and the noble savage and the innocence of toil, etc. . . . But Crèvecoeur the artist gives us glimpses of actual nature, not writ large' (p. 26). Cooper is caught between aristocratic longings and democratic lies (pp. 41–2). And in Hawthorne, '*Destroy! destroy! destroy!* hums the underconsciousness. *Love and produce! Love and produce!* cackles the upper consciousness' (pp. 83–4). Although Whitman sang the open road of his soul, 'he wasn't leaving her free. He was forcing her into other people's circumstances' (p. 174). In each study, Lawrence locates the duplicity of American art in a conflict between the blood consciousness and mental consciousness; between 'knowing' in the passional sense and knowing in the intellectual sense; between experience and rationality. He asserts his theme more dramatically in his discussion of 'Ligeia': 'You know your woman darkly, in the blood. To try to know her mentally is to try to kill her' (p. 70).

For Lawrence, literary meaning is not only different from but antithetical to what an author tries to express. It communicates itself, not its author's conscious intention; in fact, the gap between the author's conscious meaning and the realized meaning of the text widens the more resolutely an author attempts to 'point a moral' or formulate an intentional position, be it cultural (as in Crèvecoeur), moral (as in Hawthorne), or social (as in Franklin and Cooper). The text's actual meaning is not a position or idea articulated by an author through a text, but a struggle within the writer that the Lawrentian critic can discern by trusting the tale. Meaning is not, for Lawrence, an idea or concept located within the rational borders of a text; it is an activity, the operation of a writer's psyche at war with itself. In this sense, Lawrence does not allow for any stable intention, conscious or otherwise, since what a text expresses is not a stable thought or tendency articulated in a transparent linguistic medium as much as it is a collision of an express message or moral with an artist's inchoate resistance. This strategy frees Lawrence to find in American literature confirmation of his own *a priori* theory of culture and human behavior.

Since the author's expressed meaning cannot be trusted, Lawrence's theory denies the historicity of a particular writer reflecting a specific historical and social situation. He does believe that the American unconscious is a new historical development, but the tension that the unconscious registers is finally more a static opposition than a dynamic historical construct. Like other mythic and psychological critics, Lawrence locates the same struggle between blood and mental consciousness in every text, reducing a text's specific historical status to a backdrop for the primary, ahistorical drama of consciousness. To be sure, Lawrence understands man as a social creature: 'Men are free when they belong to a living, organic, *believing* community, active in fulfilling some unfulfilled, perhaps unrealized purpose' (p. 6). Lawrence renders this believing community as a social force, however, only in schematic terms, as a stable background against which the psyche of the proto-existentialist human is foregrounded. What Lawrence has done is to offer an exciting and ingenious thesis on the fragmentation of the modern psyche, one with the potential for contributing to an analysis of the impingement of modern economic and political forms on modern life (Lawrence was an avowed hater of modern technology and urbanization, though he chose a psychological model with little direct relation to social complexes). It is the self, only minimally in society, that interests Lawrence. In order to socialize that notion of self more fully, he would need to situate it more squarely in the social and historical contexts of human existence. Art-speech may prevaricate, but that prevarication is more a product of social forms than of unconscious urges in the abstract.

New Criticism and the American Renaissance:
F. O. Matthiessen

Several postulates of the older New Criticism endure in the newer, self-reflexive theories of American literature: the literary work as autonomous verbal structure rather than referential statement; as a nonrational presentation of experience rather than as a logical statement about experience; and as a sensuous texture which needs to be explored and loved rather than possessed and 'used.'

Most conspicuous, perhaps, was the New Critical formalism which posited the work of art as an autonomous verbal structure, a position anticipating recent structuralist and post-structuralist theory. The literary text, New Critics agreed, is an autonomous, organic world to be evaluated on its own terms as what it *is*, not by any 'extraliterary' concerns such as biography and the intentions of the author, the historical and social contexts of its composition, or the philosophical or moral propositions which critics may abstract from the text, or impose on it. Cleanth Brooks's discussion of 'What Does Poetry Communicate?' is representative: 'The poem is not only the linguistic vehicle that conveys the thing communicated most "poetically," ... it is also the sole linguistic vehicle which conveys the thing communicated accurately' (Brooks 1947, 74). For Brooks and most New Critics, the poem simply *is* itself; its verbal structure is an autotelic system of tensions, ironies, and paradoxes, all of which need to be grasped in their organic totality. By damning the 'heresy of paraphrase' which does 'violence to the internal order of the poem itself' by referring the structure of the poem to 'something outside the poem' (Brooks 1947, 201, 202) and by censoring the 'intentional fallacy' for restricting the poem to its author's intended meaning (however complex it may be), New Critics tried (at least in theory) to draw a rigorous boundary between the text and all extra-textual associations and determinants. Despite frequent hedgings, qualifications, and some mimetic leanings, New Critics tended to regard the text as a self-contained, self-maintaining, and, perhaps, self-consuming 'verbal icon.'

Closely related to their tendency to view the work as a self-reflexive aesthetic reality is the New Critics' view of literary language as 'poetic,' that is, nonrational and experimental, rather than 'scientific' or logical and propositional. As Terence Hawkes characterizes New Criticism, 'A poem consists, less of a series of referential and verifiable statements about the "real" world beyond it, than of the presentation and sophisticated organization of a set of complex experiences in a verbal form' (Hawkes 1977, 152). Allen Tate fuses these notions in characteristic New Critical manner when he argues that 'in poetry, the disparate elements are not combined in logic, which can join things only . . . under the law of contradiction; they are combined in poetry rather as experience, and experience has decided to ignore logic' (Tate 1955, 335). Brooks also stresses the poem as 'process,' 'experience,' or 'dramatic action': 'The poem is a dramatization, not a formula; a controlled experience which has to be *experienced*, not a logical process' (Brooks 1947, 190). Elsewhere he remarks, 'The poem, if it be a true poem, is a simulacrum of reality – in this sense, at least, it is an imitation – by *being* an experience rather than any mere statement about experience or any mere abstraction from experience' (Brooks 1947, 213). Brooks underlines the nonrational element as well, arguing that poetic 'fusion is not logical; it apparently violates science and common sense' and praising Robert Penn Warren's 'penetrating observation that all of Shakespeare's villains are rationalists' (Brooks 1947, 18, 42), as though the latter statement were both true and confirmative of his own rejection of logical discourse and rational thought. Tate and Brooks equate poetry with nonlogical experience in opposition to the lesser logic of scientific abstraction.[1]

John Crowe Ransom, too, conceived of poetic texture 'as "irrelevant" in contradistinction to prose which is logical and rational' (Morris 1972, 112). Ransom's notion of 'the world's body' and of the ideal 'disinterestedness' of poetic interpretation, like the ideas of Brooks, Tate, Richards, and others, takes scientific discourse as its adversary. It is in Ransom's work that the existential, corporeal bias of New Criticism is most evident, perhaps as the ultimate polemic against 'science,' 'positivism,' and other enemies of poetry. 'To have knowledge without desire' represented for Ransom the ideal relationship between poet and nature and, by implication, between critic and literary work. Poetic language 'is more cool than hot, and a moral fervor is as disastrous to it as a burst of passion itself' (Ransom 1941, 239). The New Critical view of poetic language as sensuous verbal texture generated in Ransom and in Brooks an erotics of art in which poetry and criticism respond sensuously and lovingly to the world, in contrast to 'science' or 'logic' which prey possessively on a passive victim. Such a loving poetics valorizes the autonomous, experiential, and nonrational being of poetic texture while eschewing all interest in utility. Ransom and other New Critics wanted to restore the concreteness of sensuous materiality in the face of scientific abstraction, to rehumanize the world which science and logic had dehumanized. Therefore criticism had to reject all approaches to poetry that tried to make poems 'mean' rather than simply 'be.' In an extreme version of Trilling's injunction against ideology, Ransom believed that 'people who are engrossed with their pet "values" become habitual killers. . . . It is thus that we lose the power of imagination, or whatever faculty it is by which we are able to contemplate things as they are in their rich, contingent materiality' (Ransom 1938, 116). Distinguishing poetry from science by its value-free acceptance of materiality, Ransom 'protected' it from any ideological content: 'The true poetry has no great interest in improving or idealizing the world. . . . It only wants to realize the world, to see it better' (Ransom 1938, x). For Ransom, poetry is 'always something magnificently chimerical' and would be 'irresponsible if it would really commit us to an action,' a degraded function of the prose language of science (Ransom 1943, 279).

D. H. Lawrence had earlier contrasted knowing passionally and knowing mentally, associating the former with a positive acceptance of the Other and the latter with abstracting, scientific coldness (Lawrence 1961, 70). Ransom, while philosophically and temperamentally different from Lawrence, reinstated this contrast in his own polarity of poetry = love versus science = lust, thus formulating what became a common preoccupation of later self-reflexive critics of American literature. From Feidelson's vision of symbolism as constitutive of concrete being to Poirier's theory of the performing self to John Irwin's assumption that hieroglyphic doubling constitutes the writer's self in visible linguistic form, self-reflexive theorists equate (or approximate) the literary text with the human self in a fusion of linguistic and corporeal criticism. Whether they view literature or writing as constitutive of an autonomous new meaning or of the human form itself, their theories draw a homologous relationship between literary and human ontology. We should approach the text as we would a human lover, for writing 'embodies' being.

To summarize: New Criticism deflected critical attention from theme to language, rejecting paraphrasable content for a direct and sensuous appreciation of the texture of poetic language. Later extensions of New Critical aesthetics alter the terms of discussion, but the predominance of language and literature as self-reflexive systems remains a constant, as does the marginalizing of literature's propositional function in favor of a view that American literature should not mean but be.

F. O. Matthiessen's *American Renaissance: Art and Expression in the Age of Emerson and Whitman* (1941) was the first study of American literature to apply New Critical analytic tools to American writing as a whole. The importance of Matthiessen's study in the history of American literature has been well documented by Richard Ruland, Wesley Morris, and Giles Gunn, and I will comment only briefly on his place among self-reflexive theorists of American literature, referring readers to these three studies for more detailed accounts.[2]

Matthiessen occupies a contradictory middle ground between the sociological and democratic criticism of the thirties and the abandonment of social considerations by later self-reflexive theorists. As Ruland points out,

> Matthiessen saw no need to reject New Criticism, but he felt
> that his contemporaries must learn from the thirties – from
> the Marxists and from V. L. Parrington. These men had
> tried, however unsuccessfully, to see life whole, to understand
> the role of economics and industrialism in the problems of
> American democracy.
>
> (Ruland 1967, 212)

In the preface to *American Renaissance*, Matthiessen balances these interests precisely:

> The avenue of approach to all these themes is the same,
> through attention to the writers' use of their own tools, their
> diction and rhetoric, and to what they could make with them.
> An artist's use of language is the most sensitive index to
> cultural history, since a man can articulate only what he is,
> and what he has been made by the society of which he is a
> willing or an unwilling part.
>
> (Matthiessen 1941, xv)

Matthiessen's emphasis on style and language in the first of these sentences is characteristic of the self-reflexive positions later advanced by Richard Poirier and Jerome Klinkowitz, who argue that the essence of American literature is a matter of language's physical presence in words, sentences, and paragraphs. Matthiessen, however, qualifies such a stress on the linguistic medium in the very next sentence, balancing the individuals' statements with their social existence, their *parole* with the cultural *langue*. Giles Gunn suggests that Matthiessen realized this balance on many levels. Horatio Greenough's works, for example, 'supported Matthiessen's conviction that literature must be appreciated in terms intrinsic to its own mode of being and yet corroborated his belief that those terms cannot be fully understood without an awareness of the historical and existential conditions that generated them' (p. 92).

In theory, at least, Matthiessen grasped the extent to which individual 'style' can also be a collective expression of the culture of its genesis. Matthiessen's distinction between an individual's willing and unwilling participation in social conventions also suggests a provocative index for distinguishing the subjective and individual from the objective and collective in literary works, of understanding how a writer's style is not – indeed cannot – be simply an individual phenomenon, but already embodies a larger perspective. Through careful consideration of a writer's works and through an informed reconstruction of the social and historical milieu of a writer's literary production, it should be possible to distinguish the objective or collective content of a text (its presentation or description of society, economics, and politics) from the subjective or individual manner in which they are reflected (an author's interpretation of characters, events, historical periods; and the tone with which they are rendered). In one sense, we already perform such an act when we discuss a particular author's divergence from literary conventions, but Matthiessen suggests that we might push farther to engage social as well as literary reality, in so far as literature embodies both.

But while Matthiessen demonstrated an interest in such a social and historical apprehension of literature, it is the New Critical side of his work that has lived on, setting a precedent for later studies that abandoned the 'background' of history, politics, and sociology for the 'foreground' of aesthetics and expression in American literature, to see 'the word one with the thing.' Matthiessen's own emphasis invites this interpretation: despite his declared intentions, he seems less interested in the democratic essence of American literature than in complex linguistic nuances of ambiguity and paradox in the works of the American Renaissance. Leslie Fiedler noted the infiltration of Matthiessen's work with New Critical methods in a 1958 essay assessing the state of American literary studies:

> But Matthiessen shows in a way that scarcely any other contributors do, the impact of twenty years of the New Criticism: that long attempt to isolate essential artistic values by close attention to the text and to reassess all literature in terms of a tradition which makes metaphysical poetry and French *symboliste* art the touchstone of merit.
>
> (Fiedler 1958, 167)

More recently, Giles Gunn argues that by opting to judge works of art by 'evaluating their fusions of form and content,'

Matthiessen reaffirmed the New Critical 'bias he had acquired from Eliot and found confirmed in the work of everyone from I. A. Richards to Allen Tate' (Gunn 1975, 72). Gary Lee Stonum stresses a similar dependence on modernist aesthetics and contextualist criticism when he notes that 'Matthiessen's contribution was to demonstrate that the Age of Emerson was best read through spectacles fashioned by the poetry of Yeats and T. S. Eliot' (Stonum 1981, 4).

Thus the aesthetic side of Matthiessen's larger accomplishment is what seems most relevant to recent critical theorists. Seeing life whole may well be what Matthiessen endeavored, yet his inherited formalist framework made a denial of his social orientation a convenient option. Without calling into question New Criticism's basic foundations, even so socially concerned a critic as Matthiessen remained clearly aligned with the metaphysical poetry and French symbolism which Eliot, Pound, and the New Critics had imported and naturalized earlier in the century. Indeed, Matthiessen's debt to Eliot seems to have so aestheticized his critical faculties that, while desiring to inculcate a socially responsible study of literature, Matthiessen could agree with Mallarmé's dictum that 'poetry is not written with ideas, it is written with words,' as well as with the assertion that 'what matters is not what a poem says, but what it is' (Matthiessen 1935, vii).[3] He continued to struggle with the social context of both poetry and the poet, but his aesthetic stance in *American Renaissance* contradicts his deep concern with social matters too fundamentally to influence later critics to pursue a balanced line of inquiry. Whereas Matthiessen remained concerned about the social contexts and origins of American literature (see, for example, his study of Dreiser), many later theorists tend to denigrate the mimetic function of American literature in favor of a purely formal, self-reflexive theory of American writing.

Making the world safe for symbolism: Charles Feidelson, Jr

Charles Feidelson's *Symbolism and American Literature* (1953), published twelve years after *American Renaissance*, is generally acknowledged as one of the seminal books on American literature and cultural history. In fact, nearly thirty years after its publication, *Symbolism and American Literature* still seems to be gaining in stature, as some contemporary theorists of American literature acknowledge Feidelson as one of the first critics to point out the self-reflexivity of American literature, as a precursor of deconstruction, a view that seems to miss Feidelson's attachment to, not deconstruction of, presence.[4] Feidelson positions his own study in the history of theorizing about American literature, invoking the names of Parrington, Winters, Wilson, and Matthiessen as his forerunners, but rejecting, in turn, their theses on the anti-aestheticism, obscurantism, romantic egoism, and political concerns of American writing. But Feidelson seems most concerned with correcting Matthiessen's inordinately 'sociological and political bent of studies.' Whereas Matthiessen argued that the 'one common denominator' among writers of the American Renaissance 'was their devotion to the possibilities of democracy,' Feidelson replaces Matthiessen's thesis with a stylistic theme: 'It is more likely that the really vital common denominator is precisely their attitude toward their medium – that their distinctive quality is a devotion to the possibilities of symbolism' (Feidelson 1953, 3, 4). It is important to note that Feidelson means to correct, not to expand or qualify, Matthiessen's sociological approach. By replacing an extrinsic with an intrinsic critical method, an interest in democracy with an interest in style, Feidelson's emphasis on the autonomy of literary language does indeed result in the first self-reflexive theory of American literature.

According to Feidelson, the writings of Poe, Emerson, Hawthorne, Melville, and Whitman constitute 'the unified phase of American literature,' which, although 'not recognized as such by the men who made it' (p. 1), was a symbolist movement. Feidelson believes that 'the relative immaturity of the American literary tradition' prevented these writers from producing any masterpieces, but asserts that their greatest contribution to literature, in fact 'their title to literary independence,' lies in their anticipation of the symbolist aesthetic central to modern literature and criticism. Feidelson locates the roots of modern symbolism in American Puritan typology and Ramistic logic and then traces the advance of symbolism through the American Renaissance to modern writers, such as Henry

James, T. S. Eliot, and R. P. Blackmur. Like modern authors such as Gide and Joyce, the American writer has tended, though often unconsciously, to view 'the task before him neither as the expression of his own feelings nor as the description of given things but rather as an adventure in discovery among the meanings of words' (p. 47).

The basic tenets of symbolist writing are its 'emphasis on literary structure, . . . and an unusual awareness of the linguistic medium itself' (p. 45). The meaning of meaning is the generative question for American symbolist writers; the symbolist method calls attention to the productive activity of writing rather than the product of that activity, the 'mean*ing* rather than the meant' (p. 53). As opposed to the logical language of science, poetic language frees itself from the burden of the material world: 'A poem delivers a version of the world; it *is* the world for the moment' (p. 57). For symbolism poetic language is a plastic medium, nonrational and alogical, concrete, and saturated with meaning (pp. 55, 56). Drawing on critics and philosophers such as I. A. Richards, R. M. Eaton, Ernst Cassirer, and Susanne Langer, Feidelson defines his method:

> To consider the literary work as a piece of language is to regard it as a symbol, autonomous in the sense that it is quite distinct both from the personality of its author and from any world of pure objects, and creative in the sense that it brings into existence its own meaning.
>
> (p. 49)

Not simply a literary practice, the symbolist enterprise is a unified epistemological stance, a profound departure in American and modern thought, a transcendence of the dualistic thinking which Feidelson feels has divided and compartmentalized our perceptual capacities for centuries.

Feidelson both traces American literature back to its Puritan origins and argues that the American tradition prefigures the triumph of modern literature and philosophy: 'The intellectual stance of the conscious artist in American literature has been determined very largely by problems inherent in the method of the Puritans' (p. 89). Although 'a properly symbolic method was denied the Puritan writer by his assumptions on method in general' (p. 84) and by his fear of the 'symbolic thinking' of a typological perspective, explicit Puritan method 'was actually at odds with itself' (pp. 88, 91). A sense of organic unity between thought and thing, sign and signified, and the proliferation of meaning inherent in the dialectical thought – 'each proposition generating its opposite' – eventually undermined the rigidity of Puritan thought, giving way to Edwards, whose 'aim was to validate the language of direct perception' and to 'affirm the basic premises of symbolism' (pp. 99, 101). Feidelson joins Perry Miller in bridging the gap from Edwards to Emerson, arguing that 'theology aside, Edwards anticipated the symbolic consciousness of Emerson' (p. 99).

Of course, it is with the 'age of Emerson' that Feidelson is most concerned:

> The symbolism of Emerson and his colleagues is a chapter in the history of modern taste. It is part of the symbolist tradition that culminates in modern literature. Hawthorne's indecision, Whitman's diffuseness, the complication of Melville's attitude, and the exaggerated unreason of Poe reflect the hazards of symbolism together with its possibilities, for each sets out from the question of *meaning*.
>
> (p. 75)

These writers all grappled with the problems posed by a new way of perceiving, of being in the world, a struggle which generated their overtures to symbolism. The world that Hawthorne seeks 'is generated by contemplation of the symbol, not by the external yoking together of two realms which by definition are different in kind' (p. 9). *The Scarlet Letter*, then, is 'a kind of exposition of the nature of symbolic perception' (p. 10) in which each character plays a symbolic role in a symbolic drama, reenacting the adventure of discovery felt by the narrator in the 'Custom House' (according to Feidelson, 'a portrait of the artist as symbolist in spite of himself'). For Feidelson, it is significant that the very focus of the book is 'a written sign,' a fact which relocates the text's significance in the question of 'not only *what* the focal symbol means but also *how* it gains significance,' the question of meaning in general (pp. 13, 10). However, since 'symbolism at once fascinated and horrified' Hawthorne, he backed off into the stability of allegorical correspondence (p. 14). The book's moral is at odds with its technique: 'The symbolism leads to an inconclusive luxuriance of meaning, while allegory imposes the pat moral and the simplified character' (p. 15).

For Emerson and Whitman, though, symbolism became an 'explicit metaphysical principle' in that 'empirical fact and rational form had no hold' on them. Emerson embodies 'the sweeping sense of poetic fusion' and 'the marriage of thought and things' that underlie the sense of the world as multiple significance and of the poet as voyager, or transparent eyeball, whose life is a perpetual creation of new meanings (pp. 16, 120). Whitman pushes Emerson's thought to its logical, poetic conclusions: 'The exploitation of Speech as the literary aspect of eternal process is the source of whatever literary value resides in *Leaves of Grass*' (p. 19). According to Feidelson, the true *subject* of 'When Lilacs Last in Dooryard Bloom'd' is 'the poetic process. . . . The art of poetizing and the context in which it takes place have continuity in time and space but no particular existence' (p. 22). Melville's great symbols – the doubloon, the sea, the whale, the voyage – and Poe's house of Usher similarly point only to themselves as aesthetic symbols, creating new symbolic meaning. 'Properly speaking,' Feidelson remarks in his representative discussion of *Moby-Dick*, 'the moment of imagination is a state of becoming, and the visionary forms simultaneously are apprehended and realize themselves' (p. 30).

Feidelson summarizes the significance of this symbolist program in his postscript:

> In brief: the affinity between large areas of American literature and of modern literature brings to light unsuspected aspects of both. In this perspective the classic American writers take on a new unity of direction, a new historical status, and a new subtlety of achievement. Modern literature becomes a less unaccountable phenomena [*sic*]; it is naturalized in a long, rather covert historical movement, of which American writing is a major phase.
>
> (p. 213)

Throughout *Symbolism and American Literature* – in his definition of symbolism, his application of symbolist theory to the texts and writers he deals with, and his vision of American literary history – Feidelson maintains a coherence of theory and consistency of practice rarely achieved in theories of American literature. But it is exactly Feidelson's 'vision' of American literature and literary history that needs closer examination, not only because it projects a unified tradition and sensibility and creates an aura of definitiveness, but also because of its influence on other theorists of American literature. As I suggested in chapter 1, Feidelson is concerned with literary history after a fashion, but only minimally concerned with the social mediation offered by American literature.

Feidelson's American literature is represented primarily by Poe, Emerson, Hawthorne, Melville, and Whitman; he mentions a few other writers – Edwards, Bushnell, Thoreau, and Eliot – but only briefly. For Feidelson, this group constitutes a unified phase of literary production, a coherent epistemological paradigm that defines American literature. Although Feidelson attempts to ground his study in a historical milieu (he argues that 'symbolism is the coloration taken on by the American literary mind under the pressure of American intellectual history' (p. 43) and that 'the isolation of the American artist in society, so often lamented, is actually parallel to the furtive and unacknowledged role of artistic method in the American mind' (p. 89)), there is an ahistorical bias at work in Feidelson's privileging of modern symbolism as the touchstone of American literary merit and in his representative exclusion of nonsymbolic writers from the American canon. Regarding symbolism as the criterion of literary value commits Feidelson to a theory of literary history that denies the importance of alien writers, texts, and literary programs. Feidelson, like many other theorists, arbitrarily denies the actual heteroglossia (to borrow a term from M. M. Bakhtin) of the American tradition by failing to acknowledge symbolism as but one historically specific literary practice among many others.

Feidelson not only imposes a rigid hierarchy on American writers, he limits the five writers he discusses in *Symbolism and American Literature* as well, isolating only those passages and texts that are approachable in symbolic terms. This species of selection led Perry Miller to accuse Feidelson's symbolic amputations as 'illegitimate, basically whimsical, and irresponsible':

Armed with this cleaver, Mr. Feidelson stretches out on his chopping block the works of Poe, Emerson, Hawthorne, Whitman, Thoreau, and Melville, slices off the symbolical tenderloin, and throws the rest into the pail of 'romanticism.' . . . Mr. Feidelson's thesis is that the portions or aspects which can be called symbolical are detachable from the others; they are the usable elements, and between them and modern writing there is an 'affinity' in view of which the modern is 'naturalized' in an American tradition. . . . That Mr. Feidelson stands in the good company of many other worshippers of the symbol does not make his amputations any less arbitrary.

(Miller 1953, 303–4)

Miller's charge seems justified in light of how much Feidelson excludes from any given author to support his thesis. For instance, Feidelson neglects in *Moby-Dick* the cetological chapters, the humor, the ethical and moral questions, and the social and political satire in order to define Ishmael's symbolic questing and Ahab's war with reason as the novel's core. Melville's motif of exploration and voyaging, along with his epistemological radicalism in *Moby-Dick* and other works, is, of course, important, but Feidelson's elimination or devaluation of all other concerns can only impoverish our response to Melville's work. Feidelson similarly writes only briefly and disparagingly of *Billy Budd* because he feels Melville acquiesced to the 'authoritarian dogmatism' (p. 212) of Captain Vere as a solace for the risky business of symbolic doubt. It would, of course, be impossible to consider all the works by even this small group of authors selected by Feidelson as the American tradition, but his method of selection is so narrow even within those works that it undermines its own claim to authority as a definition of American literature's significance.

Despite the obvious selectivity of his study, the implications of Feidelson's work are exciting, posing a strategy and a method for investigating the constitutive function of language. A historicized version of Feidelson's tactics could pursue any number of cultural inquiries. Assuming that specific discursive practices crystallize at specific moments under specific pressures, a method such as Feidelson's would be capable of revealing how and why language attempts to transcend various social determinants as well as what impact those social pressures have on cultural discourse. In other words, a historicized version of Feidelson's method would pay as much attention to the signified as to the signifier. If we assume with Feidelson that symbolic language can escape direct referential or mimetic functions and appear to exist in and for itself, could we not then work toward discerning the homologous relations that may exist between the form and the dynamics of literary texts and the social complexes of their geneses? Feidelson's historical premise – that symbolism arose at a particular historical moment – could generate semiotic analyses of the relationships between cultural texts (literature, advertising, political discourses, and so on) and social contexts, even though the texts themselves purport to transcend social determination.

Several of Feidelson's theoretical tenets, however, deflect attention from such potential. From today's vantage point, Feidelson stands midway between New Criticism and structuralism and deconstruction, the bridge being his central assumption of the work as self-reflexive linguistic artifact. While Feidelson shares the New Critical notion of the text as an autonomous, organic whole, he anticipates the poststructuralist position on the superfluity of linguistic meaning as well as its denial of a determinate point from which to begin the interpretive act, though he pulls up short of a deconstructive vision of textuality. Drawing on a large arsenal of New Critical terms and assumptions, Feidelson defines his main strategy as giving ' "language" a kind of autonomy by conceiving it as a realm of meaning, and the structure explored is discovered *in* the language, not *behind* the poem in the writer's mind or *in front of* the poem in an external world' (p. 45). Feidelson's specification of poetry's multiplicity of meaning as 'the universe of paradox' as well as his contention that poetic multiplicity of meaning results in 'no end to the process of paraphrase' (p. 63) further attest to his debt to Cleanth Brooks's 'language of paradox' and 'heresy of paraphrase.' Feidelson's 'symbol,' in fact, is difficult to distinguish from the 'poem' of New Criticism, since both aesthetics are based on ambiguity, paradox, tension, and the autonomy of the work, and are opposed to appeals either to authorial intention or to paraphrasable meaning. Like that of the New Critics, Feidelson's theory of poetry devalues the significance of a work's social and mimetic being by defining the terms of literary composition and critical analysis as a working out of the text's infrastructural tensions and ambiguity. While other elements of New Critical formalism may not persist in Feidelson's work or that of other post-New Critical thinkers, their shared denial of the referential or mimetic significance of literature constitutes a unified program adopted by most theorists of American literature.

Two other components of Feidelson's thesis – the alogicality of poetic language and the idea of poetic language as a language of process – weaken the historical potential of his theory. Feidelson defines symbolism as poetical as opposed to logical, the poetic undermining the premises of the logical, which depends on dualistic thinking, fixed categories, and a world beyond language to which language can only abstractly refer. 'Logical language is built upon the principle of discreteness. . . . Logical structure is typically atomistic,' argues Feidelson; 'we usually assume that the atoms of logical meaning antedate the proposition in which they occur' (p. 57). For Feidelson, symbolist literature does not refer to a world beyond itself; 'it *is* the world for the moment. . . . Within the poem each word is potentially a standpoint, a symbolic crossroad, from which the whole poem may be viewed' (p. 57). Feidelson sees this denial of a determinate place from which to view a literary work as the key to its nonrational, revolutionary force. By its very nature, 'literary structure . . . is logically circular. Any attempt to describe it must end in paradox' (p. 61). For Hawthorne, 'the symbol was valuable precisely because it transcended analytic thought' (p. 14). 'Empirical fact and rational form had no hold on Emerson and Whitman, whose "transcendentalism" was specifically opposed to neoclassic doctrine and method' (p. 16). Poe, of course, embodies the illogicality of symbolism most consistently: 'Poe begins where Ahab leaves off. His primary aim is the destruction of reason' (p. 35).

This destruction of fixed, logical categories is central to Feidelson's view that American literature collapses theme and technique into a literature of process, not product, a position which, strangely, seems antithetical to a symbolist aesthetic. Defining literature as productive activity (the mean*ing* rather than the meant) enables us to grasp the work as constitutive of meaning, producer of an organic world of its own. Feidelson draws on Cassirer's idea that each work contains 'a spontaneous law of generation, an original way and tendency of expression, which is more than a mere record of something initially given in fixed categories of real existence' (p. 53). Applying this notion to American writing, Feidelson notes that 'the shift of image from the contemplative eye of "establish'd poems" to the voyaging ego of Whitman's poetry records a large-scale theoretical shift from the categories of "substance" to those of "process"' (p. 17). In a typical case, 'the ambiguity of Poe's metaphysics . . . exactly corresponds to the paradox of "process,"' the paradox itself being 'the consequence of a new category, creative motion' (p. 37). Melville's *Redburn*, Feidelson argues, 'points toward the conception of experience as process. . . . The only reality, therefore, lies in the process of becoming; not in the illusory permanence of guidebooks, but in the hazards of change' (p. 180).

By severing the work from any reality outside its textual borders, and by defining the intra-textual world ahistorically, Feidelson locks American literary studies into what Fredric Jameson calls 'the prison house of language.' According to Jameson, structuralism, too, rests on a 'transformation of form into content, in which the form of Structuralist research . . . turns into a proposition about content: literary works are about language, take the process of speech itself as their essential subject matter' (Jameson 1972, 199). Jameson argues that a profound consonance exists between self-reflexive modes of linguistic criticism and 'that systematized and disembodied nightmare which is our culture today' (Jameson 1972, ix) and criticizes both formalism and structuralism in so far as they reify the linguistic texture of the work and deny not just the relevance, but the possibility of its referring to any extra-textual reality. For Jameson, insulating the text from reality is a static, undialectical enterprise that 'has the effect of reinforcing idealistic tendencies which are already at work within the material itself' (Jameson 1972, 106). Literature often does accentuate its verbal presence and call attention to its structural presence. But literature also exists in relation to the world to which its language refers; to abstract the linguistic presence from its referential function results in a form of idealism which can only fracture a work's total existence, its complexity of reflection.

With a writer like Poe, whose works often posit an escape from conventional reality as their ideal, Feidelson's readings seem quite at home, although they, of course, stop short of an analysis of Poe's positions. But when the writers themselves seem to stray outside the confines of symbolist self-reflexivity and maximize their own sociality, Feidelson explicitly deprives them of what referential, reflexive significance they intend. For example, Feidelson quotes Whitman's remark that 'no one will get at my verses who insists upon viewing them as a literary performance, or attempt at such performance, or as aiming mainly toward art or aestheticism,' and he admits that Whitman's conscious literary theory subordinates literature to sociology (p. 16). But he then evades the force of this seemingly inconsistent evidence by eliding its sense of genuine commitment and authority: 'Yet it is obvious that a larger principle governs both his poetry and his sociological doctrine; no one will get at his verses who insists upon viewing them as a sociological performance' (p. 17). By so polarizing these options (aesthetic versus sociological) Feidelson's method is incapable of allowing literature *both* an aesthetic and a social significance, even if the two are mutually reinforcing, as in Whitman's 'democratic' poetics.

In the case of Hawthorne, Feidelson defines *The Scarlet Letter*'s focus as 'a written sign,' arguing that the integral act of contemplating the symbolic scarlet letter 'opens' a new imaginative reality. While this may be true at one level, it deprives Hawthorne's imaginative reality of its material, social, theological, and moral depth: 'That it is not the material reality of nineteenth-century Salem becomes *wholly irrelevant*, since the meaning of the symbol, accreted by generations who have lived with it and in it, is continuous in time' (p. 9; italics added). Feidelson elsewhere reiterates this anti-realistic position in ways fully consistent with his view of symbolic language as autonomous and anti-referential. For example, he states that 'Puritan ministers spent their lives immersed in the meaning of words,' as though their concern with language (the trial of Anne Hutchinson is a good example) can be separated from the social reasons which prompted it, reasons such as the maintenance of political and religious stability.

Yet after all, Feidelson's symbolist theory – its stress on linguistic autonomy, on anti-referentiality, on the literature of process and exploration rather than of commentary or proposition – presupposes an implicit theory of social life and its material milieu. While Feidelson seems to adhere to the symbolist program partly because it exposes the paucity of a positivist view of reality, his own view of what reality exists outside of the aesthetic work is actually positivistic. He can only conceive of subject and object in the abstract, one irreducibly opposed to the other, the former a disembodied spirit, the latter an alien and hostile material cipher.

Feidelson's monism attempts to bridge this gap between language and reality along with other dualisms – word and thing, theme and technique, mean*ing* and meant – by substituting the act of writing as constitutive of meaning. Part of Feidelson's defense lies in his rigid distinction between poetic and logical languages, a distinction central to his precursors, notably I. A. Richards and Cassirer. The language of logic desires to 'possess' and 'use' both language and the world to which it refers, while the language of poetry celebrates its transcendence of material and scientific contamination. For Cassirer, 'science means abstraction, and abstraction is always an impoverishment of reality,' but art is 'an interpretation of reality – not by concepts but by intuitions; not through the medium of thought but through that of sensuous forms' (Cassirer 1944, 144, 146). Behind these dualisms lies Kant's original distinction between art as 'another nature' and 'pure disinterested satisfaction' as opposed to logical or scientific judgments 'bound up with an interest' (Kant 1971, 397, 383). Feidelson's transcendence of the literary and philosophical dualism between romanticism and naturalism, idealism and materialism, and between 'thinking ego and brute fact' (p. 50) is a new starting point for literary analysis 'designed to recapture the unity of a world artificially divided' (p. 51). Regarding the world not as subjective expression or as objective description but rather as 'symbolic fact' is to grasp that 'the real world . . . is known in symbolic form; to know is to symbolize in one way or another' (p. 52). Feidelson properly tries to abolish arbitrary distinctions in search of a more dynamic analysis of human consciousness in the material world, but his notion of symbolism as autonomous, self-reflexive production of meaning tends to deny the dialectical relation between subject and object that he elsewhere affirms. In fact, Feidelson's understanding of the 'thinking ego and brute fact' grants the polarized terms the very validity he wishes to deny; he sees them in a static opposition rather than in a dynamic contradiction wherein one side inhabits the other. Feidelson's argument that we need to transcend both poles actually collapses them into a new dualism between the subjective creation of symbolic meaning and the scientific or logical commentary on a given meaning, still an *a priori* valorization of the former as humane opposed to the sterility of the latter.

Feidelson's own dualistic thinking thus prevents him from acknowledging the interpenetration of experience and ideas about experience. He values pure experience itself as authentic and meaningful, while devaluing 'ideas about experience' as secondary and sterile. Of course, it is only poetic or symbolic language, meaning the language created by 'poets' or 'symbolists,' that can recapture the unity of mind lost in the dissociation of sensibility. Here Feidelson's argument echoes Cleanth Brooks's assertion that 'it is not enough for the poet to analyze his experience as the scientist does, breaking it up into parts. . . . His task is finally to unify experience. He must return us to the unity of the experience itself as man knows it in his own experience.' For Brooks, as for Feidelson, the poem is a simulacrum of reality 'by *being* an experience rather than any mere statement about experience or any mere abstraction from experience' (Brooks 1947, 212, 213). Both Feidelson and Brooks, then, regard experience as an end in itself, outside of who is experiencing, what is experienced, and under what historical and social conditions an experience occurs. In this sense, Feidelson's organicism idealizes a lost unity, a thing of the past. By viewing literature as the totality of experience itself rather than as a reflection on experience (which is necessarily an experience itself in so far as the act of commenting on experience is a new, though derivative, experience as well), Feidelson also remains attached (though, perhaps only in retrospect, as he remains troubled by his description of American symbolist technique) to what Derrida rejects as 'an ethic of presence, an ethic of nostalgia for origins, an ethic of archaic and natural innocence, a purity of presence and self-presence in speech' (Derrida 1970, 264). In this sense as well, Feidelson suggests a positivistic isolation of human subjectivity, which fetishizes and sentimentalizes (thus polarizing rather than synthesizing) both consciousness and experience. Feidelson deprives litera-ture of its status as anything other than the documentation of a moment of transcendence which, by definition, occurred in the past. The symbol can only present the momentary union, with no stability, no context, and no particular claim to importance.

It is on these grounds that Feidelson's theory of symbolism asserts its anti-social bias most strongly. While claiming to return literature to the concrete specifics of lived experience, Feidelson actually denies the social and material contexts which alone are capable of anchoring a reflection of existence. Jameson believes Saussure formulated his own anti-historical notion of language (a notion which Feidelson's theory of sym-bolism and history closely resembles) 'out of increasing dissatis-faction with his experience of history itself' (Jameson 1972, 7). Philip Rahv also touches on this metaphysics of contempt when he finds in 'the exaltation of symbolism' in critical practice (he mentions Feidelson by name),

> an attitude of distaste toward the actuality of experience – an attitude of radical devaluation of the actual if not downright hostility to it; and the symbol is of course readily available as a means of flight from the actual into a realm where the spirit abideth forever. . . . Hence the effort we are now witnessing to overcome the felt reality of art by converting it into some kind of schematism of spirit; and since what is wanted is spiri-tualization at all costs, critics are disposed to purge the novel of its characteristically detailed imaginative working through of experiential particulars.

> (Rahv 1956, 285)

Rahv remarks on problems inherent in many of the theories we have studied, such as the anti-realistic bias which appears again in the work of Richard Poirier. Feidelson and others do not deny the existence of reality, or materiality, or politics, but they often declare them empty of meaning, in need of transcendence or spiritualization. They assume that the world of social, political, and material reality is barren, a mere dead weight ('brute fact' as Feidelson terms it), devoid of significance. Herein lies a partial reason as to why symbolism appealed to postwar American criticism. In the midst of cold war paranoia and a society increasingly committed to technology and 'instrumental reason,' all of which were perceived as dehumanizing and destructive, Feidelson, like Marcuse and other members of the Frankfurt School, attempted to protect human freedom via a notion of literary autonomy by divorcing it from both material and political contingencies. One problem of such a program is that it trivializes literary production and consumption by placing them in an ersatz opposition to the very forces they are *meant* to contravene. The significance of art is not to be found in an imaginative rendering of life in society, but in its purging itself of the specificity and fixity of materiality and its formulation of a symbolic world elsewhere.

Worlds elsewhere: Richard Poirier

In a 1981 *Salmagundi* interview, Richard Poirier countered the critics, especially Gerald Graff, who accuse him of declaring writers and writing free from history and materiality, by defining his own critical interests in frankly political terms:

> I regard myself as more of a realist than [Graff] or the critics he seems to prefer, inasmuch as I always do see literary expressions as bound in by politics, by history, and by biological givens. My work is never about the autonomy of style, but instead about the way style is always bound to struggle against immitigable pressures of place, time, and nature and against literary form as a product of these.
>
> (Taylor 1981, 112)

Indeed, Poirier does punctuate that interview with intriguing remarks about literature's homologous relationship to society at large, as when he remarks that Henry James was surprised by World War I because 'he just did make the connection between the modern author's inadequacy to the task of reproducing or containing modern life and the inadequacy of modern life itself to the task of controlling its unprecedented forces' (Taylor 1981,

116). Poirier's is an important project, and the historical and political insights he brings to the study of American literature have great potential. It is for these reasons that his method needs to be examined for the kinds of inconsistencies and biases that mitigate against its declared intentions.

Poirier's *A World Elsewhere: The Place of Style in American Literature* (1966) argues that 'American books are often written as if historical forces cannot possibly provide such an environment [of freedom], as if history can give no life to "freedom," and as if only language can create the liberated place' (Poirier 1966, 5). But this American tradition has been trivialized by many critics who tend to 'treat experiences in fiction as if somehow they existed independently of the style which creates them' rather than 'through the media of language,' which transcends all the 'baggy categories of "romance," or "myth," "realism," or "naturalism"' (p. 11). Poirier argues that 'the crucial problem for the best American writers is to evade all such categorizations and to find a language that will at once express and protect states of consciousness that cannot adequately be defined by conventional formulations even of more sophisticated derivation from Marx, Freud, or Norman O. Brown' (p. 11). Since traditional criticism has 'pacified and explicated away' the 'marvelous and eccentric vitality of American writing' (p. viii), Poirier refocuses our attention on the stylistic performances of American literature, 'the sounds, identities, and presences shaped by these technical aspects [grammar, syntax, etc.] of expression.' Poirier feels that such an approach, even to the most familiar writers and passages, will defamiliarize American writing for us, resensitizing us to the 'grotesque variety of shapes' and the very 'discomforting agitations of style' we miss by being too historical about American writing (p. viii).

Poirier understands the American tradition as one of struggle for individual, verbal consciousness in the face of the deadening conventions, literary and social, that ultimately quash the individual's freedom. Style, for Poirier, is individuality, 'is the man,' so to speak. His study of this struggle to displace existing environments by creating a stylistic world elsewhere focuses on the individual author's or protagonist's entrapment by conventional social forms and historical inertia, their momentary transcendence of those strictures, and the ways in which those flights of stylistic freedom radically disrupt our expectations about reality and literature. Central to Poirier's project, then, is freedom from oppression, a freedom of expression and of individual consciousness. No other recent theorist of American literature (since, perhaps, Hicks and Parrington) has defined that literature in such political and ethically progressive terms.

Like many other theorists, Poirier derives his view of a world elsewhere from Emerson's declaration of stylistic independence from Europe:

> It could be said that the theories of literary and stylistic independence, articulated if not originated by Emerson, were gradually transmuted into an ideal of heroic character asserting its independence of oppressive environments and of prefabricated social styles. So, too, the difficulties of Cooper and Emerson in achieving stylistic independence are translated ... by Hawthorne, and increasingly by American novelists after him, into the central dramatic situation of their works. ... Salinger's Holden Caulfield is a merely stock character enacting the American hero's effort, more significantly illustrated by Isabel Archer, to express the natural self rather than merely to represent, in speech and manner, some preordained social type.
>
> (p. 27)

Poirier's definition of American selfhood resembles R. W. B. Lewis's myth of Adamic innocence and inviolable individuality. For Poirier, though, the Adamic self is victimized not by the moral evil of experience but by the fictional environment in which it is placed. Furthermore, Poirier feels that even fictional environments cannot grant the protagonists total, or lasting freedom, because the authors, too, are victims of an oppressive American social scene and, thus, are incapable of imagining such an environment of freedom. The protagonists, then, reflect the frustrations their authors register before repressive social and literary conventions.

Poirier's analyses pivot on the dialectic of freedom and submission, flight and failure, relinquishment and possession. The protagonist 'drops out' of society in order to reconstitute

authentic selfhood and then to repossess the world imaginatively. Emerson's 'transparent eyeball' is the prototype of Poirier's
American hero who takes 'possession of America, in the eye, as
an Artist.' Cooper's Deerslayer is another embodiment of the
American self as style. While at home and invincible in the
wilderness, Deerslayer fails when he must 'express his worth
within social situations made familiar by the novel of manners'
(p. 76).[5] Thoreau, too, fought stylistically against conventions,
his puns on social usage freeing him from those norms, enabling
him to 'walk over' the 'premises' not only of neighboring farms,
but of conventional logic as well (p. 86). Of course, Huck Finn's
moments of freedom with Jim on the raft clash sharply with the
society on shore, 'nothing but artifice, tricks, games, and disguise' (p. 194). Poirier says that Mark Twain's work 'discovers
that the consciousness it values most cannot expand within the
environment it provides, that the self cannot come to fuller life
through social drama' (p. 195). Poirier regards *Huckleberry Finn*
as 'a kind of history of American literature, . . . altogether
superior to most of what passes for histories of American
literature' (p. 16); his comments on that novel are critical.
'*Huckleberry Finn*,' he argues, 'is an instance of what happens to a
novel when society, as the author conceives it, provides no
opportunity, no language, for the transformation of individual
consciousness into social drama' (p. 193).

This struggle for freedom, because it is waged against these
overwhelming 'forces' of society, history, and biology, can win
only momentary battles in a losing war against 'conventions.'
In the *Salmagundi* interview, Poirier makes this explicit: 'It's an
illusion that any writer's personal way with words can do more
than negotiate between self and environment, that it can become a sufficient environment unto itself, a displacement of the
world' (Taylor 1981, 111). Poirier's literary history, then, focuses
on the brief passages in which the dream of freedom is compel-
lingly rendered in the 'transcendentalist experience of style'
(Taylor 1981, 111). He justifies his selection of brief, well-
known passages by arguing that they carry the same 'inner
authority' which William James attributed to drunken or
mystical experiences, despite their brevity and seeming marginality: 'What we remember about a book or a writer —
and this is notably true in American literature — is often the

smallest, momentary revelations that nonetheless carry . . . an "enormous sense of inner authority"' (Poirier 1966, 14). These moments can only be glimpsed in 'style,' he argues; this stylistic intoxication is what the books 'truly offer' (p. 13). Thus, although Huck and Jim spend less than one-tenth of the novel on the raft, the style in which those moments are rendered grants them an authority surpassing their brevity. *Moby-Dick*, to offer a slightly different example, grasps the reader's attention 'less by images or the significances attached to them, both being usually obvious and often banal, than by the peculiar archness with which they get expressed' (p. 36). Poirier further argues that Lambert Strether's failure to 'be in touch with reality' should not be reduced and criticized with 'sophisticated moralisms' because, in celebrating the conversion of life into art and pleasure, Strether's liberation creates 'some of the most exalting beatifications of things and people anywhere in fiction' (p. 136). These 'moments,' Poirier insists, actually *are* the works and can only be trivialized by making them cohere with a 'theme' that a critic might extract from the text. 'They are . . . pure art in being freed from the pressure of any environment but that of the mind from which they issue' (p. 128). The 'style' in and of these passages communicates the giddiness of defiance experienced in the act of transcending conventional restraints of theme, narrative, society, or history.

Liberating us from conventions and transporting us beyond the world we live in to the world elsewhere that we crave, moments of stylistic transcendence expand our sense of self by challenging our assumptions about literature and reality. The best American literary performances, according to Poirier, are 'known for their intricacy, their opaqueness, even to the point where they are discussed not as books but as "problems for interpretation"' (p. 77). This domesticated brand of 'estrangement' or 'defamiliarization,' Poirier believes, is the true accomplishment, if not the goal, of the best literature. 'Ideally,' he writes, 'the result of such writing . . . is the displacement of many of the reader's assumptions about reality, and a change in our expectations about the probable duration and sequence of events' (p. 78). Faulkner's 'The Bear,' for example, strips us of our conventional notions and forces us to renew our perceptions 'as open, mysterious, and expectant as that of someone newborn' (p. 82).[6] The great dilemma for American literature is its inability to sustain these moments in the face of social relationships. Eventually the 'newborn' babies must enter society, compromising the very freedom they struggled to attain. 'Emerson's "I" could not exist in a novel at all,' Poirier argues, '– he simply would not be interested in social dialogue for a sufficient length of time' (p. 151). The American failure to conceive of individual freedom in society, like Mark Twain's inability to prevent Huck from lighting out for the territories, reaches its furthest limits in the writings of Dreiser, Wharton, and others of the realist/naturalist school in whose works the individual is a cipher, mute in company, denied freedom of any sort by the author's conceptions of reality, and simply dispersed, alone, into inhuman landscapes.

Poirier's critical ideal, viewing transcendent moments within texts as 'pure art . . . freed from the pressure of any environment but that of the mind from which they issue' (p. 128), is akin to Feidelson's ideal of symbolist literature as constitutive of its own reality. Poirier's method, in general, pivots on many of the same distinctions and biases as does Feidelson's: their views of literary history, of society, of the freedom of literary significance from 'extraliterary' pressures, of literature as process (Poirier usually refers to 'performance'), and of literature as sensuous, trans-rational experience needing a sensuous criticism to render its 'truth' adequately. Poirier's self-declared sensitivity to the 'political,' 'social,' and 'historical' contexts of literary production and reception needs to be reexamined in this light.

Like Feidelson, Poirier uses history in a way that denies historicity. Reversing the popular view that American culture was too thin for a mature literature to develop, Poirier argues that, while American artists 'ask us to believe that the strange environments they create are a consequence not of their distaste for social, economic, and biological realities but of the fact that these aren't abundant enough in American life,' their fictional achievements in style undermine these assertions. Like Lawrence, Poirier trusts the tales, not the authors. He feels that American authors did intend to promote eccentricity both in the heroes of their works and in the environments provided for them, but suggests 'that they wanted to hide what they most

wanted to do, and to hide their true intentions under disin-
genuous complaints that they are victims of historical necessity'
(p. 9). Poirier also notes that he intends to treat his materials 'as
scale models of America':

> For if in American history some ideal national self has had
> to contend from the outset with realities of time, biology,
> economics, and social custom, so in American literature the
> individual self has had to struggle into life through media of
> expression shaped by these realities.
>
> (p. 4)

Here and in the *Salmagundi* interview, Poirier lays claim to a
complex approach to American literature and history. In practice, however, Poirier betrays a different bias. After freeing
himself from any historical responsibilities on the ground that
the struggle for expanded states of consciousness 'exists
throughout American literature, and shows even less respect for
chronology than I have' (p. x), Poirier defines his method in
expressly ahistorical terms:

> My demonstrations involve none of the usual connections
> between historical events and literary events, since I question
> the possibility of knowing what these are in relation to one
> another. Instead, I propose to measure this struggle for
> consciousness, personal and national, within the language of
> particular works.
>
> (p. 4)

The idea of a 'national consciousness' is never developed, as
Poirier subjectifies the American dream of independence and,
like Feidelson, declares American social or material history
ancillary to literary history. As Warner Berthoff complains,
'America,' for Poirier, remains 'an almost completely unanalyzed historical integer, and American literary history floats in a
strange isolated medium where only English is heard or spoken
and, except for the odd preachment by Emerson or Whitman,
only novels and stories are written' (Berthoff 1967, 111). In her
1981 study, *Seeing and Being*, Carolyn Porter accuses Poirier,
along with R. W. B. Lewis, whom she feels Poirier closely
resembles, of an 'American ahistoricism' which blends a theory
of American exceptionalism with an emphasis on Adamic

innocence to 'yield a reading of that tradition in which an "end to the memory of history," along with a faith in the transcendent sovereignty of the individual, are seen as definitive' (Porter 1981, xiii). Granting the subtlety of Poirier's argument, Porter finds him arbitrarily elevating the myth of innocence 'to the status of a given, fostering our desire to examine the linguistic environment in which he finds himself' and perpetuating the delusive 'self-regenerating myth of American ahistoricism' (Porter 1981, 5). Porter's own important study exposes in thorough and informed readings the *a priori* assumptions which enable many critics to project a personal dissatisfaction with history *onto* American history.

What enables Poirier to project an ahistorical myth onto American literary history is his acceptance of the myths of 'the American Adam' and of the 'virgin land.' Perhaps the clearest example of such a substitution of myth or ideology for reality is Poirier's assertion that 'to take possession of America in the eye, as an Artist, is a way of preserving imaginatively those dreams about the continent that were systematically betrayed by the possession of it for economic and political aggrandizement' (p. 51). The dreams that Poirier refers to, those of freedom for a new start in a new land, however, are historically inseparable from the 'economic and political aggrandizement' Poirier so disdains. Whether the dream was the pristine 'Citty upon a Hill' of the Puritans or the geographic and vegetative luxuriance advertised by promotional literature, the dream was not prior to economic reality or to theological and political systems but part of a colonial rhetoric common to the age of European expansion. The dreams served political, theological, and economic purposes; only the 'myth of America' tries to deny this reality, and even that myth is logically and ideologically implicated in the conquest of the American continent, just as the myth of the South is inextricable from southern slavery and modern capitalism.

Like Feidelson's 'brute facts,' Poirier's environment, whether social or material, is simply alien and hostile to the integrity and individuality of 'style.' Poirier argues that American literature's strangeness stems from contempt for society, and yet Poirier defines society in only the simplest terms – as 'forces' which seem to have no connection with humane values or human activity. In doing so he denies the possibility of taking 'society' seriously enough to transform it. By reifying the notion of the social, Poirier denies any dialectical dynamism between self (and dreams) and society (brute facts). He offers yet another ideological prop to the very system he criticizes. Poirier cannot admit that many American writers may have meant their works to criticize, not simply to displace, existing environments. Neither Emerson, nor Thoreau, nor Hawthorne, to refer to writers Poirier does discuss, meant their works simply as 'performances' or as 'stylistic worlds elsewhere.' Hawthorne's moral insights and Emerson's and Thoreau's ethical and political writings make no such claims to freedom from social questions; much of their work can indeed be understood as 'political,' even in the strictest sense – meant to improve society and the quality of human life.

For Poirier's criticism to have the social significance he wants to attribute to it, it would be necessary for him to take the idea of 'society' or 'politics' more seriously, to define and analyze them in terms more penetrating than vague notions like 'conventions' or 'social forces.' One can hardly expect to formulate a politically viable criticism of society (Poirier's own goal) without engaging social facts on a deeper level. Poirier argues that it is American writers who have shirked their responsibility, substituting clichés for analyses. But Poirier himself chooses to define American literature in transcendental terms, granting tacit authority to that strain in American writing and excluding an entire tradition of social ideas and criticism in American literature. Neither Winthrop nor Mather, neither Franklin nor the Connecticut Wits, neither Emerson (especially in works like 'Wealth,' 'Experience,' 'Fate,' or *Society and Solitude*, all of which Poirier does not discuss) nor the major writers of the American Renaissance, neither Eliot nor Williams, nor scores of even the most canonical writers can be understood adequately as projecting imaginative environments to protect the expanded states of their protagonists' consciousnesses. In short, it is Poirier who privileges the world elsewhere as the Ur-theme of American literature.

Poirier's reduction of the idea of society distorts American literature both by excluding texts which do not expand and protect individual consciousness and by misrepresenting the texts he does discuss. For instance, 'building one's own world' becomes for Poirier a solipsistic trope of definitive power in the American tradition. He argues that 'by an act of building [a house] . . . it is possible to join forces with the powers of nature itself, to make its style your style. But this conjunction is possible only if the imagination and space are freed from the possessive power of all that is not nature: from systems of any kind that derive from society and history' (p. 18). Such a conception, however, already rules out the importance of 'social structures' in American literature. Poirier neglects Winthrop's 'Citty upon a Hill,' Hawthorne's custom house and house of the seven gables, Henry Blake Fuller's skyscraper in *The Cliff-Dwellers*, and Silas Lapham's new house as significantly American edifices, presumably because they compromise the individuality and originality of their builders and occupants by stressing the social nature of identity. Poirier must also ignore the buildings that house the many 'diminished things' in American literature such as Wakefield's 'home away from home,' Emily Dickinson's haunted chambers, the tiny 'pigeon house' that accommodates Edna Pontillier's new-found sense of self in *The Awakening*, and, most significantly, James's Jolly Corner and Gardencourt – complete with their ghosts whose recognition signals the attainment of 'some miserable knowledge' about the possibilities of liberated selfhood. Society, or history, or conventions can only ring of some 'prefabricated' cheapness for Poirier; they cannot represent in fiction, as they do in 'real life,' the very ground on which individuals come into being, not simply through negation of society but in complex interaction with it.

Poirier concedes the complexity of this issue in his discussions of Hawthorne and James. He grants both that Isabel's romantic egoism is Emersonian, not Jamesian, and that 'in one sense [James's] novels are about the disaster of assuming that within the environments provided by society there can be any allowance of space for the free expansion of the inner self' (p. 32). None the less, Poirier interprets Isabel Archer as a stock character in American fiction, one dedicated to expressing the natural self rather than some 'preordained social type' (p. 27); her ideas express 'James's tenderness for ideals of *self*-expression as against expression by which the self is filtered through representation or acquired styles' (pp. 31–2). In other words, there are two ways in which Poirier can make a text which seemingly refutes his thesis actually support his position: by portraying 'society' or 'environments' as the stereotypical villain (it is 'society' that always victimizes individuals, and Poirier assumes James shares this sentiment), and by collapsing any instance of an individual's expression of self into an endorsement of the struggle for expanded consciousness, regardless of what the author may have been trying to express. Poirier thus argues that Miles Coverdale's isolation in his 'hermitage' is typical of a recurrent American theme 'precisely that we may see it as a significant variation': 'The account of his retreat from society into an "ideal" community and from there into sequestered landscape has affinities with those scenes in American literature of which the opening of Emerson's *Nature* is a paradigm' (p. 119). Such assertions pose an interesting question concerning Poirier's method. According to Poirier, the central American tradition consists of American authors' trying to free their characters from the rigidity of social definitions and historical circumstances, regardless of the admittedly inevitable failure of such an attempt. The problem is this: a persistent strain in American literature beginning with the Puritans' struggle to achieve an equipoise of individual and society, of internal belief and external conduct, and finding full expression in the works of Hawthorne, James, and even Eliot, suggests a tradition exactly the opposite of Poirier's. Hawthorne and James are, perhaps, the clearest examples. Who could argue that characters like Goodman Brown, Wakefield, Reuben Bourne, the man of adamant, Ethan Brand, and the numerous other Hawthorne characters alienated from humanity or some of James's solipsists such as John Marcher, Spencer Brydon, George Stransom, and a host of other artists, aesthetes, and egotists divorced from human connections do not suggest that American writers, contrary to Poirier, are actually very concerned with exposing, not endorsing, the posturings of solipsistic characters? In other words, the *real* American tradition could just as well be to socialize American characters, not to create a world elsewhere for them. Actually those two lines exist in dialectical unity, and Poirier merely outlines another nuance on the theme of American individualism pervasive in many theories of American literature. But in abstracting one side of the struggle and arguing that American literature *is* this struggle *away from* society and *for* individual consciousness, Poirier simplifies the complexity of the theme. His statements privilege individuality and devalue social being where no such priority exists in the literature itself.

Much of Poirier's ahistoricism and anti-realism is implicit in his critical presuppositions. Like Feidelson, Poirier defines literature as process or flux, not as something to be clarified but as a 'problem for interpretation.' He defines Thoreau's as an 'aesthetic so devoted to the *activity* of creation that it denies finality to the results of that activity, its objects or formulations. Art is an action not a product of action' (p. 21). Likewise, 'Emerson's theories and recognitions must not . . . be confused with his performances' (p. 65). Poirier defends James's aestheticism, arguing that 'art conceived as an activity rather than as a product is now, as before, a direct challenge to those who believe in the fixed realities of our physical environment or our moral life' (p. 142).

Poirier expands this aesthetic into a dogma in *The Performing Self* (1971), in which he argues that 'life in literature is exhibited by the acts of performance that make it interesting, not by the acts of rendition that make it "real,"' and that literature 'should be construed more properly as another dimension of action, of performance, with language as its medium' (Poirier 1971, 33, 69). These statements and many others like them support Poirier's larger thesis on the study of literature:

> What I want to suggest is that all the elements in what is called English study are, or ought to be, in motion, including the student and the teacher. A beautifully liberating instability, a relativity rather than a 'relevance,' should be all we know and all we need to know about English studies.
>
> (p. 67)

Poirier applies this thesis by criticizing those who think that 'the study of literature is supposed to have some effect on the quality of life' (p. 67), citing as main offenders black critics 'with their hangup on literature as "relevant"' (p. 6). Like Feidelson, Poirier defines the reality and significance of literary works in opposition to the fixed categories and dualistic, rational (they equate these two terms) forms of knowledge, echoing the old split and specious privileging of the language of poetry over the language of science. They differ in that while Feidelson argues that the entire work frees us from conventional perceptions of reality, Poirier argues that it is only isolable 'scenes' and 'passages' (p. 90) that transport us to the world elsewhere. It would be impossible to deny the appropriateness of Poirier's aesthetic to some major works of modern literature, but his claim to an authoritative definition of American literature and, more important, the adequacy of his 'politics' are other questions. Poirier's own narrowing of the American canon to isolated passages of stylistic transcendence of a contemptible reality can only reinforce the putative alienation between human mind and material environment.

Poirier's antinomianism gets underscored when he asks us to 'assume with Hegel that "freedom" is a creation not of political institutions but of consciousness' (p. 4) without grasping that, for Hegel, the mind cannot be abstracted from environment, history, or, most important, other minds. 'Reality' and 'consciousness' for Hegel are collective entities, not inversions or displacements of collectivity by the individual. As J. N. Findlay writes, 'True freedom, [Hegel] came more and more to think, can be found only in the laws and usages of some concrete community, in which the individual can "find himself"' (Trachtenberg 1967, 58–9). Poirier, however, forgets this basic truth of dialectics, viewing individuals only in opposition to some hostile, alien, inhuman environment. Poirier places the equation (à la David Riesman) of style = individual = authentic = experience = inner-directed = good in simple opposition to convention = society = inauthentic = analytical = other-directed = bad. Like the Puritan antinomians, Poirier refuses to grant that the 'individuality,' the soul, of a character or author can possibly be realized or recognized in any social manifestation. For Poirier the individual is always the enemy of, always victimized by, fellow humans. Poirier may couch his literary writings in terms like 'politics' or 'realism,' but for anyone who thinks of social significance or politics as issues deserving careful analysis rather than jargon and collective effort rather than individual transcendence, Poirier's own strategy for a social or political criticism needs revision.

Myths of American origins: post-structuralism

Post-structuralism has bestowed new authority on the study of American literature as self-reflexive writing. Many recent discussions of American literature have pushed to new extremes Feidelson's and Poirier's assumptions about literature as the process of meaning rather than the meant product, as alogical transcendence of rational categories, and as self-reflexive linguistic structure incapable of referring outside its inscribed borders. For many contemporary theorists, the question of American literature's social or historical significance is not so much engaged and transcended as it is ignored; the 'Americanness' of American writing, then, becomes a new set of critical assumptions concerning the origins of 'man' and 'language' and the self-deconstructing foundations upon which any such search for linguistic origins rests. Whereas 'building one's own world' represented the essential tradition for Poirier, more recent theorists find dismantling such structures more to the point.

Kenneth Dauber's 'Criticism of American Literature' (1977) reviews the tradition of textualist criticism and celebrates an anti-mimetic counterstrain. Echoing several of the critics we have considered (who have presumably 'proved' what can now be taken for granted), Dauber reifies the self-reflexive approach to American writing:

> American literature is a literature whose primary concern has always been its own nature. . . . For the poets and novelists of the classic period of American letters, the object of their work, inevitably, was its own process. Any 'problem' they might address was incorporated automatically, within their text as a 'problematic,' or principle inhering in the writing that embodied it.
>
> (Dauber 1977, 55)

Throughout the essay in which this statement occurs, Dauber denies, or 'problematizes,' not only literature as a mimetic art capable of possessing social or historical significance, but the ideas of the past, meaning, reality, events, ideas, and the self, as valid terms for any inquiry into American literature; it is writing that counts (Dauber 1977, 60–4). Accusing even the New

Critics of being too historical and too objective and material in their hypostatization of the text, Dauber offers a new relationship between critic and text capable of transcending the formalist barriers erected by 'such skilled practitioners [of New Criticism] as F. O. Matthiessen.' Extracting what he regards as an honest relativity and risky willingness to 'put himself on the line' in Van Wyck Brooks, Dauber collapses historical time and the critic into a new, contextless critical act:

> But as Derrida's own writing shows, the result need not be that we reject criticism or despair about ever finding the meaning of a work of literature. In Brooks, as in the best contemporary French critics, a certain energy or style – even a kind of self-conscious dandyism as we increasingly find – continues the energy of the text. Since meaning is not embodied in the written but is a function of writing, of the discourse proceeding between writer and critic, energetic substitution, because it keeps discourse active, keeps meaning alive.

> (Dauber 1977, 57)

Dauber's theory synthesizes numerous contemporary positions, such as Harold Bloom's theory of 'strong misreading' and anti-intentionalist theories by Richard Poirier and Susan Sontag. In Dauber, as in some of his predecessors, hermeneutical relativity destabilizes both history and meaning; the critic's job is to enter into a transaction with the text to produce whatever live meaning a contemporary mind can generate through such a transaction. What this means is that literature can no longer (indeed, never could) function in a communicative manner as a vehicle for transmitting an author's ideas. Dauber eliminates the individual author as a determining consciousness behind a text *and* the society of the work's genesis as a context for the text. He frees language, after the fashion of Poirier, from both historical or social constraints and from conventions of critical writing. The 'text' floats in a social and temporal vacuum; the study of literature becomes a potentially infinite exercise in discovering the same thing, our 'present concerns,' over and over. By implication, it doesn't matter who or what we read, whether Benjamin Franklin or Joyce Carol Oates, because any 'text' reveals only what a critic (who, according to Dauber, substitutes himself for the text) knows. Criticism reveals a critic's consciousness, not an external and historical statement of any kind. A usable past to be sure, but used only in an abstract and subjective transaction between critic and literary work.

John Irwin's *American Hieroglyphics: The Symbol of the Egyptian Hieroglyphics in the American Renaissance* (1980) ambitiously re-writes American literary history in light of the post-structuralist thought of Derrida, Foucault, and Lacan. Compared by many to earlier readings of the American Renaissance by Matthiessen and Feidelson, Irwin's study rarely strays outside the writings of Emerson, Thoreau, Whitman, Poe, Hawthorne, and Melville; it is not, strictly speaking, a theory of American literature. Irwin's work, though, does presuppose a theory of literature, thus implying a reassessment of American literature as a whole. In fact, *American Hieroglyphics* extends a theme central both to Matthiessen and Feidelson: the place of the subject in American literature. Feidelson, we recall, declared invalid the romantic egoism behind Matthiessen's master tropes of 'man thinking' and 'man in the open air' and replaced Matthiessen's subjectivism and Cartesian dualisms with an organicism of epistemological transcendence. Irwin goes Feidelson one better, replacing his cognitive theory of literature as constitutive of new meanings with a quest for the ultimate origins of language and consciousness, a quest beyond symbolism's fusion of theme and technique to a pre-symbolic abyss. Irwin's break from Matthiessen and Feidelson is only apparent, however; his continuity with the premises of self-reflexive theories of American literature suggests that *American Hieroglyphics* has simply re-arrived at its own autotelic origins in New Critical aesthetics.

Irwin's thesis that the 'common denominator' of American writing is the search for the ultimate origins of language and the self underlines his adversary relationship to Matthiessen and Feidelson in the history of self-reflexive theories of American literature. Whereas they specified essentially progressive themes such as the democracy of 'man in the open air,' and the 'open road' of symbolism's quest for meaning, Irwin inverts their approaches, offering a regressive trope – the quest for the self's origins – as the definitive American theme. Irwin, for example, grants that Whitman used the will and the insatiable desire for the 'open road' as metaphor for 'the image of limitless possibility, of an infinite "second chance" or new beginning, one of whose historical manifestations was the idea of the expanding frontier,' but argues that

> we will never quite understand Whitman's open road and the idea of an endless frontier unless we see it as one pole of an opposition whose other pole is the voyage to the abyss. For just as the idea of the open road makes man's goal the endlessness of beginning again, so the voyage to the abyss as a quest for an ultimate origin (a quest for a beginning beyond which one cannot go and thus for a beginning that is an end) reveals that quest to be *abyssos*, bottomless, nonclosable, just like the interrupted 'ending' of *Pym* that doesn't really end and that symbolizes the endlessness of the quest for origins, the limitlessness of seeking an ultimate limit.
>
> (Irwin 1980, 112, 113)

Irwin argues that this opposition lies at the heart of the American dream of achieving an ultimate earliness and of the paradoxical attempts to escape history by returning to an origin (America as Edenic, virgin land), which only commits one to an endless series of new beginnings in search of the point where all history begins. Drawing on Fitzgerald's conclusion to *The Great Gatsby*, Irwin suggests that this 'new place' is an unreachable origin, that 'the restless mobility of the American will to power is at once impelled and baffled by the irreversibility of time' (p. 114). Irwin's place in the history of self-reflexive theories is similarly paradoxical. His 'new reading' actually offers remarkably few new 'readings,' refocusing Lawrence, Matthiessen, and Feidelson through the lenses of recent post-structuralist theory, just as Matthiessen had 'used' Yeats, Eliot, and the aesthetics of French *symboliste* poetry; and Feidelson had used Cassirer, Langer, and various New Critics to re-view American literature. Irwin's remarks on Whitman, for example, echo Lawrence's argument that Whitman's seeming 'openness' and sociality function primarily to cover up his extraordinary solipsism – his quest for 'himself.'

Like Poirier, Feidelson, and the New Critics, Irwin treats the literary work as a dynamic process, as dancing rather than either the dancer or the dance. Also like Feidelson, Irwin collapses theme and technique, finding in each writer the inevitable metaphor of the quest for origins, which is both what writing *is* as well as what it is *about*. According to Irwin (via Lacan), writing as transgression against the father is 'the Promethean theft of the father's stylus and the virgin sheet,' a theft paralleling Irwin's version of writing as exploration of the self:

> This sense of writing's origin as an act of transgression accords with the mechanics of inscription, for as Emerson remarks in *Nature*, the original, 'concrete' meaning of *transgression* was the 'crossing of a *line*,' and it is precisely the crossing of lines, both vertical and horizontal, that forms one of the differential oppositions constituting the physical presence of writing. Moreover, in Poe the precariousness of narrative is characteristically associated with the crossing of previously uncrossed lines in search of an ultimate knowledge. . . . The womblike abyss that is the goal of so many of Poe's voyages bears an Oedipal prohibition.
>
> (pp. 69–70)

Poe, however, is only the heir to the romantic poets, for whom 'the investigation of man's linguistic relationship to the world frequently takes the form of literary works whose inquiry into the origin of their own written presence on the page is a synecdoche for the inquiry into the simultaneous origin of man and the world in the act of symbolization' (p. 55).

Literature as exploration of new identity, as quest for the self, is, for Irwin as it was for Poirier, Feidelson, and the New Critics, nonrational. According to Irwin, the contradictory, or alogical, essence of American literature is a function of writing itself, inseparable from the 'alogical myth' of the quest for origins:

> The myth of hieroglyphic doubling as the origin of man and language manifests its alogical core when we pursue the logical consequences of the scenario in which an act of simultaneous projection/introjection of the shadow raises a prelinguistic creature to the level of self-consciousness.
>
> (p. 136)

Again Poe, whose *Eureka* is dedicated to 'those who feel rather than to those who think,' is central, perhaps archetypal, for

American writing. The quest for the origins of thought, language, the self, or the universe are prior to human consciousness, yet paradoxically generated by that consciousness that can never achieve its quest, an echo of Hegel's 'unhappy consciousness,' yet a singularly perplexing conundrum that Irwin feels none the less unites American writers:

> In *Eureka*, then, Poe presents us with the paradox of a 'unified' macrocosmic body that is without a totalizing image – an alogical, intuitive belief whose 'truth' rests upon Poe's sense that cosmologies and myths of origin are forms of internal geography that, under the guise of mapping the physical universe, map the universe of desire. Like the other writers of the American Renaissance, Poe finds himself in the uncertain region between knowledge and belief, waking and dreams, between what compels him intellectually and what moves him emotionally; and like his contemporaries Poe has begun, in the very act of asserting his beliefs, to subordinate those beliefs in crucial and irrevocable ways to his knowledge by allowing that knowledge to dictate the discursive form and logical status of his assertion.
>
> (pp. 222–3)

Just as Feidelson and Poirier followed the New Critics in devaluing literature's social or historical significance as well as its mimetic potential, Irwin denies literature any socially mimetic or referential status. Although these critics use different, sometimes seemingly antithetical strategies, their conclusions and the implications of those conclusions are similar. Eliot and later New Critics may argue that the poet's personality and biography and intentions are irrelevant, that the poet is not in the poem, while Irwin argues that the text can never reveal anything other than the author's split or doubled self, but, in any case, there is nothing outside of the work of art; there is only language. Even when writers seem to be 'mapping the physical universe,' Irwin argues that such an overture to social, historical, or geographic reference is a sham, for writing can only map an 'internal geography,' 'the universe of desire.' Irwin's literal denial of writing's capacity to refer to anything other than itself, then, mirrors his assumption that the self can never transcend its subjectivity. Writing can only project the self, the split image of which doubles back upon itself. One questions which comes first for Irwin, the 'prison house of language' or of the self, although he would deny the question's grounds, arguing that self and language arise simultaneously as mutually constitutive oppositions. For Irwin, a text, a writer's 'corpus,' can only embody the author, in fact, *is* the author writ large. And it is Irwin's model of writing as inescapably subjective that makes *American Hieroglyphics* representative of self-reflexive theories of American literature.

According to Irwin, the hieroglyph suggested the problematic dialectics of appearance and reality, inner and outer, sensible form and hidden meaning, the one and the many, compelling concerns for Emerson in *Nature*, Thoreau in *Walden*, Hawthorne in *The Scarlet Letter*, Melville in *Moby-Dick*, *Pierre*, and *The Confidence-Man*, and Poe in *The Narrative of Arthur Gordon Pym* and *Eureka*. In a remark on Thoreau's emblematic technique, Irwin suggests the appeal of the hieroglyph for these writers in general. Thoreau's description of his activities at Walden

> depicts all of these things as hieroglyphic emblems whose meanings are hidden from the majority of men because the petty concerns and busyness of life have degraded their powers of intellect and observation. Thoreau's descriptions of the external shape of his world are at the same time explications of the world's inner significance.
>
> (p. 14)

Thoreau does, of course, express such an attitude toward 'the majority of men,' as do Hawthorne, Melville, and Poe, so many of whose protagonists distinguish themselves from their society by taking hidden spiritual reality seriously and scorning the landlocked comfort of the bourgeoisie. In fact, the writers of the American Renaissance can be understood in part, as Perry Miller understands Edwards and Emerson, as rejecting the rampant materialism of nineteenth-century America by reaffirming moral, ethical, or aesthetic reality in the face of a growing positivism that defined what was as what was right. In this sense, then, Irwin's argument suggests that the Puritan dilemma's extremes of antinomianism and Arminianism had not, by the 1850s, been resolved, and that American writers

played Anne Hutchinson to mass culture's Arminian identifi-
cation of appearance with reality.

Whereas antinomianism existed in a context with its polemical adversary in Puritan theological debates, however, Irwin
abstracts this subjective idealism, offering it as a definition of
writing itself, a peculiar strategy considering Irwin's own insistence on the logical inseparability of binary oppositions and the
inevitability of their mutual cohabitation. Irwin's psychologiz-
ing of literature's significance and writing's 'meaning' actually
grounds his entire study. On one level, Irwin suggests that it is
the origin of man in the abstract which preoccupied these
writers: 'For the writers of the American Renaissance, the
hieroglyphics and the question of man's origin are implicit in
one another; if you start with one, sooner or later you will be led
to the other' (p. 61). More fundamentally, it is the individual
writing and the written self that, Irwin argues, define American
writing. Citing Whitman's line 'In the best poems re-appears
the body,' Irwin asserts that 'certainly part of the immense
symbolic importance of the Egyptian hieroglyphics for the
writers of the American Renaissance is that the hieroglyphics
represent the archetypal form of writing in which the outline of a
body is rendered visibly present' (p. 98). This visible body turns
out to be that of the individual author. For Poe, 'the doubling of
Poe and Pym suggests the constitutive opposition between the
writing self and the written self, the problematic doubling of the
writer and his book' (p. 120). The many images of veiling in
Hawthorne's stories and, particularly, *The Scarlet Letter* suggest
to Irwin that 'what Hawthorne intends is a veiled unveiling of
"the inmost Me," not a drawing back of the veil, but an
imprinting on the veil's surface of a hieroglyph of what lies
"behind" it, a pictographic cipher addressed to "the few who
will understand him"' (p. 267). Furthermore, this revelation of
'the inmost Me' involves an androgynous persona building an
identity in retaliation against the past:

> By figuring his expulsion from the customhouse as a symbolic
> decapitation/castration, Hawthorne carries out an ironic
> revenge upon his Puritan forefathers, for it is the public self
> . . . that is the victim of this patriarchal punishment adminis-
> tered by the 'inmost Me,' the artistic self who provides the

specific image of the guillotine for his loss of office. It is not surprising that Hawthorne should associate this self-inflicted ... decapitation with the 'idea of committing suicide,' nor surprising that if such a symbolic castration evokes the figure of the feminized male as representative of the artist's feminine role, this figure should, in a scenario of death and resurrection, give birth to the reborn literary man recovered from the creative impotence of the customhouse and wielding once more the phallic pen.

(p. 280)

Given Irwin's reasoning in this passage, true as it is to Lacanian theory, it is hardly surprising that he also suggests that 'the enigmatic letter A may also signify "author"' (p. 283).

The self, for Irwin, can only recognize itself as self when it is either split or doubled, externalized as reflected image or inscribed in writing, and no longer whole. Like a Möbius strip, this mutually constitutive opposition of writing self and written self 'involves the same bewildering interpenetration of one and two, so that it is felt at once to be both one and two, and neither one nor two' (p. 122). Such also, Irwin argues, was the fate of Narcissus, and both the erotic and thanatoptic constituents of that myth are present in American writers, for whom narcissistic doubling is synonymous with hieroglyphic (pictographic) writing. According to Irwin, the artistic form of the narcissistic impulse is 'the artist's forever frustrated desire to make love to the work of art' (p. 159). In a system of binary oppositions such as Irwin's, eroticism, of course, implies its opposite (annihilation in the abyss) and writers write to achieve a kind of immortality: 'A writer – who wills fictive worlds into existence, who creates himself in the act of writing and endows that written self with the power to survive death – is particularly subject to such presentiments of immortality' (p. 227). As Irwin argues, however, the only immortality that writing can confer on the author's self is 'an indefinite repetition of the author's inscribed self through the act of (re)reading' (p. 197). Irwin finds such a narcissistic impulse in *Moby-Dick*: 'The whale's ubiquity is but the self's own sense that, look where it will, it sees only some aspect of itself' (p. 287). We should remember, however, that much of Ishmael's narrative lobbies strenuously against the confusion of self and other. Ishmael can grant the complexity of a decentered self (as he does in 'The Monkey Line') while still situating the question of selfhood in the social world of the Pequod and in the centrality of human labor and communality.

Irwin's subjectivist bias, however, would seem to deny any significance in literature other than that of the individual self's linguistic splitting and doubling. The self is an inscribed, a written, entity. The mutual constitution of self and writing brings the maxim 'style is the man' to its logical conclusion. Irwin's focus on the writing and the written self as constitutive of the self at large nevertheless rests on reductive, asocial assumptions. The 'real' self, Irwin argues, is only what is inside and hidden, not what is or can be socially visible and verifiable. He also abstracts the acts of writing and reading, which could be viewed as pre-eminent examples of the self's sociality, its impulse toward communication with others, even in moments of seeming solitude. There is only the 'self' and 'writing' outside of any analysis of what and why writers write and readers read and of the extent to which both writing and reading are mutually constitutive of a complex social act involving writer and reader in a transaction of social and cultural significance. Irwin's view of 'writing,' however, predictably doubles his theory of the self, transforming self-consciousness from a social phenomenon into an epistemological given, somehow free of social existence. Irwin, like other self-reflexive theorists, ignores the probability that epistemological doubt and obsession with the self's origins and 'true' identity are symptoms of alienation in a relatively homogeneous social class which are felt under changing social and economic conditions. The doubt and ambiguity in writers such as Hawthorne and Melville is undeniable, yet to argue that it stems from private thematics or from the inevitable and timeless context of artists creating themselves in art rather than from the internalization of historically specific contradictions of American culture reduces the complexity of the actual dialectic between self and society. Irwin's internalization of hieroglyphic writing simply transports it to the timeless realm of myth and mystifies the significance of American literature as a partial index to social reality. Whereas Poirier's American self tries to escape social and historical determination by transcending such forces in a homemade world, Irwin's 'selves' seem already free from society or, more accurately, incapable of seeing anything other than their projected images.

In this respect, there exists a crucial distinction between Feidelson's perception of American symbolist language and Irwin's of linguistic doubling and indeterminacy. Feidelson, we need to remember, regarded the turn toward self-reflexivity in American literature as a specific historical problem as well as a literary problematic. Like Trilling and other cultural theorists, Feidelson struggled to see American culture whole. From his basic historical premise that 'the intellectual stance of the conscious artist in American literature has been determined very largely by problems inherent in the method of the Puritans' (Feidelson 1953, 89), to his assertion that 'symbolism is the coloration taken on by the American literary mind under the pressure of American intellectual history' (Feidelson 1953, 43), Feidelson labors to establish a historical ground for his critical method (one 'designed to recapture the unity of a world artificially divided' (Feidelson 1953, 51)) and for the significance of certain American texts. Feidelson delineates the 'unhappy consciousness' he perceives tending toward solipsism and collapse, but one, like Hegel's vision of the unhappy consciousness, which could be transformed dialectically to a higher level of philosophical unity.

For Irwin, on the other hand, language as such generates the endless, if not happy, free play of the signifier in a linguistic realm in which subjects, objects, and history are all themselves fictions, 'beyond' the kind of historical analysis Feidelson might attempt to bring to them. Feidelson perceives symbolist discourse, as Walter Benjamin perceives allegory, as a symptom of cultural crisis. Irwin understands language as primarily, if not wholly, intrapsychic and trans-historical. As one critic remarks,

> There can be in Irwin's telling only one Quest, continually repeated, continually balked, and continually subverting the grounds of language and consciousness that make the Quest possible. Irwin's problematic is thus so general that it either transcends historical particularity or renders secular history an idle pursuit.
>
> (Stonum 1981, 10)

At a time when post-structuralism has also challenged us in productive and exciting ways to re-historicize and re-politicize literary theory by acknowledging, even insisting on, the ideological nature of all discourse, critical and literary, Irwin's position, accurately defined, I think, by Stonum, seems an anomaly, though perhaps no more so than other critical attempts to assess the social significance of American literature which also undermine their own historical assumptions.

For Feidelson the past may figure primarily as a prelude to a modernist, symbolic technique, but notions like the past, the present, and history are still issues of social *and* literary relevance, even though Feidelson might deny their presence within symbolist texts. What I have suggested as ahistorical in Feidelson is a method that proposes an account of historically specific literary phenomena but finally de-historicizes its own assumptions. Feidelson's work remains an attempt at social and historical engagement. Irwin's text privileges those very features with which Feidelson wrestles as metaphysical givens, mirroring, in their own anti-mimetic and ahistorical essences, a vision of life and literature inseparable from the sliding and indeterminate contexts of textuality.[7] Irwin, thus, disengages literary studies from the very frames which Feidelson and Poirier, for that matter, argue generate their own work. Feidelson bemoaned Melville's literary voyaging toward a self-contained abyss as the final collapse of symbolic practice; Irwin celebrates the same tendency as the definitive mode of American literature without addressing the very contexts which Feidelson would argue call symbolist writing into question. Poirier, like Feidelson, may depict the inevitable failure of attempts to construct fictional worlds elsewhere, but he maintains that struggles between selves (fictional and authorial) and environments (again, fictional and social) generate the great moments in American literary texts. These moments, Poirier suggests, strike us as they do largely due to their consonance with social and historical struggles for liberation in a realm beyond textual borders.

By erasing those borders, Irwin seems to typify Frank Lentricchia's charge that 'American poststructuralist literary criticism tends to be an activity of textual privatization, the critic's doomed attempt to retreat from a social landscape of fragmentation and alienation' (Lentricchia 1980, 186). It would seem as though Feidelson's insistence on American symbolist literature as a historically determined practice would distinguish him from Irwin's practice and distance him from Lentricchia's charge. His differences *are* important, but Feidelson's study is not, as my earlier discussion argues, without contradictions. While he suggests a specific historical basis for American literature, his reliance on the linguistic philosophies of Langer and Cassirer suggests an ahistorical, essentialist theory of language. Can symbolist discourse both represent 'the coloration taken on by the American literary mind under the pressures of American intellectual history' (Feidelson 1953, 43) *and* embody a timeless, literary and linguistic essence? I suggest not, and I think Feidelson's many explicit denials of the importance of historical contexts signal the effects his theory has on his practice. Barbara Foley addresses this inconsistency in Feidelson's work in provocative terms:

> Because it evinces no awareness of its own genetic relation to this philosophical tradition [New Criticism's epistemological assumptions], however, Feidelson's book is finally less a literary study than it is a work of ideology: that is, it proposes an analytical framework for comprehending a historically unified set of materials, but then it dehistoricizes that framework, converting what is a temporarily specific scheme into a presumably timeless attribute of literature itself. While rooted in historical and philosophical imperatives character- istic of a particular moment, the ideological text, to borrow the formulation of Marx and Engels, 'has to give its ideas the form of universality, and represent them as the only rational, universally valid ones.'
>
> (Foley 1984, 63)

Defining *Symbolism and American Literature* as an 'ideological text' doesn't necessarily help us understand how Feidelson's study is unique among theories of American literature, many of which, according to Foley, could be considered ideological texts. I agree that there is an ideological identity among the theories, namely the denial of literature as a form of social knowledge, but I also feel we need to grant the important differences that characterize so diverse a body of works. Foley is interested in establishing Feidelson in a critical lineage leading up to deconstruction and stresses his continuities, ideological and methodological. Nevertheless, the contradictions in Feidelson's work can also be viewed as separating him from later celebrants of self-reflexivity. While Feidelson *can* be so situated as a forerunner of contemporary critical practice, we need also to acknowledge the significant, though admittedly contradictory, distance between his attempt to situate American writing historically and Irwin's explicit denial of any determinants beyond the boundaries of the self.

'The world's body'

It is necessary to understand these self-reflexive theories of American literature in a broader context, as many of them are as much theories of the autonomy of the individual human being as they are theories of the autonomy of literary language. Feidelson, Poirier, and Irwin all abstract the 'self' from society just as they abstract literary texts from social and historical contexts. In each of their theories, the autotelic text parallels the autonomous individual, and the 'self' in 'self-reflexive' suggests the isolation of not only the texts but the self as well from social existence. Contrary to Feidelson's and Poirier's assertions that stylistic freedom is tantamount to political or cultural freedom, the selves that such critics celebrate in literature and society are diminished things, plagued by a nostalgic longing for a lost wholeness. For Feidelson, a moment of symbolic freedom can exist only retrospectively, as in a lost moment of unity amidst the anarchy of material existence. Poirier's world elsewhere is similarly belated and tragic, as social forces inevitably thwart the self's ephemeral moments of stylistic transcendence. Irwin most radically (and most enthusiastically) underscores the impossibility of the unity of consciousness: the quest he takes to be central to American literature is, to borrow a phrase from Poe, 'some never-to-be-imparted secret, whose attainment is destruction.' The self for these critics is an Ishmael floating alone on the dirge-like main, deprived of the ultimate knowledge of self attained by bolder water-gazers like Narcissus and Ahab.

Such pronouncements about the self's isolation from ultimate knowledge of itself suggest a kinship between self-reflexive theories of American literature and an existentialist view of Self. Hazel Barnes echoes Feidelson's view of symbolic form as constitutive of dynamic meaning when she notes that 'when Sartre speaks of the Self, he speaks of it as that which is forever pursued but never attained. This is because man is a self-making process' (Barnes 1967, 15). Short of death, the Self is never self-identical; it is always in the past or the future. 'The Self cannot exist as a fixed entity, for it changes with each new act of consciousness,' Barnes argues. Furthermore, 'as consciousness contemplates its own products, its very reflection alters that which it contemplates. Thus we have that play of mirrors, that impure reflection or never quite effected scission of consciousness by self-reflection which Sartre has compared to a game of musical chairs' (Barnes 1967, 247, 248). Barnes's commentary on the Self always distanced from itself and from the world as it knows it anticipates Irwin's later re-vision of the Self as a complex hall of mirrors, knowing itself only in fragmented reflections.

The relationship between existentialism's autonomous individual and New Criticism's autonomous text has been traced by Murray Krieger in 'The Existential Basis of Contextual Criticism' (1971).[8] This existential basis consists of the constants we have observed in self-reflexive theories, including the transcendence of dualistic rational thought, the view of poetry as dynamic and experimental as opposed to stable and propositional, the privileging of the language of poetry over that of science, and the corporeal equation, text = body. Drawing on Ransom's metaphor of 'the world's body,' Krieger rejects the 'ruthlessness of Platonism,' which neuters language, uses it as a 'tool,' prohibits the free play of language, and results in 'ideological, even propositional, poetry.' In place of such a 'predatory,' 'loveless,' 'totalitarian,' and 'puritanical' denial of the sensuous thusness of language, Krieger, like Poirier, offers a view of poetic language capable of 'lingering wastefully in order to cherish at leisure the richness of the body' with 'very little less than erotic love,' and of initiating 'a democratic state of nearly autonomous elements (of objects and words) instead of the coldly marshaled totalitarian state of nonpoetry' (Krieger 1971,

1226, 1227). In such remarks, Krieger sums up major constituents of self-reflexive theories of American literature. He equates poetic texture with human form and linguistic freeplay with erotic foreplay, both focusing almost exclusively on the isolated and autonomous individual.

Such an emphasis on autonomy – whether of literary language or of the individual human being (a unified *or* a decentered self) – links self-reflexive theories. These theorists all abstract literary texts and human beings from their social environments, regardless of the contradictions they fall prey to as a result of their strategies. But a different line of thinking, one which grants the historical and social milieus of language, selfhood, and literary production as its starting point, presents an alternative to the self-reflexive view of literature as autotelic.

We should return briefly to Matthiessen's remark on style: 'An artist's use of language is the most sensitive index to cultural history, since a man can articulate only what he is, and what he has been made by the society of which he is a willing or unwilling part.' Matthiessen's understanding of language, individuality, and society grants an interpenetration among the three terms not recognized in the subsequent self-reflexive theories we have examined. Whereas Matthiessen sees the self as both individual and social, later theorists either regard selfhood in increasingly isolated and inflated terms, or they reduce the social to language or psychology. Matthiessen's notion of society, too, is balanced, encompassing elements which an individual may willingly adhere to, consciously reject, or unconsciously reflect. For Feidelson and Poirier, on the other hand, society is irreducibly other and hostile; while, for Irwin, it seems to disappear altogether into an abyss of textuality. 'Facts' or 'forces' occupy an alien, material sphere antithetical to 'mind' or 'individuality,' or they are absorbed into symbols, imaginative processes, or textuality. Feidelson, Poirier, and Irwin all polarize the terms, never granting the interpenetration of social and creative activity. More important, Matthiessen recognized the desirability, indeed the inevitability, of regarding language as a social medium and as an 'index to cultural history,' as difficult and as general as that term may be. Feidelson, Poirier, and Irwin all believe language either struggles toward or actually succeeds in constituting its own world.

Warner Berthoff, like Matthiessen, points to the contradiction inherent in such a view when he criticizes Poirier's ideal of pure art 'freed from the pressure of any environment but that of the mind from which [the works] issue.' 'Such a thing,' Berthoff argues, 'cannot be (though it is the great dream of Symbolism) so long as the writer uses language, which remains the most thoroughly collective and environmental pressure the creative mind can know' (Berthoff 1967, 114).

While specifying exactly the relationship between individual and society or between style and convention may be difficult, it is equally difficult, if not impossible, to deny literature the mimetic and referential function which the linguistic medium, as the foundation of human communication, possesses. M. M. Bakhtin insists that

> the living utterance, having taken meaning and shape at a particular historical moment in a socially specific environ- ment, cannot fail to brush up against thousands of living dialogic threads, woven by socio-ideological consciousness around the given object of utterance; it cannot fail to become an active participant in social dialogue. After all, the utter- ance arises out of this dialogue as a continuation of it and as a rejoinder to it – it does not approach the object from the sidelines.
>
> (Bakhtin 1981, 276)

George Steiner also locates literature both historically and socially in a manner reminiscent of Bakhtin:

> A speech act is embedded in the conventions, social and philosophic inferences, contingent emphases of the moment. . . . It carries the manifold impress of the social and professional milieu. There is an idiom above and below stairs, an argot in the ghetto and a *lingua franca* of the marketplace. The circumstantial pressures on speech are, in a strict sense, immeasurably diverse, and literature embodies that plurality.
>
> (Steiner 1972, 28)

For Bakhtin and Steiner, monologue (what Feidelson, Poirier, and Irwin posit as the goal of literary language) is an illusion;

'languages do not *exclude* each other, but rather intersect with each other in many different ways' (Bakhtin 1981, 291).

Just as a writer's style is social, so the individual, even in the seeming extremes of individual literary 'performance,' formulates and consolidates a sense of self with and within a social community. Some writers find a voice in a cultural and social context more obviously than others, but a complex dialogic network underlies any 'individual' work of literature, making the desirability (not to say the possibility) of drawing a meaningful line between individual voice and cultural context extremely doubtful. I do not mean to suggest that there is nothing individual about specific writers and texts, but rather that to define a particular author's work's individuality outside of the contexts capable of rendering that individuality meaningful only (and ultimately) reduces the importance of an individual's contribution to a cultural dialogue. Like Hegel's seemingly 'individual' and 'concrete' moment of sense-certainty, the self-reflexive theories communicate an alienated understanding of 'the individual' that contains the seeds of its own dialectical undoing and renders only the most abstract and general notions of self or of text, or of American literature.

5
What is to be done?

Recent literary theory offers some promising directions for theoretical work on American literature. If we assume that our theories are already striving for a more social or cultural appreciation of American literature, then the primary obstacle deflecting them into various modes of derealization is an inadequate method, or vocabulary, for understanding literature as a reflection of American society. As I suggest in chapter 1, other problems may also exist. If many theories of American literature are a form, conscious or not, of American cultural imperialism functioning to consolidate and define the cultural dominance of the United States, as its economic and political hegemony are themselves solidified; or, if certain critics aim to define and defend the postwar status quo (a charge leveled by many at Lionel Trilling), then a rigorously social approach to American literature may seem too compromising. As Langston Hughes remarks, poems about the moon (or abstract critical theories) perturb no one, but social poems (and perhaps, social criticism) that expose poverty, oppression, and racism are another matter. But these questions, important as they are, demand another study. To return to the primary problem – what tack could a social theory of American literature take, and how could it correct the tendencies toward abstraction characteristic of the present theoretical corpus?

Part of the answer lies in correctly identifying the problem. Different theories advance different theses about American literature's minimal connection with American society. Most, however, partake of Lionel Trilling's early remarks concerning the 'tangential' relationship between American literature and American reality. 'American writers of genius,' we recall Trilling asserting, 'have not turned their minds to society.' David Hirsch locates a weakness in Trilling's work that, I think, is of primary importance. In attacking V. L. Parrington's simplistic and arrogant belief that 'reality is always reliable, always the same, always easily to be known,' Trilling himself, according to Hirsch, 'winds up making the same assumptions about "reality" that Parrington makes' (Hirsch 1971, 35). As a result of Trilling's empirical reduction of reality (his belief that only 'manners' are capable of reflecting 'reality'), Trilling denigrates 'the artistic legitimacy of any other kind of representation of reality' (Hirsch 1971, 36). The result: 'a total disregard not only of the social but of the physical world as well, and an uncurbed flight into a world of fancy totally unrelated to the ordinary facts of human existence' (Hirsch 1971, 36).

Hirsch's accusations are not all accurate – it seems particularly unfair to define Trilling's reality simply as 'a world of fancy.' Trilling was, after all, a 'cultural' critic. The problem is not Trilling's narrow conception of reality, but, more important, his expectations as to how the *social* is to be represented in the *aesthetic*. In this respect, there may be a positivist tinge to Trilling's theory, which leads to an overly simple analysis of American literature. Since the literature he values is not the type which creates a direct and recognizable reflection of a knowable world, Trilling is able to conclude that literature is, at best, only 'tangential' to social reality in the United States. This prejudice against literature that constitutes social reflection and offers social knowledge is not peculiar to Trilling alone, and, as I suggest above, owes at least as much to an earlier state of literary criticism as it does to individual biases.

What is the American tradition?

The practical effect that many of these theorists have, whatever their reasons, is to separate, almost absolutely, 'major' from 'minor' writers and also 'literary' from non- or subliterary texts, with the subliterary works tending to be those that reflect a direct interest in social and political concerns. One fact commonly lost sight of is that the very idea of distinguishing radically between 'major' and 'minor' writers and between literary and nonliterary texts emerged rather late in the history of criticism, in the first half of the nineteenth century. Distinctions and judgments have, of course, always been made, but the consensus about who was 'major' and who was not (and the corresponding effect such a consensus had on an entire field of study) has never been so strong and should not go unexamined. This lack of historical sensitivity concerning our critical tastes and methods results in the canon of American literature seeming not only unquestioned and obvious, but natural as well, despite three major transformations of the American canon in the twentieth century alone.

No canon is ever obvious or natural. 'The selection of literarary constructs,' as Alastair Fowler argues, is inherently selective and timebound:

> Merely to talk about some works rather than others involves commitment to a canon. Not that the canon need be enumerative as is Johnson's choice of 'the poets' for his *Lives*, Leavis' *Great Tradition*, . . . and the less obviously exclusive Oxford *History of English Literature*. Indeed, canonical hints in the tones of quotations, or in reversions to stock examples, possibly impose a more effective, because less oppressive, limitation. Nor do the dangers of an unexamined canon decrease with the vogue for prepacked source collections, casebooks, and the like, which make it easier to fancy one's mind stored with comprehensive, unselective information such as can only be arrived at through individual, freely-ranging, first-hand exploration among unfashionable as well as fashionable authors.
>
> (Fowler 1975, 51)

These dangers of an unexamined canon are exactly those which result in many theorists of American literature rehearsing similar approaches to predictable authors, texts, and even, as Richard Poirier admits, passages. As we have seen, however, theorists of American literature are united not only by who and what they do include, but by who and what they exclude as well. Raymond Williams, like Fowler, argues that although the information of any tradition is inevitably a conscious, purposive, and 'radically selective' activity, this selectivity often betrays unrecognized biases:

> From a whole possible area of past and present, in a particular culture, certain meanings and practices are selected for emphasis and certain other meanings and practices are neglected or excluded. Yet . . . this selection is presented and usually successfully passed off as 'the tradition', 'the significant past'. What has then to be said about any tradition is that it is in this sense an aspect of *contemporary* social and cultural organization, in the interest of the dominance of a specific class. It is a version of the past which is intended to connect with and ratify the present. What it offers in practice is a sense of *predisposed continuity*.
>
> (Williams 1977, 115–16)

While he fails to offer guidelines for determining *what* class benefits from a certain interpretation of a literary tradition or *how* it may do so, Williams, I believe, accurately identifies the ways in which a selective, biased vision of the past is imposed upon a broad body of works, ostensibly in an attempt to communicate continuity and coherence. He argues, as I have argued, the unnatural, arbitrary nature of any static tradition, especially one so narrowly defined as that offered by many theorists of American literature.

To escape the 'dangers of an unexamined canon,' theorists of American literature should first reassess the very idea of an American canon, especially one which has remained relatively static since shortly after World War II. The realist canon before that had replaced the acceptable poets canonized by the genteel tradition with a new, vigorously anti-genteel canon, including Mark Twain, Walt Whitman, Theodore Dreiser, and other cultural iconoclasts. The American canon once did serve a progressive, liberating function (we should remember that Brooks and others championed Melville and Whitman for their vigor and honest commitment to life). But under the current paradigm, even the survivors of the realist canon have been denatured, and the canon has been reduced to dogma, a composite of theoretical assumptions which, though formulated to combat the rigid authority of one approach to American literature, now serves mainly as a prescriptive structure itself.

Of course, any theory eliminates areas of significance (words, lines, texts, authors) for the sake of its own formulation. But, as in any reading of a poem, the worth of a theory lies in its ability to account for as much of its subject as possible. In this simple sense, a theory of American literature that can incorporate twenty authors is better (other things being equal) than one that deals with five, ten, or fifteen writers. Historical, economic, and pedagogical matters limit the number of authors that a theory can conceivably incorporate, and I am not suggesting that the next theory necessarily address the place of Jacqueline Susann, though I would not deny the worth of such a decision. On the other hand, theorists who focus primarily on the writers of the American Renaissance have given us not theories of American literature, but explications of themes, styles, and concerns in the writings of a few, admittedly 'major,' authors. We can, however, only learn so much about American literature as a whole from reading after reading of Hawthorne or Melville, no matter how rich their writings are and how important critical inter-pretations of them have been and still are. It is not surprising that, in these American writers, the New Critics found an American tradition preoccupied with ambiguity and irony, myth critics found myths in abundance, psychological critics find undercurrents of psychological meaning, and deconstruc-tors are finding a self-reflexive exorbitance defining American literature. It has been critical trends, not necessarily the writers and the texts themselves, that have dominated the history of theoretical writings on American literature. Without an expan-sion of the canon, there can be no real opening, no freshness, no democratization of American literary studies – there will only be new critical tools applied to the same old texts.

The expansion of the American canon should be carried out on two fronts: by abandoning the 'major author' bias and by broadening the conceptual focus of literary study to include the social significance of American texts. This does not mean merely replacing the now 'major' writers with 'minor' ones or casting aside current critical interests in myth, romance, or style with social criticism, but rather enlarging the very idea of the aesthetic and of who and what constitutes American literature. Though an appreciation and understanding of the aesthetic nature of literature is necessary, a primarily aesthetic apprehension of literature – if such a thing is even possible – is antithetical to any study postulating a theory of American literature. Also vital to this expanded conception of literature is a necessary acceptance of change within the canon. The canon of American literature since World War II has, however, remained more or less closed to new texts, new authors, and changing literary concerns. Changes have been made, and new authors have influenced these theorists, but notable figures such as Kate Chopin and Ralph Ellison still gain value primarily in so far as they relate to firmly entrenched authors and themes. They have not been allowed to shed new light of their own; they have simply been enlightened by others.

In some sense, the need for expansion has been a continuing concern for critics of American literature. In 1918, Van Wyck Brooks criticized the 'professorial mind' that denatured and devitalized American literature, discouraging American writers from confronting the actualities of American life. Brooks suggested that the 'real task for the American literary historian . . . is not to seek for masterpieces . . . but for tendencies,' with the express purpose of bringing literary studies closer to life (Sprague 1968, 221, 224). Speaking of the student of American letters in 1928, Norman Foerster wrote, 'if his learning is to have clarity and thoroughness, it must prepare him for a real confrontation with the nature of American culture' (Foerster 1928, xii). Arthur M. Schlesinger wrote in 1928:

> What first impresses the social historian is that his fellow delver in the literary field has been mainly interested in the picturesque, the unusual, and the super-excellent; the same preoccupation, it is well to recall, was the dominant complex of the historian himself a generation ago. . . . The point of view has changed from the heavens above to the earth below. It is now recognized that many of the mighty movements that have affected the destiny of man had their origins in obscure places; they gathered strength in hidden valleys and along dusty highways, and were carried through to success by the united efforts of hordes of nameless men and women.
>
> (Foerster 1928, 160–1)

In 'The Responsibility of the Critic' (1952), F. O. Matthiessen commented:

> Today we can take no tradition for granted, we must keep repossessing the past for ourselves if we are not to lose it altogether. . . . The proper balance, even for the critic who considers his field to be the present, is to bring to the elucidation of that field as much of the art of the past as he can command.
>
> (Matthiessen 1952, 7)

More recently, in 1970, Malcolm Cowley advised that 'the first of [the critic's] functions is to select works of art . . . that are new, not much discussed, or widely misunderstood. Incidentally this task has been neglected by academic critics, most of whom prefer to write about works already regarded as canonical' (Cowley 1970, 250). Brooks, Foerster, Schlesinger, Matthiessen, and Cowley all argue that the actual problem hampering literary studies is the perspectives brought to bear on American literature by its critics.

In fact, a critical 'rage for order' has obscured much of the heterogeneity and the social significations of American literature. Philip Rahv made the point as early as 1950 in a *Partisan Review* symposium on 'Religion and the Intellectuals.' Addressing the issue of a religious revival among American intellectuals, Rahv remarks:

> In certain literary quarters the idea of tradition has lately taken on an honorific meaning that empties it of all content. Thus '*the* tradition' – as it is spoken of in some of our literary reviews, with the definite article stressing an exclusiveness staggering in its presumption and historical naivete – has been transmogrified into a patent ideological construction. It has come to stand for a special kind of higher reality, no less, bristling with magico-religious associations on the one hand and promises of aristocratic investiture on the other.
>
> (*Partisan Review* 1950, 240)

Reviewing Richard Poirier's *A World Elsewhere*, Warner Berthoff criticizes Poirier and other theorists for their imposition of order. 'Perhaps,' suggests Berthoff, 'American literature is, very simply, *not* an organic or dialectical whole' (Berthoff 1967, 111) Frank Lentricchia applies a Foucaultian model to make much the same point:

> Whether it comes from Harold Bloom or traditional historians of American poetry like Hyatt Waggoner and Roy Harvey Pearce, the isolation of Emerson and an Adamic 'tradition' (in Foucault's sense) running through Whitman, Stevens, Roethke, and Ginsberg produces a repetitious continuity which celebrates the individual authorial will . . . and which dissolves, in the process, the myriad, changing forces, poetic and otherwise, that shaped the identities of figures as culturally separated as Emerson and Roethke. . . . The habit of historians of American writing is to distinguish a single defining theme (the Adamic, the romance, the pastoral, the symbolic, the world elsewhere); this strategy tends to result in a forcing of widely dispersed events of our literary history into a single container.
>
> (Lentricchia 1980, 202–3)

Michael J. Colacurcio concludes a review essay on recent books attempting to define the American tradition with a related criticism. However skeptical our tempers, Colacurcio remarks,

> however bitter our patriotism, the uncritical investment in a 'totalized' American meta-text commits us to the substitution of America for the Church, and the various texts of American literature for the successive books of Sacred Scripture. . . . But the time for its deconstruction seems long overdue. . . . The literary history of 'America as an Ordinary Country' will be difficult to write. But the other sort, however exciting, have come to seem a little too easy.
>
> (Colacurcio 1978, 130)

While Colacurcio's immediate focus is the questionable historical methods employed by American literary historians, his criticism of the lures *and* the inadequacies of the implicit belief in America as a metaphysical entity is relevant to our discussion of the 'American tradition' as suggested by the theories. Williams's political criticism and Colacurcio's historical remarks *both* point to the need for, at very least, an examination and testing of the premises on which theorists of the American tradition operate.

Just as conventional forms of criticism, in Terry Eagleton's words, smooth 'the troubled passage between text and reader' by domesticating contradictions within individual texts, theorists which offer American literature in a 'single container' suppress contradictions within the entire canon (Eagleton 1976a, 42). Like latter-day Henry Adamses, these critics (albeit of diverse ideological perspectives) call our attention to the illusion of unity in a field characterized more by multiplicity, perhaps chaos. Given the range of American writings that theorists force into a single container, devalue, or exclude altogether, one feels that they flatten American literature more than they elucidate its essence. Abandoning the notion of American literature or a coherent American tradition may explode all existing senses of continuity in American literature, maybe even the possibility of a 'theory of American literature.' But, more important, it may also enable us more accurately and more inclusively to trace the development of continuity or struggle and diversity in American writing and the extent to which that writing responds to social and political pressures.

New directions

Style organically contains within itself indices that reach outside itself, a correspondence of its own elements and the elements of an alien context. The internal politics of style (how the elements are put together) is determined by its external politics (its relationship to alien discourse). Discourse lives, as it were, on the boundary between its own context and another, alien context.

M. M. Bakhtin, *The Dialogic Imagination*

Recent literary theory has expressed similar dissatisfaction with the general state of literary studies, pointing the way beyond such major/minor and aesthetic/social dualisms and providing some guidelines for theories of American literature, which, to a large extent, hinge on the broader question of 'what is literature?' and what is a theory of literature, questions that are becoming increasingly problematic. In his 1973 article, 'The Notion of Literature,' Tzvetan Todorov casts 'doubt upon the legitimacy of the very notion of literature,' finding both structural and fictional (literature should *instruct* and *delight*) definitions of literature inadequate and erasing convenient discriminations of the literary from the nonliterary.

Anticipating the now familiar post-structuralist assault on the privileged literary text, Todorov declares:

> Instead of a simple notion of literature we now have a number of different types of discourse, each equally deserving attention. If the choice of our object of study is not dictated by purely ideological reasons (which would then have to be spelled out), we no longer have the right to limit ourselves to purely literary subspecies, even if we are employed by the 'Department of Literature.'
>
> (Todorov 1973, 5, 6)

Coming from a different critical direction, E. D. Hirsch, Jr, similarly questions whether there is anything intrinsically literary in literature. For Hirsch, 'literature has no independent essence, aesthetic or otherwise. It is an arbitrary classification of linguistic works which do not exhibit common distinctive traits, and which cannot be defined as an Aristotelian species' (Hirsch 1976, 135). Tony Bennett also addresses this issue in *Formalism and Marxism* (1979), situating the question within the development of academic literary studies:

> Written texts do not organize themselves into the 'literary' and the 'non-literary'. They are so organized only by the operations of criticism upon them. Far from reflecting a somehow natural or spontaneous system of relationships between written texts, literary criticism organizes those texts into a system of relationships which is the product of its own discourse and of the distinctions between the 'literary' and the 'non-literary' which it operates. As we shall see, this contention is fully substantiated by the history of the term 'literature', which finally achieved the range of meaning discussed above only during the nineteenth century, side by side with the consolidation of literary criticism and aesthetics as autonomous and academically entrenched orders of inquiry.
>
> (Bennett 1979, 7)

Terry Eagleton makes much the same point, albeit in a more politically combative way: 'Literary value is a phenomenon which is *produced* [as opposed to *immanent*] in that ideological appropriation of the text, that "consumptional production" of the work, which is the act of reading. It is always *relational* value: "exchange-value"' (Eagleton 1976a, 166–7). By 1983, Eagleton was simply denying the existence of literature and declaring literary theory a 'nonsubject.' That 'literature' in the restrictive sense is a recent phenomenon inseparable from the academic study of texts, however, does not adequately account for the terms of exclusivity. Any discipline tends to distinguish and consolidate itself by the specificity of its definitions and through some degree of exclusivity. Thus, the question for theorists of American literature is the rigidity of their definitions and exclusions, how they have successfully eliminated from consideration works which the preceding critical paradigm valorized as essentially 'American.' Bennett and Eagleton underline the necessity of a social and political study of *why* social and political literature have been devalued. While I only speculate on this matter (see chapter 1), a thorough consideration of the issue will be necessary before we can fully comprehend the conception of American literature projected by these theorists in the specific social and political climate of postwar America.

Todorov, Hirsch, and Bennett call into question the aestheticization of literary studies, suggesting that criticism, in the name of objectivity, has projected its own theories of aesthetic autonomy onto heterogeneous texts. And both Todorov and Hirsch question the adequacy of definitions of literature for a purpose – the integration of 'minor' or subliterary (and conceivably non- or antiliterary) linguistic works into literary studies. Todorov asserts that 'there is no longer any reason to confine to literature alone the types of studies crystallized in poetics: we must know "as such" not only literary texts but *all* texts, not only verbal production but *all* symbolism' (Todorov 1981, 71). In *The Aims of Interpretation* (1976), E. D. Hirsch, Jr similarly calls for integration:

> One of the most important tasks of criticism at the present time is the reintegration of plain prose, even plainest prose,

into the canon of literature. The first step would be to regard
literature as verbal discourse, not merely as verbal artifact.

(Hirsch 1976, 142)

What is needed is a situating of authors, texts, genres (of
discourses, as Todorov and Hirsch would have it) in a milieu
capable of accommodating diverse, often radically disjointed,
linguistic works and of generating new appreciations of what
might emerge as 'American' about American writings. The
categories of major/minor, aesthetic/social, and text/context
need not be scrapped so much as reevaluated to determine, once
the wide range of American writing is accepted for the plurality
of voices that it is, where, if anywhere, distinctions between the
terms may lie. We can provisionally accept some such distinctions, but only if we understand how loaded such polarities as
aesthetic/social are and how they can block effective evaluation
from ever taking place.

As we have seen, however, theorists of American literature
not only operate on a limited canon and definition of literature,
but also deny or minimize American literature's status as a
social discourse. Many theoretical definitions of American literature or of *the* American tradition labor under both brands of
narrowness. It is to the question of literature's relation to the
society of its genesis that some theorists, especially those working under the rubric of Marxism, are turning. An exhaustive
account of recent advances in 'new literary history' is beyond
the scope of this project. I would like to cite a few examples
(neither new nor complete) of work indicative of profitable
directions for criticism of American literature to take. Theorists
of American literature have been limited by a textual bias, one
capable of integrating psychological, philosophical, and occa-
sionally political data, but not of synthesizing a fully cultural
theory of literary production and reception. Fredric Jameson,
Thomas E. Lewis, and Thomas Metscher advance different, yet
compatible theories of literary reflection that point beyond the
impasse to a fully social fundamental point: literature not only
potentially, but *inevitably* refers in profound ways to the society
of its origins.

According to Jameson in *The Political Unconscious*, politics
is the 'absolute horizon of all reading and interpretation'

(Jameson 1981, 17). Jameson echoes David Hirsch's charge against Trilling's narrow interpretation of reality, seeing such denials of political and social significance of literature as 'a symptom and a reinforcement of the reification and privatization of contemporary life':

> Such a distinction reconfirms that structural, experiential, and conceptual gap between the public and the private, between the social and the psychological, or the political and the poetic, between history and society and the 'individual,' which – the tendential law of social life under capitalism – maims our existence as individual subjects and paralyzes our thinking about time and change just as surely as it alienates us from our speech itself.
>
> (Jameson 1981, 20)

The only liberation from these constraints, Jameson argues, 'begins with the recognition that there is nothing that is not social and historical – indeed that everything is "in the last analysis" political' (Jameson 1981, 20). Thus, the 'political unconscious,' while usually not articulated *in* the text, is the ultimate horizon *of* the text, rather like Althusser's 'absent cause' or the 'Real' of Lacan. In recasting a theory of mediation, Jameson offers an important corrective to theorists' denial of literature's mimetic significance. He cautions against separating two essential dimensions of the literary symbolic act – 'the active way in which the text reorganizes its subtext' and 'the imaginary status of the symbolic act.' To exaggerate the former (the ideology of structuralism) attempts to obliterate the referent, while to emphasize the latter (the ideology of vulgar materialism) reifies the text's social ground as a passive object of reflection and denies its more active (present) significance as a subtext. As we have seen, many theorists of American literature tend to one of these extremes and haven't yet grasped the literary act in its social context. Jameson's assertion that 'there is nothing that is not political' itself poses problems, for if everything is political we may not be much closer to determining how politics are *significantly* present or to distinguishing among opposing politics than we are if we declare that nothing is political. In either case, we have an all or nothing situation which only creates the need for yet another mode of definition and evaluation. Jameson does, however, pose a potent alternative to the prevailing theorists, who too readily simplify or ignore the question of social and political reflection.

In 'Notes toward a Theory of the Referent' (1979), Thomas E. Lewis fuses a semiotic, cultural notion of the referent with a Marxist interpretation of the referent as an ideological unit. His purpose is to deny the possibility of any literature's having only a 'tangential' relationship with society. Arguing, like Eagleton, that 'the notion of a direct, spontaneous relation between text and history . . . belongs to a naive empiricism which needs to be discarded,' Lewis defines the literary referent as necessarily social:

> The literary referent is a cultural ideological unit that, by virtue of its unrepresented relation to other non-identical cultural units, furnishes in the mode of a dialectical absence the materials requisite for a conceptual understanding of both certain properties of the text and the structure of the historical reality to which the text alludes.
>
> (Lewis 1979, 472–3)

Lewis applies this synthesis of semiotics and Marxism to the 'so-called non-referential modernist text.' Since many theorists of American literature operate from certain *a priori*, modernist assumptions about literature and tend to define American literature as an anticipation of modernist aesthetics, Lewis's remarks are germane:

> Far from bearing no relationship to the referent, the modernist text registers in its very form the phenomenological fact of those highly resistant barriers to human cognition – monopoly capitalism, global political structures, and mass-media information systems – that characterize the social reality of our complex world.
>
> (Lewis 1979, 465)

Lewis's significant point is that referentiality cannot be determined or evaluated by a simple calculation of how much reality a text duplicates; the question is how texts signify the world as a cultural ideological unit. The 'reality' is not a given entity (Lewis is clear in his attack on the idealist ramifications of a metaphysics of the referent). It is rather produced, and its production is achieved within the signifying conventions and ideological horizons of a specific, historical society. Social reality in literature, then, is the reality of social relations. And social relations don't always take on the easily identifiable, reified form many theorists of American literature seem to expect.

Thomas Metscher situates the concept of aesthetic cognition in such a way as to transcend the polarization between the aesthetic and the social, enabling us to grasp them in their inevitable unity. Literary criticism has not yet comprehended the centrality of the social to the aesthetic, Metscher suggests, because it falsely distinguishes not only the social and aesthetic, but the individual and the social as well. Metscher counters such distinctions by arguing that art is 'an objectification of social consciousness, . . . a function of the intellectual appropriation of the world by the social subject.' The concept of aesthetic form ('*the constitution of social consciousness as aesthetic form* in art'), then, 'refers to the *total complex of historically developed and ever-changing artistic forces of production* through which and in which reality is appropriated, which are at the disposal of the artist, and in which the acts of aesthetic cognition, interpretation and evaluation occur' (Metscher 1979, 25, 28). Granting the historical gap that may separate author from reader, Metscher none the less rejects entrapment in the hermeneutic circle. Simply stated, the author articulates a mediated rendition of reality in the work of art; the recipient, then, appropriates the aesthetic reality previously appropriated by the author. In any case, reality – the 'total content of our existence' (Hegel); 'the total social object' (Lenin); i.e., the 'totality of our economic, social, cultural, and ideological processes' – is the absolute basis for either literary production or aesthetic reception. As a result of the social basis of art, 'a literary text can be related to the social processes underlying it, and its adequacy to reality can . . . be ascertained. This is a *historicizing* procedure' (Metscher 1979, 22–5, passim).

Metscher reiterates a dissatisfaction with empiricist reductions of reality when he notes, 'Art reflects not a rigid world of objects but social processes and relationships.' Reality, then, is not simply reproduced in a work of art. Rather, the aesthetic work opens up or discovers its own reality, which is none the less that of a specific historical era: 'The production of art is an *active* discovery of reality. . . . The world is brought to consciousness, the interrelations of reality are revealed' (Metscher 1979, 22, 35–6). That literature actively works up reality is an important corrective to many theories of American literature. We have seen many critics take note of the apparent tangentiality of American literature and conclude that the absence of a dense social fabric in, say, *The Scarlet Letter* or *Moby-Dick* means that Hawthorne or Melville have cut the cable, to borrow James's metaphor, between their art and their social world. Even Charles Feidelson, who, like Metscher, argues for art's *constitutive* function, devalues the social and historical importance of the world created by American symbolist literature in favor of its more narrowly epistemological significance. Metscher would counter that what may seem *merely* 'tangential' or 'allegorical' is actually the *mode* of art's relationship to reality, not some unbridgeable gap between art and the real. Metscher mentions three such possible modes: mimetic affirmation, negation, and anticipation, all functioning as interpretive strategies for reflecting the social substratum of artistic production.

Metscher concludes with a discussion particularly pertinent to our concerns. Since art is an *interpretation* of reality, the various aspects revealed by art are perspectively (or ideologically) revealed. 'Every work of art in a social-historical period,' he offers, 'opens up a view of the same reality different from every other work of art.' The essential differences among various perspectives stem from the 'social standpoint from which reality is apprehended' (Metscher 1979, 37). He also argues that the quality of the worldview among various artistic interpretations

> results from the interplay of the emotive, cognitive, ethical, political-ideological, and specifically aesthetic moments. It is the living synthesis of all the factors which are reflected in the aesthetic product, a synthesis which is realized in the course of the artistic process.
>
> (Metscher 1979, 38)

Theorists of American literature tend to limit the possible range of social perspectives and thus flatten the 'interplay' or 'synthesis' of the various moments of literary reflection by positing a homogeneous (or, at least, seemingly so) tradition of New

England literature and by defining literature so as to exclude texts and genres of a frankly social cast.

According to M. M. Bakhtin, there are 'new worlds of verbal perception' to be won through such an opening of literary studies. Bakhtin, Todorov, Hirsch, and Foucault, to name just a few, have dealt with the necessity of such an integrated, 'dialogized,' to use Bakhtin's term, perception of literature; theorists of American literature can benefit from their insights. Bakhtin and others (however diverse their perspectives may be) push us toward a greater understanding of the social and ideological implications of language. Bakhtin's work provides the basis for a new appreciation of the heterogeneity of American literature, a heterogeneity often blurred or denied by the polarization of canonical/noncanonical, major/minor, aesthetic/social. Language, for Bakhtin, is inherently dialogic, inherently social. He uses the term 'heteroglossia' (in opposition to 'monoglossia' or a unitary, holistic language) to suggest the fundamental interaction between self and other and the necessary intermingling of diverse points of view – aesthetic, political, or otherwise – implicit in language. Language, perhaps because of its communicative function, always transcends an absolute, individual, *mono*logic isolation. Despite attempts to formalize it into a rigid, closed system, and however impervious one may be to such a dialogized essence, 'there can be no actual monologue' (Bakhtin 1981, 426, 7).

Bakhtin's work has important implications for literary criticism in general and for theories of American literature in particular. He formulates his notion of the 'dialogic imagination' with specific reference to the history of novelistic form. Despite the richness of his approach, Bakhtin's intra-textual bias is also his chief limitation. True, he elucidates the heteroglossia within any given text, but he fails to extend his awareness of dialogism beyond any specific novel into the 'novelization' of literary traditions or critical paradigms. If the novel integrates diverse generic voices, could we not expand Bakhtin's notions in order better to account for the ideological diversity of any one literary period or canon? Bakhtin is correct in highlighting the heteroglot essence of novelistic form – how much more diverse, however, is the literary production of any given period (the American 1890s, or the American Renaissance, for example).

The struggle to find and establish a voice, then, is not simply a matter of generic or stylistic importance, but also one of ideological necessity. We need, in short, to 'novelize' Bakhtin's method, to use it to expand and to re-accentuate the idea of an American tradition or canon, much as Bakhtin himself uses it to analyze the generic fluidity inherent in novelistic form.

Bakhtin's model has the potential to de-factionalize critical thought, not by denying all boundaries of traditions, schools, or genres, but by marginalizing rigid distinctions which falsify both what is inside and privileged as well as what gets excluded by critical paradigms. According to Bakhtin,

> At any given moment of its historical existence, language is heteroglot from top to bottom: it represents the co-existence of socio-ideological contradictions between the present and the past, between differing epochs of the past, between different socio-ideological groups in the present, between tendencies, schools, circles and so forth, all given a bodily form. These 'languages' of heteroglossia intersect each other in a variety of ways, forming new socially typifying 'languages.' ... Therefore languages do not *exclude* each other, but rather intersect with each other in different ways.
>
> (Bakhtin 1981, 291)

Since both literature and criticism constitute social communities striving to articulate meaning, to unmask or support ideologies, and to debate these issues publicly, who could draw the line at which one writer or critic's ideas begin or cease to be 'individual' or 'original' and at which they can be grasped only in their dialogic (or dialectical) contexts? Should we not rather admit diversity and struggle for the sake of reassessing the history and theory of American literature? With Henry James, Hamlin Garland, Kate Chopin, Edward Eggleston, and Frank Norris all writing simultaneously, from different ideological and even geographical perspectives, a theory of American literature should consider these and other writers and texts together, looking for interrelationships and intersections as well as differences rather than canonizing one (James), marginalizing others (Chopin and Norris), and casting the other two into theoretical oblivion. Given market pressures and the ease with which a writer or text can go out of print, isn't it important for theorists of American literature to preserve and integrate (to make 'usable') as much of the American literary past as is possible? If literary and critical communities do or are going to play an ideological role, whether adversary or not, in a culture, this opening and dialogizing of the American canon is an essential project. The split between canonical and noncanonical fixes the term in an influential hierarchy, not only monopolizing attention, but defining the very terms of investigation. The dialogizing of inadequately examined divisions in the American canon would yield a new understanding of the interrelationships of now nearly mutually exclusive writers, themes, and world-views. What such a method provides is not only a means of dissolving dualisms now obstructing critics and historians of American literature from grasping literature (and criticism) as social to the core but the rationale as well for decentering such concepts as 'major' and 'literary' and placing them along with their opposites (opponents?) in dialogue.

Raymond Williams points out further implications of tradition maintenance and canon formation. For Williams, the 'residual' comprises cultural elements which cannot be eliminated, integrated, or appropriated by a dominant cultural class, but none the less remain active in a culture, posing oppositional and often antagonistic alternatives:

> A residual cultural element is usually at some distance from the effective dominant culture, but some part of it, some version of it – and especially if the residue is from some major area of the past – will in most cases have had to be incorporated if the effective dominant culture is to make sense in these areas. Moreover, at certain points the dominant culture cannot allow too much residual experience and practice outside itself, at least without risk. It is in the incorporation of the actively residual – by reinterpretation, dilution, projection, discriminating inclusion and exclusion – that the work of the selective tradition is especially evident. This is very notable in the case of versions of 'the literary tradition,' passing through selective versions of the character of literature to connecting and incorporated definitions of what literature now is and should be. This is among several crucial

areas, since it is in some alternative or even oppositional versions of what literature is (has been) and what literary experience ... is and must be, that, against the pressures of incorporation, actively residual meanings and values are sustained.

(Williams 1977, 123)

I believe we can draw not too simple an analogy between Williams's notion of residual and the texts, writers, and genres commonly excluded from consideration by theorists of American literature. Many authors and texts have either been expelled or never granted admission into the American canon, though they have played significant roles in the development of American writing and have been involved and often instrumental in transitions from one literary period to another. As we discussed above, this is especially true of the social realist tradition in American literature. The so-called schoolroom poets, to cite an example of a different nature, at least provided a coherent enemy for advocates of literary realism, naturalism, and modernism and are thus present, if only as antitheses to the tradition, in subsequent writers. The same dialectic informs the 'tradition' of American criticism. The theorists I have examined have almost unanimously written against the social criticism of Parrington, Hicks, and Calverton. Future critics and theorists of American literature would do well to address the struggle of American criticism to suppress the social and political significance of American texts.

Bakhtin's distinction between 'canonization' and 're-accentuation' (a concept similar to the 'defamiliarization' of Russian formalism) highlights his ideas on dialogization of a canon and bridges the gap between his theory proper and its applicability to the specific problem of the American canon I have been discussing. Canonization and re-accentuation relate dialectically: canonization blurs heteroglossia; re-accentuation, not surprisingly, reintroduces it.

Bakhtin carefully adds that such a re-accentuation is not simply an imposition of new priorities upon the literature of the past. In a passage which echoes Van Wyck Brooks's idea of a 'usable past,' yet without the relativizing implications, Bakhtin historicizes the process of re-accentuation:

Every age re-accentuates in its own way the works of its most immediate past. The historical life of classic works is in fact the uninterrupted process of their social and ideological re-accentuation. Thanks to the intentional potential embedded in them, such works have proved capable of uncovering in each era and against ever new dialogizing backgrounds ever newer aspects of meaning; their semantic content literally continues to grow, to further create out of itself. . . . New images in literature are very often created through a re-accentuating of old images, by translating them from one accentual register to another (from the comic plane to the tragic, for instance, or the other way around).

(Bakhtin 1981, 420–1)

Considering the recent work by Metscher, Lewis, and Jameson on the social, historical, and ideological significance inherent in what has been specified as 'the aesthetic,' the prospects for a new re-accentuation of the American tradition are promising. Not only will we be able to investigate the aesthetic significance of such commonly excluded writers as Frederick Douglass, Theodore Dreiser, or Tillie Olsen; the social and ideological significance of such purportedly metaphysical or 'tangential' writers as Hawthorne, Dickinson, and Stevens will also become more vital an inquiry.

The American scene

New backgrounds, new images, new aspects of meaning are what theorists of American literature have begun to discover and elucidate through a new literary history/criticism. Such horizons of meaning are discoverable on many levels: in works rarely regarded as literary, in works once canonical but for various reasons now exiled as sub- or nonliterary, and in canonical texts indicative of present aesthetic/critical assumptions. We have questioned two varieties of narrowness in the American canon – the smaller number of authors treated by the theorists, and the asocial themes regarded as constituting the majorness of 'major' figures. Both the so-called American authors and the American themes, once thrown against newly appreciated backgrounds – composed largely of authors and themes usually beyond the pale of critical taste and anthological space – can themselves gain in significance as the writers and writings of different interests, different styles, and different politics elucidate elements in, say, Hawthorne or Melville, that have gone largely unnoticed or unexamined for want of a context capable of foregrounding their significance.

Nina Baym and Paul Lauter have criticized the exclusivity of the American canon on both sexual and racial grounds. Baym's 'Melodramas of Beset Manhood: How Theories of American Fiction Exclude Women Authors' offers a feminist critique of male control over American literary studies. Noting such practical facts as the commercial and numerical domination of women as producers and consumers of American literature since the middle of the nineteenth century, as well as the typecasting of women as 'enemies' by males – Hawthorne's contempt for those 'scribbling women' is an obvious example – Baym formulates an insightful reading of the American critical tradition. Granting that the *standards* of most theorists are not intentionally sexist, she argues that their *practice* – including their definitions of literature, their overwhelming emphasis on male authors, and their language (note Leslie Fiedler's tacit assumptions of a male audience, for instance, or Eric Sundquist's remarks about the notion of 'fathering a tradition' being central to American writers) – definitely *is*. Baym's most important contribution, however, is to push her insights beyond sexual politics toward a more comprehensive grasp of the problems many theorists present, that is, their reluctance to situate American literature in its social context. The situation, Baym suggests, is complex. Somehow the American literary establishment has come to view 'society' as a monolithic and destructive pressure on individuality (Poirier's *A World Elsewhere* is the most explicit articulation of what Baym terms the 'American myth'). In addition to so simplistic a reduction of so complex an issue, theorists (and, perhaps, male writers as well) have mythicized women writers as assenting to the dominant culture, and thus have marginalized them in favor of a more 'manly,' nay-saying lineage of male figures. Neither component of this scenario can withstand serious scrutiny, yet the program continues to inform even recent studies of the American tradition. Baym's conclusion sums up the ramifications of these 'melodramas of beset manhood' that have passed as theories of American literature:

> In pursuit of the uniquely American, [male theorists of American fiction] have arrived at a place where American-ness has vanished into the depths of what is alleged to be the universal male psyche. . . . What a reduction this is of the enormous variety of fiction written in this country, by both women and men.
>
> (Baym 1981, 139)

Baym could, perhaps, have elaborated more on how the recognition of women in American literature would revise the reigning theoretical paradigm. How would it alter the definition of Americanness? of literature? of society? While Baym's focus is the imposition of 'maleness' onto the study of American literature, she suggests, though she doesn't fully pursue, the connection of a white male hegemony over the field with the larger issues of nationalism and the inescapable contradictions of defining what is uniquely 'American' in universal terms. Baym's work over the past two decades, however, presents a formidable challenge to the prevailing theorists, more concerned, perhaps, with the sins of the *fathers* than with the fullness of the American literary past.

Addressing the question of race and gender in the shaping of American literature, Paul Lauter has worked out a more thoroughly political analysis of the canon. Reminding us that 'the literary canon is . . . a means by which culture validates social power,' Lauter argues for the centrality of revising the canon, a task possible 'only by conscious literary and organizing efforts' (Lauter 1983, 435–6). After surveying trends in anthologies and literary histories throughout the twentieth century, Lauter specifies three factors responsible for the exclusion of women and minorities: the professionalization of the teaching of literature; an aesthetic theory that privileges certain texts; and the chronological organization of the canon into periods or themes.

First, the professionalization of the teaching of literature ensconced as educators, critics, and arbiters of taste 'college-educated, white men of Anglo-Saxon or northern European origins' from a relatively small, élite, and homogeneous social base (Lauter 1983, 442). This group, according to Lauter, projected their own values as well as their own fears of recent immigrations from Southern and Eastern Europe onto the field of American literature. In a sense their 'usable past' was meant to validate and bolster their own social positions, which they feared to be eroding beneath them. Second, two aesthetic systems – one celebrating a nationalistic usable past and the other emphasizing *belles-lettres* – had the mutually reinforcing effect of narrowing the canon to either a particular vision of American culture or a definition of literariness. As Lauter demonstrates, the defense of class characteristic of academic teachers of literature informed their definitions of literature as well, granting credentials of 'literary interpreters' to an élite collection of literary intellectuals while excluding the lives and works about which others wrote. Like the white couple in Langston Hughes's 'The Slave on the Block,' white critics, Lauter implies, valued minorities primarily as exotica, 'like a taste for Pernod or jazz' (Lauter 1983, 451). The third factor Lauter elaborates, the tendency toward periodicity, provided further support for an academicized élite. Whether around a chronological division such as 'Puritanism' or a category such as 'frontier spirit,' literary critics perpetuated a history reflecting the hegemony of white males. It is necessary, Lauter maintains, to understand that male dominance was won (or stolen) from women, blacks, and native Americans. In his furthest reaches, Lauter argues that the very conception of periodicity accentuates the discontinuities over the continuities of life and is 'something like imagining the world as it is presented in a tabloid newspaper, with its emphasis on the exceptional, rather than upon the commonplace, the ongoing' (Lauter 1983, 456). In other words, literary histories and theories that succumb to a chronological or thematic organizational system bias not only the literary texts they include, but also the notion of history those texts are meant to communicate.

Though Lauter himself doesn't advance such a critique, his juxtaposition of the problems of periodicity and the sensationalistic overtones of such a method with his concluding remarks on the economics of 'heavily capitalized' anthologies and mass-marketed texts and on the star-system impact of popular critics suggests a profound political dilemma for American literary studies. If literary study is subject to forms of racial and sexual discrimination different only in degree from their more brutal manifestations, and if the dynamics of literature and criticism as commodities are little different from the shallow hype of Madison Avenue, does this not point toward the co-optation of literary and cultural studies by the very system they are often meant to oppose and criticize? As mentioned earlier, a great many of the theorists proposing theories of American literature do so in an explicit attempt to cast American texts as nay-saying statements against a yea-saying culture, characterized (perhaps too simply) by its urge for consensus and conciliation. If my reading of Lauter is correct, not only do these theorists and the canons they support fail to mount an effective criticism of American culture, but they actually contribute a subtle ideological brace to the very system they claim to challenge. In *Literature Against Itself*, Gerald Graff argues that, contrary to the avant-garde posturings of modern and postmodern literary criticism, 'the real avant-garde is advanced capitalism, with its built-in need to destroy all vestiges of tradition, all orthodox ideologies, all continuous and stable forms of reality in order to stimulate higher levels of consumption' (Graff 1979, 8). The context of Graff's remarks differs from that of Lauter's discussion, but I would suggest that they both imply an abstract, yet authoritative complicity between 'advanced capitalism' as Graff takes it, and literary culture, which both Graff and Lauter agree either does, claims to, or should criticize the fragmentation and alienation essential to the cultural hegemony of capitalism.

I am not convinced that Lauter's solution of abandoning 'the very conception of periodicity' is a very potent corrective for the problems he describes. In fact, the practice of both the Macmillan and the Norton anthologies of American literature, which have abandoned thematic and period labels in favor of a simple chronological sequence of authors, might well escape the pitfalls Lauter criticizes, but does it point to any more egalitarian or representative a canon? Not necessarily. Given Lauter's politicized discussion, would it not be more productive to re-thematize and re-periodize anthologies on more accurate grounds? Even given his example of Puritanism as a sexually and racially discriminatory label, I would argue that granting the term by which 'a narrow group of male divines construed

and confirmed their dominant roles in New England society'
(Lauter 1983, 453) doesn't necessarily implicate us in their
dominance. Once granted, the term Puritan, denoting as it does
the socioreligious monopoly of the Massachusetts Bay settlement by white male clergy, provides a valuable context against
which suppressed or marginalized voices – women, native
Americans, blacks, and dissenting religious sects – can be
understood. Religious and political debates, and the importance
of figures such as Anne Hutchinson, Anne Bradstreet, Roger
Williams, John Woolman, and others, I would argue, need to be
approached within the general context of Puritanism. To discard Puritanism as a descriptive phrase on the ground that it
reflects the dominance of a repressive regime would also grant a
monolithic, ideologically impervious presence to the Puritans,
while the reality of the era is far more complex, contradictory,
and unstable than such an attribution of power suggests. I
would argue that the integration of 'the broader contexts of
New England family, political, and business life [and the]
comparisons with cultural development in other English as well
as non-English settlements' that Lauter claims the label Puritan
implicitly discourages *is* possible, and offers more dialectical
and productive a corrective than the abandonment of period
labels. The integration of such texts would force an enlargement
of the meaning and authority of Puritanism, and a possible
refinement of our historical sense of the entire range of colonial
America.

More specifically than Baym or Lauter (in these remarks at
least), critics of American literature have begun revising our
understanding of major authors as they recognize previously
neglected ranges of literary work. Let us examine the case of
Hawthorne. For many critics, Hawthorne's isolation, his
strange detachment from his times, enables him to transcend
historical and cultural determination in the way 'great artists'
tend to. And yet his career, the context of his writing, his genius
were all rooted in his experience as a historical person.
Hawthorne needs to be understood as one voice among many
others in a cultural, historical, and literary debate (moment).
Hawthorne's relationship to that 'damned mob of scribbling
women' is a case in point. Hawthorne's scorn for the sentimental pulp fiction churned out by women for a wide audience

is well known. What is not well known, however, is how great
Hawthorne's debt to them may have been. Although Hawthorne's contempt for their brand of generic fiction aroused
him to write 'against' them, he was also positively influenced by
them. In *Faith in Fiction: The Emergence of Religious Literature in
America* (1981), David Reynolds discusses the historical novel as
one of five subgenres of religious fiction which emerged between
1820 and 1850. Including such forgotten works as Harriet V.
Cheney's *A Peep at the Pilgrims* (1824), Lydia Child's *Hobomok*
(1824), and John L. Motley's *Merry-Mount* (1849) among early
novels about the Puritan era, Reynolds summarizes their plots
in suggestive terms:

> In these novels, admiration for the heroism of New England
> forefathers was usually qualified by a distaste for their in-
> tolerance, gloom, and logical rigidity. . . . Unlike Nathaniel
> Hawthorne, who would exploit Puritan gloom to contravene
> optimistic views of human nature, the liberal historical novel-
> ist typically portrayed a cheerful, ethical protagonist (often a
> young woman) who wins either a moral or an actual victory
> over dour Calvinist antagonists. The liberal rebellion against
> tyranny and enigma that earlier had been veiled in Oriental
> guise became in these novels more directly anti-Calvinist.
> Threatened with imprisonment or death by stern Puritans,
> the protagonist customarily survived by adhering to a simple
> outlook of good works, aesthetic imagination, and hope.
>
> (Reynolds 1981, 106)

Although Reynolds calls attention to Hawthorne's departures
from this scheme, the similarities between *The Scarlet Letter* and
these earlier works are more significant for this study. The
intolerance, gloom, and logical rigidity of the Puritan rulers and
the young woman who counters her dour adversaries with good
works, aesthetic imagination, and hope do, with some qualifications, point to the likelihood that Hawthorne was working
consciously in a familiar mode, to which he added his own
touches. Reynolds's depiction of the Puritan autocracy in
popular fiction reminds us of Hawthorne's portrayal of it not
only in *The Scarlet Letter*, but in short stories such as 'The
Maypole of Merry Mount,' 'The Man of Adamant,' 'Young
Goodman Brown,' and 'The Minister's Black Veil' as well.

Hester Prynne's dedication to good works (her community service prompts some townspeople to interpret the 'A' as 'able'), her aesthetic imagination (many comment on the fineness of her embroidery), and the hope which Hester harbors throughout the novel are among the traits placing her in the tradition of the novels Reynolds discusses. Hawthorne's elaborations on the earlier, formulaic works – the sexual relationship between Hester and Dimmesdale, the moral ambiguity and depth complicating a simple opposition of cheerful, female protagonist versus dour Calvinist rulers – distinguish Hawthorne's work from the others. But the mere presence of moral ambiguity, complexity, and an ironic 'dark vision' do not justify elevating *The Scarlet Letter* out of the context of its predecessors. Hawthorne's work may well be the best of these novels, but it should not be theoretically abstracted from a context capable of shedding light both on *The Scarlet Letter* and on the other novels Reynolds discusses, as well as on the development of American literature as a whole. Isolating Hawthorne's work and themes from these other writers and texts falsifies and simplifies Hawthorne's achievement by assuming that he wrote in a relative vacuum, relying primarily on his original genius and private reflections on American history and morality. By considering these works together, theorists of American literature could discern new areas of significance in *A Peep at the Pilgrims* and *The Scarlet Letter*. Studying Hawthorne in light of thematic relationships with other 'major' American writers (his symbolistic technique, his world elsewhere, the machine in his garden, etc.) yields interesting and valuable insights into his works and his place among these other figures, but it denies the immediate, cultural context of Hawthorne's career in favor of large themes of intellectual history. For a theory of American literature, both areas of investigation are necessary, yet only the latter has been pursued. Jameson offers a pertinent analysis of American criticism's reluctance to engage Hawthorne in his full historical context:

> If the modern reader is bored or scandalized by the roots such texts [Hawthorne's, Milton's and others'] send down into the contingent circumstances of their own historical time, this is surely testimony as to his resistance to his own political

unconscious and to his denial (in the United States, the denial of a whole generation) of the reading and the writing of the text of history within himself.

(Jameson 1981, 34)

The primary purpose of viewing *The Scarlet Letter* in the context of such 'minor' works as *A Peep at the Pilgrims* is not simply to clarify some arcane historical significance or to strengthen Hawthorne's place among American writers, though any new knowledge of *The Scarlet Letter* that such comparisons reveal is undeniably important. 'Minor' works cannot just be used as raw material for the further aggrandizement of 'major' works. What such minor texts elucidate enhances their own importance, not simply that of Hawthorne's work.

Jane Tompkins has advanced a compatible thesis in 'The Politics of Hawthorne's Literary Reputation.' Noting that 'the novels of sentimental writers like Susan Warner and Harriet Beecher Stowe were praised as extravagantly as Hawthorne's, and in exactly the same terms' (Tompkins 1984, 627), Tompkins argues that the subsequent canonization of Hawthorne and the related marginalization of sentimental novelists needs to be studied as a 'political matter,' especially in terms of what cultural criteria were the dominant ones for literary evaluation and, equally important, what powerful literary and publishing connections authors had through friendships, family ties, and the like. Arguing against the popular notion that literary reputations testify to writers' works transcending specific historical determinations and standing as monuments to eternity, Tompkins notes certain contradictions regarding Hawthorne's critical reception and suggests that we 'need to study the interests, institutional practices, and social arrangements that sustain the canon of classic works' (Tompkins 1984, 642). Not least among the benefits from such a critical intervention would be opening the way to recuperate noncanonical texts that the 'literary establishment ... has suppressed' (Tompkins 1984, 642). For both Reynolds and Tompkins, decentering Hawthorne has the important effect of recognizing writers and texts that need the kind of careful study we have traditionally reserved for such entrenched authors as Hawthorne.

While Reynolds's study codifies an immense range of American religious literature, much of it previously ignored, and provides invaluable contexts for situating 'major' American writers in a dense literary and cultural milieu, Jane Tompkins's essay on *Uncle Tom's Cabin* (1981) poses another, more radical, challenge by privileging that novel and other so-called sentimental texts usually denigrated by theorists of American literature. Tompkins's clearest targets are American critics, Ann Douglas foremost among them, who trace a complex of cultural evils to sentimental women writers of the nineteenth century and who, by so doing, provide a subtle rationale for a traditional and 'hidebound' canon of major, male American authors, again to the virtual exclusion of women. But Tompkins also raises several other issues of theoretical importance that remain more or less in the background of her essay. Most engagingly, she identifies the ideological subtext of theories of American literature: the de-socializing of the American canon. For instance, she locates the power *and* the popularity of *Uncle Tom's Cabin* (as well as its continuing critical neglect) in its explicitly public program. 'The inability of twentieth-century critics either to appreciate the complexity and scope of a novel like Stowe's, or to account for its enormous popular success,' Tompkins asserts, 'stems from their assumptions about the nature and function of literature':

> In modernist thinking, literature is by definition a form of discourse that has no designs on the world. It does not attempt to change things, but merely to represent them, and it does so in a specifically literary language whose claim to value lies in its uniqueness. Consequently, works whose stated purpose is to influence the course of history, and which therefore employ a language that is not only not unique but common and accessible to everyone, do not qualify as works of art.

> (Tompkins 1981, 82)

What Tompkins here assigns to 'modernist thinking' is an array of those tendencies we have traced in their American context. Tompkins asks her readers to 'set aside' standard criteria for literary evaluation – 'stylistic intricacy, psychological subtlety, epistemological complexity' – in order to read *Uncle Tom's Cabin*, 'not as an artifice of eternity answerable to certain formal criteria and to certain psychological and philosophical concerns, but as a political enterprise halfway between sermon and social theory, that both codifies and attempts to mold the values of its time' (Tompkins 1981, 83). In fact, challenging critics – Douglas by name, but a number of theorists by implication – who reject *Uncle Tom's Cabin* for its sob-story sentimentality and who would define an event such as little Eva's protracted death-bed scene as impotent and decorative because it 'does nothing to remedy the evils it deplores' and 'leaves the slave system and the other characters unchanged' (Tompkins 1981, 84), Tompkins turns the tables on modern critics by posing that those arguably maudlin scenes operate within 'a pervasive cultural myth which invests the suffering and death of an innocent victim with just the kind of power that critics deny to Stowe's novel, the power to work in, and change, the world' (p. 86). Furthermore, she adds, 'if the language of tears seems maudlin and little Eva's death ineffective, it is because both the tears and the redemption they signify belong to a conception of the world that is now generally regarded as naive and unrealistic' (Tompkins 1981, 87).

This discrepancy between *Uncle Tom's Cabin*'s original reception and influence and its subsequent critical reception, Tompkins suggests, highlights, if not the inadequacy of American literary theory, at least its historical, political, and genderized limitations. In a trenchant passage, Tompkins remarks that Sacvan Bercovitch's disregarding Stowe's novel in *The American Jeremiad*, despite that novel's constituting 'the most obvious and compelling instance of the jeremiad since the Great Awakening,' provides 'a striking instance of how totally academic criticism has foreclosed on sentimental fiction; since, even when a sentimental novel fulfills a man's theory to perfection, he cannot see it' (Tompkins 1981, 93).

Bercovitch's ignoring of *Uncle Tom's Cabin* can be traced, Tompkins implies, either to the male-centered canon Bercovitch labors within, or to the negative inertia obscuring the power of Stowe's text. As significant as either of these possibilities, however, are the political strategies of *Uncle Tom's Cabin*. Tompkins can't charge Bercovitch with evading political texts; his work is centrally concerned with the ideological operations performed by American writers. Instead, she returns to Ann

Douglas, who claims that sentimental writers were disenfranchised, disaffected, and 'cut off from any "awareness of class and interest, of societal structure, which genuine political consciousness fosters"' (Tompkins 1981, 84). According to Tompkins, Douglas (and Bercovitch by implication) simply misunderstands 'the relationships between discourse and power which the jeremiad presupposes' (Tompkins 1981, 94), essentially those of defining social reality. The crucial similarity between *Uncle Tom's Cabin* and 'accepted' jeremiads is their rhetorical shaping of reality to a political design and their attempt to construct history by selling a vision of the world assumed to be true. The crucial difference, however, is that the jeremiad à la Bercovitch 'represents the interests of Puritan ministers, while the sentimental novel represents the interests of middle-class women' (Tompkins 1981, 94). Thus, Tompkins attempts to redefine social and political reality from a feminist perspective.

Again rejecting Douglas, who defines the American cult of domesticity as a 'mirror phenomenon,' Tompkins asserts the centrality, the reality even, of Stowe's previously marginalized vision. The home, the hearth, and the women who preside therein (a scenario best depicted in Rachael Halliday's Quaker kitchen) represent, not a haven from a heartless world, but rather 'an economic *alternative* to that world, one which calls into question the whole structure of American society' and which reflects 'the real communitarian practices of village life, practices which had depended upon cooperation, trust, and a spirit of mutuality' (Tompkins 1981, 97). What might, then, appear as a conservative return to 'an age of homespun,' Tompkins argues, 'is precisely what gives [Stowe's] novel its revolutionary potential' (p. 98). The impossibility of integrating a domestic economy into a capitalistic mercantile one highlights the necessity of one triumphing at the expense of the other. The continuing popularity of *Uncle Tom's Cabin* testifies, for Tompkins, not only to its power for Stowe's time, but to its political promise for our own.

Tompkins turns the tables not only on Douglas and Bercovitch, but on many theorists of American literature as well. For her, a feminine point of view and social program is most clearly and potently in touch with the sources of mass political power in the United States. *Uncle Tom's Cabin*'s popularity assures Tompkins of this suppressed fact, just as certainly as does its neglect by American critics won to a masculine political vision (even Ann Douglas, Tompkins argues, indicts women writers because they aren't *more like* the canonical male authors (Tompkins 1981, 81)). For Tompkins, the male hegemony over American criticism has resulted in the imposition of an abstract political bias which, however sound in theory (albeit a *male* theory), is *only* an abstraction compared to the powerful alternative represented by suppressed writings by sentimental women writers. It is crucial that Tompkins links an arguably aesthetic issue – the denigration of a certain kind of text on aesthetic grounds – to a political issue – the suppression or, at least, trivialization of a feminist politics and domestic economy in favor of a masculine political vision and exchange economy.

In this diagnostic respect, Tompkins's reading is exemplary of what American criticism needs to pursue, interventions at the critical and practical level. While her analysis of the problem involves both sexual/political and aesthetic/institutional components (she rejects a set of aesthetic criteria that have canonized a largely male tradition), her solutions fail, I feel, to get American literary thinking much beyond a *genderized* impasse, which could become as exclusionary as the one it supplants. Just as Tompkins locates the revolutionary potential of Stowe's text in the impossibility of its politics being integrated (they resist through their very conventionality full male appropriation), her implicit vision of American literary history is one which defies an acceptance of heterogeneity. That 'Stowe relocates the center of power in American life, placing it not in the government, nor in the courts of law, nor in the factories, nor the marketplace, but in the kitchen' (p. 98), is a credible description of Stowe's vision and its revision of American politics. What, however, is the potential of such a reading for revising American literary history? In Tompkins's essay, it is a 'new matriarchy' that 'constitutes the most politically subversive dimension of Stowe's novel, more disruptive and far-reaching in its potential consequences then [*sic*] even the starting of a war or the freeing of slaves' (p. 96). In this new matriarchy, Tompkins argues, 'the removal of the male from the center to the periphery of the human sphere is the most radical component of this millenarian scheme which is rooted so solidly in the most traditional values—religion, motherhood, home, and family' (p. 98). The woman-centered political structure displaces rather than supplements or revises the male-dominated marketplace as the 'dynamic center of activity, physical and spiritual, economic and moral' (p. 98). 'And that means,' Tompkins announces, 'that the new society will not be controlled by men but by women' (p. 98).

It would be impossible to argue that Tompkins has not offered a potent alternative to simplistic reductions of *Uncle Tom's Cabin* as either a work of literary value or as a coherent political/social text; her contribution is an important one. However, it does seem contradictory for Tompkins, who suggests that part of Ann Douglas's 'inordinately narrow view of politics' is related to her inverse sexism (she condemns women because they aren't more like men), to conclude by suggesting that men must either cease to function *or* become more like women, arguably as sexist and exclusionary a reading as those against which Tompkins positions herself. What her reading exposes is the inadequacy of a gender-specific literary aesthetic, and one might suppose that her solutions don't do much more than reverse the roles without solving the underlying problems of genderized values. What her reading offers, I would argue, is an antithesis to male hegemony, both within the antebellum South of Stowe's text and within the contemporary American critical establishment. She neither advances nor implies, however, what kind of dialectical synthesis the critical establishment could forge. A world in which *either* sex dominates seems to be the problem we need to address.

I do not mean to suggest that Tompkins has 'misread' *Uncle Tom's Cabin* or that her remarks aren't exciting and important. What does concern me is that, in an essay subtitled 'The Politics of Literary History,' Tompkins doesn't suggest what the larger theoretical implications of her revision of Stowe's text may be. Tompkins correctly addresses the abstract perspectives brought to American literary studies by a largely male establishment. Are we to assume, though, that centering women and feminist concerns in American literary studies while marginalizing the place of masculinity will result in a more representative canon? Or are we to expect that by correctly understanding the politics of domesticity that Stowe articulates and Tompkins defends we can re-politicize American literary studies and correct the abstract, anti-social paradigm that has rejected *Uncle Tom's Cabin*? My guess is that Tompkins suspects so. Her essay is strangely contradictory, though, because she may, by presenting a political analysis of *Uncle Tom's Cabin*, simply further guarantee its exclusion by the critical community which she defines as hostile to overtly political writing. The problem is that Tompkins offers no coherent revision of the American critical enterprise which renders her own reading peripheral. I also feel that we need to get beyond the sexual politics on which Tompkins focuses to those issues which she drops rather quickly, namely the larger denial of all politicized concerns by theorists of American literature.

H. Bruce Franklin's reading of Melville through the work of Frederick Douglass provides another example of how a revision of a 'major' author can transform our understanding of an entire tradition. Franklin's reading is extreme, but so extreme an approach may well be necessary to counterbalance the critical consensus over Melville's work and his significance in the American tradition. Franklin's discussion, in fact, demonstrates how the exclusion or suppression of certain areas of significance impoverishes, not to say falsifies, our conception of American literature. Not willing to subordinate the literature of American prisons to the acceptable canon, Franklin performs two preliminary operations meant to reorient literary study. First, he situates American literature in the context of American history, in this case that of racial oppression:

> A literature that was consciously 'American' first came into being in the eight decades between the Revolution and the Civil War. During this period most white Americans thought of Blacks as anything from funny childlike creatures to animals of a distinct subhuman species. Fundamental to the outlook of most of the new Republic's writers, this view was implemented throughout American society and was codified into the founding Constitution and subsequent legislation.

> (Franklin 1978, 3)

This codification of racist stereotypes, Franklin suggests, permeates the writings of Hawthorne (whose pro-slavery remarks Franklin quotes), Poe, and other American authors.

Franklin's second strategy is to assert the centrality of a countertradition among American slaves:

> In opposition to this view [racism] and to the system it defended, there emerged a literary genre whose form and content is uniquely American – the narrative of the escaped slave. . . . The racist mentality of William Gilmore Simms and Nathaniel Hawthorne, of Edgar Allan Poe and James Fenimore Cooper, is not uniquely American; it was and still is, generally characteristic of European societies and the colonialisms exported from Europe to the Americas, Asia, and Africa. The slave narrative, however, is truly American. In fact, it was the first genre the United States contributed to the written literature of the world.
>
> (Franklin 1978, 4–5)

After citing examples of slave narratives and the Reverend Ephraim Peabody's article 'Narratives of Fugitive Slaves' (1849), in which Peabody declares 'America has the mournful honor of adding a new department to the literature of civilization – the autobiographies of escaped slaves,' Franklin adds that 'in less than a century, however, this literary achievement had been effectively expunged from the study of American literature' (Franklin 1978, 4–5).

Franklin's remarks on the narrowness of the American canon, the 'Americanness' of slave narratives, and their suppression from literary study all corroborate the themes we have been considering. Some may object to the political animus behind Franklin's project or to his apparent attempt to replace the traditional canon with one based on the literature of oppressed slaves. Such a revision, like that offered by Jane Tompkins, could simply usher in a new narrowness. Franklin's contribution need not, however, result in another form of canonical tyranny. It is Franklin's method, not his conclusions, that is important. He establishes an important precedent for a principled expansion of the American canon, capable not only of introducing new writers and genres, but of correcting our understanding of traditional writers in light of a more egalitarian approach to American writing.

In practice Franklin achieves exactly that, reading the *Narrative of the Life of Frederick Douglass, An American Slave: Written by*

Himself in order to show 'that individual early Afro-American works of literature merit the kind of close attention we usually reserve for works of the canon' (Franklin 1978, 7). That Franklin must resort to traditional methods of literary criticism – close scrutiny of details and the tracing of image patterns – need not trouble us; we must work with traditional means as new approaches to literary study are being formulated. Franklin's crucial contribution is his broader application of textual analysis to demonstrate that a body of commonly suppressed writings can bear close scrutiny, even by acceptable methods.

When Franklin bases a reading of Melville on Douglass's work, we perceive new areas of literary significance. Again, this is not to subordinate Douglass to Melville; the *Narrative* emerges as a 'major' text capable of illuminating significance in Melville as well as in the American tradition as a whole. Placing Melville in the context of Douglass, whose work foregrounds the specific historical and social milieu of his times and the primacy of human labor to human identity, reveals in Melville a strikingly similar materialist epistemology contrary to the abstract essence frequently imputed by theorists of American literature. Reading Melville primarily as a 'proletarian artist' may seem perverse, but Franklin's approach does emphasize elements in Melville's work that are arguably important, though often overlooked and, as Franklin demonstrates, sometimes suppressed.

Franklin acknowledges 'that Melville has been released from the silence and obscurity imposed on him by the petty-bourgeois authorities of the cultural world of his own time' as well as Melville's undisputed importance in American literature and culture, but none the less asserts that 'what is most vital and relevant about Melville is still largely suppressed and buried.' According to Franklin, 'despite the deepening understanding of many teachers awakened by the historical events of the last decade, the Melville that is taught is still predominantly a denatured Melville, an academic Melville' (Franklin 1978, 38). Such an appreciation might not be unwarranted if Melville were a dramatist of afternoon tea, but Franklin, rightly I believe, argues that any approach to *Moby-Dick* (and most of Melville's fiction) from any direction 'other than one that follows Melville's own path through the brutal but ennobling labor of the whaleman is not just to distort but fundamentally to misrepresent *Moby-Dick*' (Franklin 1978, 44). Defining the novel's central ethic as proletarian solidarity, Franklin posits two indispensable assumptions about Melville's work: first, 'that its underlying power comes from the reality of whales and whaling, the ocean and the men who sailed it,' and, second, 'that it is a celebration of the transcendent dignity and nobility, in fact divinity, of the most oppressed members of the proletariat' (Franklin 1978, 44–6, passim).

The presence of labor and solidarity in Melville's work as in Douglass's, then, becomes a new touchstone for literary significance. The suppression of explicitly political passages from *Typee*; the oppression of sailors aboard Melville's ships; Melville's own desertion from ship (recounted in *Typee*); White Jacket's flogging and humiliation by his captain; Ishmael's meditation on solidarity in 'The Monkey-Rope'; his being cheated by the *Pequod*'s owners; the racial equality aboard ship; Bartleby's imprisonment for the crime of vagrancy; Israel Potter's life of exile, obscurity, and manipulation; and countless other examples of prisoners and outcasts in Melville's writings all assume a new importance in light of a materialist perspective.

Granted, these passages and themes may not immediately strike us as significant in the same way as do Ahab's assault on ultimate good and evil, the ambiguities of Pierre's identity, or *The Confidence-Man*'s deconstruction of a stable human character. Such themes are indeed of enduring importance, but they have been overemphasized, just as explicit political and social themes have been minimized by a primarily asocial approach to American literature. The important point is not that we must reject other readings, but that we can perceive a Melville different from the obscurantist of Winters, the symbolic voyager of Feidelson, or the aesthetic politician of Leo Marx. Furthermore, once we establish the presence and importance of a more overtly social tradition in American writing, the works of other authors such as Thomas Paine, George Lippard, Theodore Dreiser, and Tillie Olsen naturally and properly grow in stature.

6

Conclusion:
the significance
of Frederick Douglass

One need not, as H. Bruce Franklin does, situate Frederick
Douglass so narrowly or base a new theory of American literature on the centrality of labor, however, to grant his significance. Douglass's place in the American canon has, over the
past decade, grown increasingly more secure. Less certain,
however, is just *how* Douglass's *Narrative* is to be situated in
American literary history. Douglass's *Narrative* can, in fact,
stand on its own merits, even given the standards of an accepted
and traditional humanistic canon. Douglass's text is an intelli-
gent, humane, and aesthetically coherent inquiry into perhaps
the most significant of all questions: what is a human being?
Douglass refuses to grapple with such a question in the abstract,
and, true to his own lived experience – his oppression and
economic degradation as a slave – poses his questions and
wrenches his answers in the material and historical context of a
racist society. Unlike his transcendental contemporaries,
however, Douglass grasped questions such as 'where I lived'
and 'what I lived for' as matters of life and death, not as issues
for philosophical reflection. And Douglass's answers, unlike
those of Emerson and Thoreau, could not be formulated in
living 'experiments' near Walden Pond or in the scholar's study
or orator's pulpit. Douglass had to win human freedom in a
physical battle with his owner.

I would like to suggest that Douglass occupies an important, though unexamined, place among the major writers of the American Renaissance. Three thematic concerns – Douglass's complex perspective on the relationship between individual and community, his fusion of theory and practice, and his own method of defamiliarizing conventional perceptions of reality – link him with his American contemporaries as a literary artist and thinker of the first rank and establish his *Narrative* as perhaps the first literary, political, and epistemological extension of ideas advanced in Emerson's major early essays. Situating Douglass squarely within the context of the 'major' writers of the American Renaissance illumines not only his work, but the works of Emerson, Thoreau, Hawthorne, and Melville as well.

One of Douglass's major thematic concerns (and in the *Narrative* theme never suggests only a literary motif) that reiterates a prevalent motif among Emerson, Thoreau, Hawthorne, and Melville is his complex working out of an individual's relationship with his community. For Douglass, that already difficult dialogue between self and other is complicated by the racial and political barriers that set black against white. Douglass's sense of community and of family, for example, must also be realized in opposition to the conventions of a slave system that separates children from parents and siblings and friends from friends. Friendship and community, thus, have little or no support from traditional biological, domestic, or social contexts. Even in this sense, Douglass anticipates the themes of isolation, orphanage, and alienation that pervade so many texts of the American Renaissance. But for Douglass, this is the point from which he begins to construct an identity, not an existential given. Douglass's historical and experiential biases may well represent his greatest significance within this period of American literary history. He repeatedly *grounds* in the economic and cultural contexts of his own life as a slave thematics that subsequent American writers address, though rarely in so material and antagonistic a milieu.

It is in his relationships with other slaves, however, that the dialectic between self and community takes its most decisive form. Although Douglass adopts the slogan of 'Trust no man!' when he first escapes from slavery, and although his earliest plan to escape was betrayed by a fellow slave, he remains committed to a communal philosophy. While Douglass's feelings on this issue are sometimes expressed as fear of separation, they usually take a more positive form, as a paean to brotherhood and community. For example, Douglass attributes much of the relative ease of life under Mr Freeland to the society of his fellow slaves, 'noble souls,' he calls them, with loving and brave hearts.

> We were linked and interlinked with each other. I loved them with a love stronger than any thing I have experienced since. It is sometimes said that we slaves do not love and confide in each other. In answer to this assertion, I can say, I never loved any or confided in any people more than my fellow-slaves, and especially those with whom I lived at Mr. Freeland's. I believe we would have died for each other. We never undertook to do any thing, of any importance, without a mutual consultation. We never moved separately. We were one; and as much so by our tempers and dispositions, as by the mutual hardships to which we were necessarily subjected by our condition as slaves.

> (Douglass 1968, 91)

But Douglass does not leave this intense communal consciousness unexamined or uncomplicated as a romantic myth. Much as Hawthorne might, Douglass renders his feelings toward community in all their complexity. Most notably, on the eve of his departure, Douglass registers a somber, almost debilitating, note:

> It is impossible for me to describe my feelings as the time of my contemplated start drew near. I had a number of warm-hearted friends in Baltimore, – friends that I loved almost as I did my life, – and the thought of being separated from them forever was painful beyond expression. It is my opinion that thousands would escape from slavery, who now remain, but for the strong cords of affection that bind them to their friends. The thought of leaving my friends was decidedly the most painful thought with which I had to contend. The love of them was my tender point, and shook my decision more than all things else.

> (p. 110)

Thus the very force which inspires Douglass and enables him to conspire an escape is *also* the force which inhibits many slaves from enacting their own escapes. It is in this relational context that Douglass forces us to consider nearly every element of life under a slave system. Few things are what they seem, nothing remains self-identical, and polar opposites eventually cohabitate. In a thoroughly transcendental context, Douglass performs a fusion of theory and practice coherent with some of Emerson's most famous articulations of such reintegrations in 'The American Scholar,' 'Self-Reliance,' and 'The Poet,' as well as with Thoreau's extrapolation of those Emersonian exhortations. Douglass's remarks on his educational history relieve his frequently violent narrative with a reflective, almost philosophical, commentary. We need only recall some of Douglass's earliest remarks about himself to grasp the intellectual gaps he needed to bridge. In his first paragraph, Douglass presents the issue starkly:

> I have no accurate knowledge of my age, never having seen any authentic record containing it. By far the larger part of the slaves know as little of their ages as horses know of theirs, and it is the wish of most masters within my knowledge to keep their slaves thus ignorant. I do not remember to have ever met a slave who could tell of his birthday. They seldom come nearer to it than planting-time, harvest-time, cherry-time, spring-time, or fall-time. A want of information concerning my own was a source of unhappiness to me even during childhood.

> (p. 21)

This lack of information concerning even his own past (he was also, we need remember, kept apart from his parents) suggests that the problem of ignorance for Douglass involves not only a lack of self-knowledge, but of history – personal and communal – as well. Douglass's comparison of the status of slaves to that of horses, and the seasonal register for slaves' birthdays indicate that his own biography, like that of most slaves, was a naturalistic, not a social or historical, matter. Douglass projects the insights he gains into the workings of slavery throughout the text, remarking, for example, that, after he heard Mr Auld chiding his wife, Sophia, for teaching Douglass the alphabet, he

'now understood what had been . . . a most perplexing difficulty
– to wit, the white man's power to enslave the black man' (p.
49). Sophia Auld, too, soon learned 'that education and slavery
were incompatible with each other' (p. 53). While Douglass first
rhapsodizes that 'from that moment [his realization that knowledge was the key to freedom], I understood the pathway from
slavery to freedom' (p. 49), this initial optimism is soon
squelched by his realization that knowledge in the abstract is
ineffectual.

Douglass's love of reading, which follows hard on Sophia
Auld's preliminary lessons, soon sours, even as his reading fills
in crucial social and historical gaps concerning slavery, and he
plunges into a state of despair.

> The more I read, the more I was led to abhor and detest my
> enslavers. . . . As I read and contemplated the subject, be-
> hold! that very discontent which Master Hugh had predicted
> would follow my learning to read had already come, to
> torment and sting my soul to unutterable anguish. As I
> writhed under it, I would at times feel that learning to read
> had been a curse rather than a blessing. It had given me
> a view of my wretched condition, without the remedy.
> It opened my eyes to the horrible pit, but to no ladder
> upon which to get out. In moments of agony, I envied my
> fellow-slaves for their stupidity. I have often wished myself a
> beast. I preferred the condition of the meanest reptile to my
> own.
>
> (p. 55)

Douglass's perceptions here can be traced to three different
problems informing his own educational history. The extent of
his ignorance (obliterating even a sense of familial origins)
could account for the perceived failure of knowledge to set him
free. Perhaps equally significant is the very source of Douglass's
learning. Though kind, Sophia Auld may pose more problems
for Douglass than she answers. As he enters his new 'home,'
Douglass remembers,

> here I saw what I had never seen before; it was a white face
> beaming with the most kindly emotions; it was the face of my
> new mistress, Sophia Auld. I wish I could describe the

rapture that flashed through my soul as I beheld it. It was a new and strange sight to me, brightening up my pathway with the light of happiness.

(p. 46)

This recollection suggests a crippling discrepancy at the core of Douglass's first learning experience. Inherent in *what* he can learn from Sophia Auld are the limitations of her context and its foreignness to Douglass's own experience. Still present are the social relations of slavery – she is, after all, his new 'mistress.' Her knowledge, furthermore, resonates with classical significance, as suggested by the allegorical implications of her name. Sophia Auld might as well be Lady Philosophy who can console Boethius *within* his prison but can't free him materially from its confines. Sophia's knowledge is also white, a point stressed by Douglass as he refers to her face as white, beaming, and brightening (the whiteness associated with Douglass's early learning recalls the dilemma faced by Phillis Wheatley, who found whiteness or purification of some sort inextricably bound with her notions of self, salvation, and poetic conventions). The racial and social differences that polarize Douglass and Sophia Auld could vex Douglass more than liberate him. Like Jim, whom Tom Sawyer forces to adopt the rhetoric of romanticized white prisoners, and like Invisible Man, who must forget his name, deny his past, and accept a world of whiteness before he can be given a *clean* bill of health, Douglass is imprisoned by the notion of literacy that he hopes will liberate him.

A third possibility, which might simply be a culmination of the first two suggestions, involves the abstract and reflective nature of Douglass's 'knowledge.' Derived exclusively from his reading, Douglass's knowledge makes him a passive recipient of information transmitted through a process mediated by Sophia Auld's white presence. As Emerson's famous remark in 'The American Scholar' asserts, 'Books are the best of things, well used; abused, among the worst' (Emerson 1982, 88). Douglass isn't exactly *abusing* his sources, but at this early stage he is more the bookworm than the Emersonian Man Thinking. Douglass is still pinned down by books; he has not yet learned that 'each age ... must write its own books' (Emerson 1982, 87). However,

Douglass concludes his despairing meditation (which returns him to an animalistic state and during which he goes so far as to suggest that he wishes himself dead (p. 56)) by asserting 'I would learn to write' (p. 59). His decision to move from a receptive reading mode to the more productive activity of writing soon, however, meets with a crushing blow at the hands of Mr Covey. As Douglass notes, 'Mr. Covey's *forte* consisted in his power to deceive. His life was devoted to planning and perpetrating the grossest deceptions' (p. 74). Nicknamed 'the snake,' Covey uses a repertoire of surprise visits, religious hypocrisy, and, of course, violence. Covey's unpredictability, his power to make work go 'on in his absence almost as well as in his presence' (p. 73) reintroduces a gap between the world as it appears and as it actually is, a problem of signification that Douglass's reading and writing had attempted to bridge. Douglass's response to Covey's reign of deceptive terror is couched in significant terms:

> I was somewhat unmanageable when I first went there [his education has already rendered Douglass an insurgent], but a few months of this discipline tamed me. Mr. Covey succeeded in breaking me. I was broken in body, soul, and spirit. My natural elasticity was crushed, my intellect languished, the disposition to read departed, the cheerful spark that lingered about my eye died; the dark night of slavery closed in upon me; and behold a man transformed into a brute!
>
> (p. 75)

Thus, Douglass's carefully constructed human identity has been negated by a new form of tyranny; deception added to physical cruelty, intellectual anxiety added to bodily pain. That Douglass uses light/dark and animal imagery to signify this transformation reminds us of his initial optimism and the similarly metaphorical account he gave of his first meeting with Sophia Auld. His despair here, too, echoes that which he felt when he first sensed that learning only made him more aware of his servitude.

Douglass's physical battle with Covey thus represents a moment of personal consolidation, of transcendence, of socialization. *During* that battle Douglass's physicality is never related to his previous educational experiences; it stands on its own historical and literary merit, much like Douglass's absolute assertion of self in his struggle. In this sense, it needs no context. Douglass's reflections on that battle and its significance do, however, relate it to the passages in which Douglass's learning to read and write inspire new hopes which are almost immediately extinguished by some new and more brutal experience.

> This battle with Mr. Covey was the turning-point in my career as a slave. It rekindled the few expiring embers of freedom, and revived within me a sense of my own manhood. It recalled the departed self-confidence, and inspired me again with a determination to be free. . . . It was a glorious resurrection, from the tomb of slavery, to the heaven of freedom.
>
> (pp. 82–3)

In this best known of all passages from the *Narrative*, Douglass notes that his fight was a 'turning-point,' but whereas earlier turning points had proved illusory, the language here is more confident, even decisive. Echoing the plethora of 're' prefixes that mark the role of Emerson's poet (who among other things re-attaches words to things), Douglass asserts that the battle *re*kindled his sense of freedom, *re*vived his assurance of his manhood, *re*called his self-confidence, and *again* inspired him to be free. It is significant that at this crucial juncture in his narrative Douglass chooses to recall his earlier disappointments and to represent the physical battle consciously as the recapitulation of his earlier overtures toward freedom and as the resolution of this central issue. What Douglass dramatizes is a dialectical progression from ignorance through reading and writing to physical combat. This progression is important in several ways. First, each stage relates him to his owners. Whereas he is deprived of knowledge by white slave drivers, he is given the rudiments of literacy by Sophia Auld (herself too ignorant of slave dynamics 'naturally' to know not to teach him to read). Douglass's physical victory over Covey also frustrates 'the snake's' style of deception by refusing to accept his intellectual duplicity on its own terms. When his owners practice *primarily* physical cruelty, Douglass dramatizes himself primarily as a thinking being, but when Covey adds overt deception, Douglass is moved to physical retaliation. In dialectical terms, Douglass negates the various negations of his humanity by his masters. Second, each stage in Douglass's self-defined resurrection represents a progression toward social emancipation. Whereas his reading and writing had been private (though not privatistic) moments, his physical struggle is the objectification not only of his thoughts of freedom (inspired and clarified by his reading and writing) but of his human dignity as well. Thus, Houston Baker, Jr's assertion that 'by adapting language as his instrument for extracting meaning from nothingness, being from existence, Douglass becomes a public figure' needs some qualification (Baker 1980, 39). It is, of course, true that the publication of the *Narrative* launched Douglass's career as a 'public' figure. But, while Baker stresses language as Douglass's prime vehicle in becoming public (though he does not adhere to a simple or privatistic notion of language as such), Douglass himself renders language as an abstract medium subordinate to the externalization of that self (partially a linguistic construct) in physical battle. In an earlier essay, Baker nicely clarifies another dimension added by the experiential mode I have been stressing in Douglass's work. Stressing the mimetic verisimilitude of the *Narrative*, Baker notes that 'the world of the *Narrative* is a world of action, one in which only the strong and determined survive,' and traces much of the text's strength to Douglass's rendering of the external realities of an agrarian milieu and slave system:

> We learn, for example, the exact number of Colonel Lloyd's slaves, horses, and cultivated acres. We become acquainted with the narrator's place of residence in Baltimore in terms of the area, the street, the neighbors, and the treatment accorded to neighbors' slaves. . . . We watch harvesting and the transporting of goods by water; we witness the actions of overseers, Southern preachers, and slave breakers; we see the slave cabins, barns, and stables. There is no hothouse atmosphere in Douglass's work; never is life reduced to the taking of toast and tea.

> (Baker 1972, 74–5)

Douglass's objective rendering of an actual milieu with such material specificity should, I offer, be seen as a product of his more subjective grasp of his own identity in a densely social and historical context.

Finally, this crystallizing moment (Douglass's physical battle) recalls similar such moments in writings by other central figures from the American Renaissance. In 'The American Scholar,' for example, Emerson attacks commodity fetishism and the division of labor by asserting that man,

> this original unit, this fountain of power, has been so distributed to multitudes, has been so minutely subdivided and peddled out, that it is spilled into drops, and cannot be gathered. The state of society is one in which the members have suffered amputation from the trunk, and strut about so many walking monsters, – a good finger, a neck, a stomach, an elbow, but never a man. Man is thus metamorphosed into a thing, into many things.
>
> (Emerson 1982, 84)

Emerson proposes the reunification of this original unit in order to combat the psychological division of faculties that follows from a social division of labor. Thoreau's fusion of intellectual and physical labor in constructing his own house, in growing his beans, or in fishing pushes for the same integration of human experience, though he prefers a spiraling from *mere* physicality to philosophical reflection. Ishmael, too, argues that only by approaching the whale both intellectually and materially can humans gain any knowledge. The most grotesque representations of the whale, we should recall, have been rendered by those who have never gone before the mast and experienced the whale directly. Douglass's early intellectual overtures are not by any means grotesque, but they are ineffectual, almost counter-productive (each failure sends him into a deeper despair) because they are abstract. In affirming this experiential mode, Douglass no less than Emerson, Thoreau, and Melville (the list could go on) is not denying the potency of philosophical reflection but rather insisting that only a consolidation of human powers – intellectual, spiritual, and physical – can represent the fullest in human experience.

More thoroughly than his contemporaries, however, Douglass refuses to leave his apparent 'resurrection' unchallenged. He stresses the difficulties he faces in realizing his new sense of self while still living in a racist society. When he and a band of friends plan an escape, it is their *ignorance* of geography that intimidates them most.

> Our path was beset with the greatest obstacles; and if we succeeded in gaining the end of it, our right to be free was yet questionable – we were yet liable to be returned to bondage. We could see no spot, this side of the ocean, where we could be free. We knew nothing about Canada. Our knowledge of the north did not extend farther than New York; and to go there, and be forever harassed with the frightful liability of being returned to slavery – with the certainty of being treated tenfold worse than before – the thought was a truly horrible one, and one which it was not easy to overcome.
>
> (p. 92)

By addressing the practical consequences of ignorance (here of geography), Douglass refuses to simplify the complexity of social and historical action. Though literate, confident, and part of a group, Douglass still faces practical obstacles to his quest for actual freedom. More like Ishmael or Israel Potter than Emerson or Thoreau, who asserts the need, but not the results, of leaving Walden, Douglass grapples with the status of a human being in a problematic historical moment.

In another strategy that situates him both within major thematics of the American Renaissance as well as within a proto-modernist tradition of literary practice, Douglass dismantles the ideological structure of slave society by defamiliarizing and 'making strange' its most fundamental assumptions, usually by demonstrating that the most commonplace notions about slaves living under slavery are simply falsehoods perpetrated by slave owners. Thoreau, perhaps, represents this impetus most clearly throughout *Walden*, but particularly in 'Economy.' In a famous passage, Thoreau attempts to jar his readers into a new perception of their lives of quiet desperation:

> I have travelled a good deal in Concord; and every where, in shops, and offices, and fields, the inhabitants have appeared to me to be doing penance in a thousand remarkable ways. What I have heard of Bramins sitting exposed to four fires

and looking in the face of the sun; or hanging suspended, with their heads downward, over flames; or looking at the heavens over their shoulders 'until it becomes impossible for them to resume their natural position, while from the twist of their neck nothing but liquids can pass into the stomach;' or dwelling, chained for life, at the foot of a tree; or measuring with their bodies, like caterpillars, the breadth of vast empires; or standing on one leg on the tops of pillars, – even these forms of conscious penance are hardly more incredible and astonishing than the scenes which I daily witness.

And, more theoretically, in 'Where I Lived and What I Lived For,' Thoreau notes that 'shams and delusions are esteemed for soundest truths, while reality is fabulous.'

In a Fourth of July address delivered in 1852, Douglass rivals Thoreau in the impact of his own comparisons, if not in the allusiveness of his rhetoric:

Go where you may, search where you will, roam through all the monarchies and despotisms of the old world, travel through South America, search out every abuse, and when you have found the last, lay your facts by the side of the every-day practices of this nation, and you will say with me that, for revolting barbarity and shameless hypocrisy, America reigns without a rival.

(Douglass 1969, 445)

There is no evidence of influence between Douglass and Thoreau. The similarities between these passages suggest a deeper affinity than mere influence, however: their shared perception of America's blindness to its own darker truths. Commenting on Douglass's similarities with Melville, Henry-Luis Gates, Jr makes a pertinent point. According to Gates, both saw that in American society is to be found as much that is contrary to moral order as could be found in pre-revolutionary Europe. The novelty of American innocence is, however, the refusal or failure to recognize evil while participating in that evil (Fisher and Stepto 1979, 218).

Both Douglass and Thoreau make their points by referring to the distant (in both time and space), to the bizarre, and to the most seemingly impossible ranges of experience. For both, the truth of American life is its most terrible nightmare, that civilization, progress, or freedom, as most of their contemporaries understood these terms, are utter frauds. They both, to borrow Gates's term, force us to *re-cognize* the truths that are American existence. That Thoreau is speaking about figurative modes of slavery and Douglass about literal, economic slavery only makes their rhetorical similarities more significant by rendering the homologous relationships between these two modes in sharply etched figures.

In the *Narrative* Douglass performs similar defamiliarizing operations, though in that text's usually more literal and urgent manner, by exposing the lies that white culture has accepted in order to conceal the facts of slavery. For example, after a discussion of slave songs and how he traces his 'first glimmering conception of the dehumanizing character of slavery' (Douglass 1968, 73) from them, Douglass addresses the common fallacy that singing slaves equal happy slaves.

> I have often been utterly astonished, since I came to the north, to find persons who could speak of the singing, among slaves, as evidence of their contentment and happiness. It is impossible to conceive of a greater mistake. Slaves sing most when they are most unhappy.
>
> (p. 32)

In a similar vein, Douglass follows a graphic discussion of a slave being punished (chained, handcuffed, and snatched from family and friends to be sold down the river to Georgia) for telling the 'simple truth' concerning his treatment at the hands of his overseer with another extrapolation on common misconceptions.

> It is partly in consequence of such facts, that slaves, when inquired of as to their condition and the character of their masters, almost universally say they are contented, and that their masters are kind. The slaveholders have been known to send in spies among their slaves, to ascertain their views and feelings in regard to their condition. The frequency of this has had the effect to establish among the slaves the maxim, that a still tongue makes a wise head. They suppress the truth rather than take the consequences of telling it, and in so doing prove themselves a part of the human family.
>
> (p. 36)

Douglass's rhetorical strategy here is representative of the *Narrative*. He begins with a personal experience, moves on to a generalization about slavery, and, from there, extends to the 'human family' in general, a spiral pattern that anticipates Thoreau's work in *Walden*.

Finally, after a discussion of his own holiday between Christmas and New Year, Douglass similarly exposes the fallacy of believing that holidays are an indication of benevolence on the part of the slave owners. Rather, he affirms, they are 'among the most effective means in the hands of the slaveholder in keeping down the spirit of insurrection' (p. 81). According to Douglass,

> The holidays are part and parcel of the gross fraud, wrong, and inhumanity of slavery. They are professedly a custom established by the benevolence of the slaveholders; but I undertake to say, it is the result of selfishness, and one of the grossest frauds committed upon the down-trodden slave. . . . Their object seems to be, to disgust their slaves with freedom, by plunging them into the lowest depths of dissipation.
>
> (pp. 84–5)

The tenor of these passages is clear enough. Many people (especially Northerners, his immediate audience) maintain softer visions of the slave system because of the white hegemony over information networks and their ability to perpetrate plausible misconceptions. Douglass's rhetorical constructions in these cases place him within the mainstream of the American Renaissance as well. Like Melville, Thoreau, and Whitman, Douglass renders philosophical or ideological generalizations only after a specific personal and material instance (sometimes more than one) prepares his text for such a projection. There are few if any moments in the *Narrative* in which Douglass reasons idealistically – he, like Thoreau in his bean field or Ishmael with his hands inside the whale, works from the ground (or ocean) up.

The point at which Douglass diverges most radically from Thoreau (Emerson as well) and from the Melville of *Moby-Dick* is precisely on the question of a starting point from which to initiate any inquiry. For Thoreau there is little doubt that 'there is a solid bottom everywhere' (Walter Benn Michaels's exemplary deconstructive reading (1977) of *Walden* notwithstanding).

It is Walden's bottom, that point in nature to which human thought can be moored, that provides a *point d'appui* from which thought can emerge. And while Ishmael complicates the transcendentalist notion of nature, the sheer palpability of the whale, the reality of the ocean, and the material specificity of whaling furnish points from which Ishmael's thinking expands. It is the Melville of *Pierre* and *The Confidence-Man* (and to a lesser extent Hawthorne as well) with whom Douglass is most clearly aligned. In *Pierre* nature is absolutely a construct, a convention that provides no haven, no *point d'appui*, because it is lost to human needs as a result of its conventionality. It is a fiction, no less than Pierre's early poetry and worldview, but more deceptive and inscrutable because its conventionality is determined by the economic and cultural hegemony of the 'bladders,' Mrs Glendinning, Mrs Tartan, and the Reverend Falsgrave. In 'Benito Cereno' and *The Confidence-Man*, elements within nature cannot reflect human desire or assure human needs 'because,' as Benito Cereno despairingly remarks, 'they have no memory, . . . because they are not human.' Reality is a decisively human and social fiction in post-*Moby-Dick* Melville; nature is relegated to the nonhuman.

For all its organic metaphors, Douglass's *Narrative* anticipates Melville's assault on nature (or at least on Emerson's *Nature*). Slaves may have situated their birth dates seasonally, according to 'planting-time, harvest-time, cherry-time, spring-time, or fall-time' (p. 21), and Douglass may fill his narrative with comparisons between humans and animals, a strategy which both reproduces the white reduction of black selfhood to the level of animals *and* which suggests the corresponding diminution of white consciousness. However, nature provides no ultimate foundation for Douglass, no *point d'appui* upon which he can build either a sense of self or his narrative. Sophia Auld does not *naturally* know not to instruct Douglass in reading because

> she at first lacked the depravity indispensable to shutting me up in mental darkness. It was at least necessary for her to have some training in the exercise of irresponsible power, to make her equal to the task of treating me as though I were but a brute.
>
> (p. 52)

In other words, white treatment of blacks, regardless of their attempts to justify forms of dehumanization in notions of racial superiority, is a social construct that members of a slave society must acquire. Similarly, the strategy of separating families to keep slaves ignorant and in historical vacuums proves futile. It is not the natural unit of the family, but the socialized communal bonds formed with other slaves that enables Douglass to imagine realities beyond slavery and to conspire to attain them. Thus the naive white reliance on natural bonds (or the breaking of them) falls beneath the inertia of constructed social units among slaves. *Social* unity supplants family bonds.

These and other examples work together to focus the ultimate question of Douglass's *Narrative*, that of the nature of the self. Whereas Emerson, Thoreau, and, to a lesser extent, Melville tended to situate the self within some natural context, Douglass renders a fully social and dialectical notion of selfhood, one more diverse and elusive, and ultimately more historically potent. Douglass forces us to recognize (perhaps with Hawthorne) that any self is a social construct, not a natural integer, and it is in that sense of human sociability and in Douglass's ability to render the institution of slavery as an ideological construct subject to change that provides the *Narrative* with its final act of defamiliarization, and, perhaps, its finest moment of literary and historical power.

I would like finally to argue that Douglass's life, his works, the institution of slavery, and the struggle against slavery waged by black and white alike are the material, social, and political basis on which the works of other major writers of the American Renaissance are founded. The dynamics of slavery made the less specific (though certainly no less important) meditations of Emerson, Thoreau, Hawthorne, Melville, Stowe, and others *possible*. Their writings represent the imaginative ramifications of a slave system and focus the implications of chattel slavery in terms applicable and appropriate to all humans, slaves and transcendentalists alike. What American criticism needs to address are the homologous relationships between historical data, explicit slave discourse, and those texts by American authors not usually read as connected to the cruder facts of economic, racial, and political reality. The works of other major writers from the nineteenth century can, of course, be read without reference to slavery as an institution or to the diminution of life, white and black (and today Western and Third World), resulting from all forms of institutional oppression. However, by so abstracting text from text (major from minor, white from black, male from female) and literary text from social context are we not reading 'The American Scholar,' *Walden, The Scarlet Letter, Moby-Dick, Israel Potter, Huckleberry Finn, Uncle Tom's Cabin,* and *Uncle Tom's Children* in damagingly incomplete ways?

Not all the political and social thinking in American texts is as admirable, humane, and central as Douglass's, but we need to acknowledge its presence, not to write it off as subliterary. And we needn't, of course, concentrate exclusively on the harshest or most palpable material and political contexts for literary production. Such foci might, however, be a new beginning. Thoreau stressed the necessity of his beans being rooted firmly in the earth before they could grow toward the heavens, and both Thoreau and Melville (at least in Ishmael's voice) argue that all theoretical knowledge must proceed from the social, natural, and material contexts of its formulation. Yet theorists of American literature have tended to ignore the social foundation of American writing. Without roots in the actual social fabric of American life their theories can only give a partial sense of American literature.

Notes

Chapter 1. The unused past: theorists of American literature and the problem of exclusivity

1 Throughout this study I use the conventional phrase 'American literature' rather than the arguably more accurate (though cumbersome) alternative 'literature of the United States.'
2 Extracted from a pamphlet for the colloquium. I would like to thank A. Robert Lee, a participant in the program, for bringing it to my attention.
3 See Graff 1979, chapter 1, 'Culture, Criticism, and Unreality.'
4 See Lentricchia 1984 and Foley 1984.
5 See Metzger 1955, 413–20 for a good discussion of these years.
6 I am indebted to Metzger's article for these examples.

Chapter 2. The problem of Puritan origins in literary history and theory

1 See Ruland 1967, chapter 4, 'Exemplum: The Sherman-Mencken Debate,' for a thorough and engaging discussion of the issue.
2 For a thorough bibliography on Miller's historiography, see Crowell 1977.
3 See especially chapters 9 and 10 for Morgan's account of the antinomian crisis.
4 See also Morgan's chapter on 'Puritan Tribalism' for a fuller treatment of this.
5 In *The Puritan Family*, Morgan remarks that, for the Puritans, God

had ordained only one social relationship, that of child to parent: 'the other forms of social relations had to be filled by the voluntary actions of individuals' (p. 26); and, on marriage, he adds, 'every proper marriage since the first was founded on a covenant to which the free and voluntary consent of both parties was necessary' (p. 30). *The Puritan Family* examines many modes of Puritan voluntarism. Perry Miller, too, points out the voluntary participation of both God and humans in the covenant (see 'The Marrow of Puritan Divinity' in Miller 1956), but he often reduced the covenant to a matter of aesthetic coherence: 'It was a special way of reading scripture so that the books assembled in the Bible could all be seen to make sense in the same way' (Miller and Johnson 1963, 58).

6 Nathaniel Hawthorne, *The Scarlet Letter*, Centenary Edition, vol. II (Columbus: Ohio State University Press, 1962), p. 5. In the 1851 preface to *The House of the Seven Gables*, Hawthorne reiterates the same historical framework: 'The point of view in which this tale comes under the Romantic definition lies in the attempt to connect a bygone time with the very present that is flitting away from us.' In that same preface, Hawthorne grants that 'the reader may perhaps choose to assign an actual locality to the imaginary events of this narrative,' and admits that 'the historical connection . . . was essential to his plan.' Although Hawthorne qualifies the importance of his historical contexts, he seems more concerned with protecting his tales against too rigid and reductive a historical interpretation than with denying his works' historical reference.

7 Lovelace's study is an essential, theologically based study of Mather. See also pp. 84–5 of that study for ways in which Mather addressed different segments of his congregation with different rhetorical strategies.

Chapter 3. 'Nothing that is not there and the nothing that is': cultural theories of American literature

1 The seminal essay, 'Reality in America,' had been published in two earlier sections, one in 1940, the other in 1946.

2 While it is not my purpose to analyze the relationship between the New Left and the counter-Progressives, nor to equate the New Left with the Progressives, the New Left's reinstatement of political criteria does highlight the tension between a materialist and an idealist debate. Whereas counter-Progressives might explain American imperialism in terms of misguided moralism, New Left historians would see expansion as the inevitable result of capitalist power structures.

3 Delmore Schwartz accuses Trilling of giving 'a very limited meaning

to the word society' and of being concerned and anxious only about 'the welfare of the educated class: he is a guardian of its interests and a critic of its ideas' (Schwartz 1953, 59–60, 65, 66).

4 Mills 1973; see especially pp. 3–31 and the appendix, 'Revising the Trilling Thesis.'

5 While Trilling is critical of Eliot's autonomy theory of literature, his own overall response to Eliot was an ambivalent mixture of admiration and opposition. As William M. Chace observes,

> In having thought earlier (in 1940) about T. S. Eliot – obviously a conservative – Trilling had expressed great admiration. Eliot had once been obliged to confront Arnold's legacy, and the encounter had helped to define his criticism. And in 1940 it was Trilling who knew he could profit from the same encounter with Eliot. That profitable encounter reveals to us one side of Trilling's political stance: the conservative. Another, and opposing side, is revealed when this admiration on Trilling's part gets severely qualified in his speaking of Eliot's 'deficiencies,' his 'cold ignorance,' his 'fierce puritanism,' and his 'confusion of morality with snobbery or conformity.' Here Trilling admits his misgivings about the conservative posture.
>
> (Chace 1980, 69)

6 In *Reality and Idea in the Early American Novel*, David Hirsch criticizes both Trilling and Chase for simplistic notions of reality:

> As with Trilling, so . . . with Chase. Manners and a rigid and well defined class-structure have become the only legitimate agents which can be used to communicate reality and insofar as a work of fiction cannot be directly related to or superimposed upon an empirically verifiable, highly stratified social structure, to that extent it has veered away from 'reality' towards 'romance.'
>
> (Hirsch 1971, 39)

Interestingly, Hirsch's remarks echo Trilling's own accusation of Dreiser's and Parrington's narrow and arrogant notions of reality.

7 New Critics – I. A. Richards and Cleanth Brooks, for example – argued that various tensions *were* resolved in the poem. Chase's discussion of the *unreconciled* contradictions in American literary texts, however, differs little from the New Critical position. Even though he argues that American contradictions were not resolved in the work of art, American fiction does, according to Chase, achieve at least a balanced state of irresolution.

8 See *Opening Up the Canon* (Fiedler and Baker 1981).

9 I am indebted to Gene H. Bell-Villada (1982) for this summary of Frye. The event is recounted in Frye's *The Critical Path: An Essay on*

the Social Context of Literary Criticism (Bloomington: Indiana University Press, 1973), p. 146. Bell-Villada's paper is a lively discussion of the infusion of American literary thought with myths of American universalism and with anticommunist ideology, both of which, Bell-Villada argues, are sustained by a literary criticism which abstracts literary significance in the form of mythic archetypes.

Chapter 4. American literature should not mean but be: self-reflexive theories of American literature

1 René Wellek argues that detractors of New Criticism have missed the subtle sense in which New Criticism did not abolish rationality or correspondence to the world from poetry (Wellek 1979).

2 See Morris 1972; Ruland 1967; and Gunn 1975 for three excellent accounts.

3 See Matthiessen's entire study for a more explicit statement of his affinities with Eliot. Richard Ruland, incidentally, refers to Eliot as Matthiessen's 'lifelong master' (Ruland 1967, 212).

4 Joseph Riddel argued this approach in his course on American poetics during the 1981 Summer Session of the School of Criticism and Theory.

5 Poirier defines 'conventions' in both literary and social terms; sometimes the two work together, while at other times Poirier emphasizes one over the other, as in the case of Deerslayer, who, he argues, is trapped by an English literary mode. Edwin Fussell studies the American poet's struggle against the English poetic tradition as well: 'that dialectic can never be entirely resolved. The experimental American poet is wonderfully trapped between desire and necessity: the desire to be totally free of the English poetic tradition' (Fussell 1973, 24). For Fussell, 'the history of American poetry is the history of recurrent explosions, metrically centered, caused by the frustration of the American poet.' Fussell's notion of the American 'Lucifer' (an interesting inversion of Lewis's American Adam) bound up by language and cultural conventions, echoes many of Poirier's concerns.

6 Poirier's remarks recall some remarks by Russian formalists on 'defamiliarization.' Whereas Jameson argues that Shklovsky's definition of art as defamiliarization had 'profound ethical implications,' Poirier's version seems to offer only psychological or existential freshness (Jameson 1972, 50–3).

7 My thinking about Feidelson has been sharpened by conversations with Barbara Foley.

8 It should be noted that an existential position would replace the New Critical definition of the text as autonomous object with one that

emphasized the experiential dynamics of literature. As Gerald Graff argues, this 'corresponds to the difference between treating human beings as *persons* rather than as *things*' (Graff 1979, 131). The point at issue in this case is the *autonomy* imputed to either text or individual.

Works cited

Allen, Gay Wilson and Pochman, Henry A. (1969) *Introduction to Masters of American Literature.* Carbondale and Edwardsville: Southern Illinois University Press.

Baker, Houston A., Jr (1972) *Long Black Song: Essays in Black American Literature and Culture.* Charlottesville: University of Virginia Press.

—— (1980) *The Journey Back: Issues in Black Literature and Criticism.* Chicago and London: The University of Chicago Press.

Bakhtin, M. M. (1981) *The Dialogic Imagination.* Ed. Michael Holquist. Austin and London: University of Texas Press.

Barnes, Hazel E. (1967) *An Existentialist Ethics.* New York: Vintage Books.

Baym, Nina (1979) Review of *The Puritan Origins of the American Self,* by Sacvan Bercovitch. *Nineteenth-Century Fiction* 34: 348–52.

—— (1981) 'Melodramas of Beset Manhood: How Theories of American Fiction Exclude Women Authors.' *American Quarterly* 33: 123–39.

Becker, John E. (1971) *Hawthorne's Historical Allegory: An Examination of the American Conscience.* Port Washington, New York: Kennikat Press.

Bell-Villada, Gene H. (1982) 'Northrop Frye, Modern Fantasy, Anti-Marxism, Centrist Liberalism, Passing Time, and Other Limits of American Criticism.' Paper delivered at the International Association of Philosophy and Literature, Spring Session. Evanston, IL.

Bennett, Tony (1979) *Formalism and Marxism.* London: Methuen.

Bercovitch, Sacvan (1975) *The Puritan Origins of the American Self.* New Haven: Yale University Press.

—— (1978) *The American Jeremiad.* Madison: University of Wisconsin Press.

Berthoff, Warner (1967) 'Ambitious Scheme.' *Commentary* 44 (October): 110–14.

Bewley, Marius (1959) *The Eccentric Design: Form in the Classic American Novel.* New York: Columbia University Press.

Bourne, Randolph (1956) *The History of a Literary Radical and Other Papers by Randolph Bourne.* New York: S. A. Russell.

Breen, T. H. (1980) *Puritans and Adventurers.* New York: Oxford University Press.

Brodhead, Richard H. (1976) *Hawthorne, Melville, and the Novel.* Chicago: University of Chicago Press.

Brooks, Cleanth (1947) *The Well Wrought Urn: Studies in the Structure of Poetry.* New York: Harcourt, Brace and World.

Brooks, Van Wyck (1951) *The Confident Years.* New York: Dutton.

Bryer, Jackson R. (ed.) (1969) *Fifteen Modern American Authors.* Durham: Duke University Press.

Cassirer, Ernst (1944) *Essay on Man.* New Haven: Yale University Press.

Chace, William M. (1980) *Lionel Trilling: Criticism and Politics.* Stanford: Stanford University Press.

Chase, Richard (1957) *The American Novel and Its Tradition.* Garden City: Doubleday.

Colacurcio, Michael J. (1978) 'Does American Literature Have a History?' *Early American Literature* 13 (Spring): 110–32.

—— (1984) *The Province of Piety: Moral History in Hawthorne's Early Tales.* Cambridge, MA: Harvard University Press.

Cowley, Malcolm (1970) *A Many-Windowed House.* Ed. Henry Dan Piper. Carbondale and Edwardsville: Southern Illinois University Press.

Crèvecoeur, J. Hector St John de (1957) *Letters from an American Farmer.* New York: Dutton.

Crowell, John C. (1977) 'Perry Miller as Historian: A Bibliography of Evaluations.' *Bulletin of Bibliography* 34: 77–85.

Dauber, Kenneth (1977) 'Criticism of American Literature.' *Diacritics* 7: 55–66.

Davis, Robert Gorham (1960) 'Freud and Faust in American Letters.' *New Leader* (16 May): 11–13.

Derrida, Jacques (1970) 'Structure, Sign, and Play in the Discourse of the Human Sciences.' In *The Structuralist Controversy*, ed. Richard Macksey and Eugenio Donato, 247–65. Baltimore and London: Johns Hopkins University Press.

Douglas, Ann (1978) *The Feminization of American Culture.* New York: Avon Books.

Douglass, Frederick (1968) *Narrative of the Life of Frederick Douglass, An American Slave: Written By Himself.* New York: New American Library.

—— (1969) *My Bondage and My Freedom.* New York: Dover Publications.

Eagleton, Terry (1976a) *Criticism and Ideology.* London: New Left Books.

—— (1976b) *Marxism and Literary Criticism.* Berkeley: University of California Press.

—— (1983) *Literary Theory: An Introduction.* Minneapolis: University of Minnesota Press.

Eggleston, Edward (1957) *The Hoosier Schoolmaster.* New York: Hill and Wang.

Emerson, Donald (1972) 'The Remaking of "American Literature."' *Transactions of the Wisconsin Academy of Sciences, Arts and Letters* 60: 45–51.

Emerson, Ralph Waldo (1982) *Selected Essays.* Ed. Larzer Ziff. New York: Penguin.

Erikson, Kai T. (1966) *Wayward Puritans: A Study in the Sociology of Deviance.* New York: John Wiley.

Feidelson, Charles, Jr (1953) *Symbolism and American Literature.* Chicago: University of Chicago Press.

Fiedler, Leslie A. (1948) *An End to Innocence: Essays on Culture and Politics.* Boston: Beacon Press.

—— (1958) 'American Literature.' In *Contemporary Literary Scholarship: A Critical Review,* ed. Lewis Leary, 157–85. New York: Appleton-Century-Crofts.

—— (1960) *Love and Death in the American Novel.* New York: Stein and Day.

—— and Baker, Houston A., Jr (eds) (1981) *Opening Up the Canon.* Baltimore and London: Johns Hopkins University Press.

Fisher, Dexter and Stepto, Robert B. (eds) (1979) *Afro-American Literature: The Reconstruction of Instruction.* New York: Modern Language Association of America.

Foerster, Norman (ed.) (1928) *The Reinterpretation of American Literature.* New York: Harcourt, Brace.

Foley, Barbara (1984) 'The Politics of Deconstruction.' *Genre* 17: 113–34.

—— (1984) 'From New Criticism to Deconstruction: The Example of Charles Feidelson's *Symbolism and American Literature.*' *American Quarterly* 36 (Spring): 43–64.

Foster, Stephen (1971) *Their Solitary Way: The Puritan Social Ethic in the First Century of Settlement in New England.* New Haven: Yale University Press.

Fowler, Alastair (1975) 'The Selection of Literary Constructs.' *New Literary History* 7: 39–55.

Franklin, H. Bruce (1978) *The Victim as Criminal and Artist*. New York: Oxford University Press.

Fussell, Edwin (1973) *Lucifer in Harness*. Princeton: Princeton University Press.

Gottesman, Ronald, *et al.* (eds) (1979) *The Norton Anthology of American Literature*. New York: W. W. Norton.

Graff, Gerald (1979) *Literature Against Itself*. Chicago: University of Chicago Press.

Green, Martin (1963) *Re-Appraisals: Some Common Sense Readings in American Literature*. London: Hugh Evelyn.

Green, Philip (1958) 'Radicalism for Rotarians.' *New Republic* 139 (20 October): 17–20.

Gruber, Carol S. (1975) *Mars and Minerva: World War I and the Uses of the Higher Learning in America*. Baton Rouge: Louisiana State University Press.

Gunn, Giles (1975) *F. O. Matthiessen: The Critical Achievement*. Seattle and London: University of Washington Press.

Hall, David D. (1971) 'Understanding the Puritans.' In *Essays in Politics and Social Development: Colonial America*, ed. Stanley Katz, 32–50. Boston: Little, Brown.

Halttunen, Karen (1978) 'Cotton Mather and the Meaning of Suffering in the *Magnalia Christi Americana*.' *Journal of American Studies* 12 (December): 311–29.

Hawkes, Terence (1977) *Structuralism and Semiotics*. Berkeley and Los Angeles: University of California Press.

Heilbroner, Robert (1980) *Marxism: For and Against*. New York: W. W. Norton.

Henderson, Harry (1974) *Versions of the Past: The Historical Imagination in American Fiction*. New York: Oxford University Press.

Herbert, T. Walter, Jr (1980) *Marquesan Encounters: Melville and the Meaning of Civilization*. Cambridge, MA: Harvard University Press.

Hicks, Granville (1933) *The Great Tradition*. New York: Macmillan.

Hirsch, David H. (1966) 'Reality, Manners, and Mr. Trilling.' *Sewanee Review* 72 (Summer): 420–32.

—— (1971) *Reality and Idea in the Early American Novel*. The Hague: Mouton.

—— (1977) '"Hermeneutics" as Free-Floating Fantasy.' *Sewanee Review* 85: lxxii–lxxix.

Hirsch, E. D., Jr (1976) *The Aims of Interpretation*. Chicago and London: University of Chicago Press.

Howard, Leon, Wright, Louis B., and Bode, Carl (eds) (1955) *American*

Heritage: An Anthology and Interpretive Survey of Our Literature. 2 vols. Boston: D. C. Heath.

Howe, Irving (1960) 'Literature on the Couch.' *New Republic* (5 December): 17–19.

Irwin, John (1980) *American Hieroglyphics: The Symbol of the Egyptian Hieroglyphics in the American Renaissance*. New Haven and London: Yale University Press.

James, Henry, Jr (1883) *Hawthorne*. London: Macmillan.

Jameson, Fredric (1972) *The Prison-House of Language: A Critical Account of Structuralism and Russian Formalism*. Princeton: Princeton University Press.

—— (1981) *The Political Unconscious: Narrative as a Socially Symbolic Act*. Ithaca: Cornell University Press.

Jones, Howard Mumford (1948) *The Theory of American Literature*. Ithaca: Cornell University Press.

—— (1967) 'American Studies in Higher Education.' In *Essays on American Literature in Honor of Jay B. Hubbell*, ed. Clarence Gohdes, 7–19. Durham, NC: Duke University Press.

Kant, Emmanuel (1971) *Critique of Judgment*. Reprinted in *Critical Theory Since Plato*, ed. Hazard Adams, 379–99. New York: Harcourt Brace Jovanovich.

Karanikas, Alexander (1966) *Tillers of a Myth: Southern Agrarians as Social and Literary Critics*. Madison: University of Wisconsin Press.

Karcher, Carolyn L. (1980) *Shadow Over the Promised Land: Slavery, Race, and Violence in Melville's America*. Baton Rouge: Louisiana State University Press.

Kartiganer, Donald M., and Griffith, Malcolm A. (eds) (1972) *Theories of American Literature*. New York: Macmillan.

Kelly, Ernece B. (ed.) (1972) *Searching for America*. Urbana, IL: National Council of Teachers of English.

Kirsch, James (1961) 'The Problems of Dictatorship as Represented in *Moby Dick*.' In *Current Trends in Analytical Psychology*. London: Tavistock.

Klein, Marcus (1981) *Foreigners: The Making of American Literature, 1900–1940*. Chicago: University of Chicago Press.

Klinkowitz, Jerome (1980) *The Practice of Fiction in America*. Ames, IA: Iowa State University Press.

Krieger, Murray (1971) 'The Existential Basis of Contextual Criticism.' Reprinted in *Critical Thought Since Plato*, ed. Hazard Adams, 1224–31. New York: Harcourt Brace Jovanovich.

Krupnick, Mark (1986) *Lionel Trilling and the Fate of Cultural Criticism*. Evanston: Northwestern University Press.

Lasch, Christopher (1967) *The New Radicalism in America, 1889–1963*. New York: Random House.

—— (1968) 'The Cultural Cold War: A Short History of the Congress for Cultural Freedom.' Reprinted in *Toward a New Past: Dissenting Essays in American History*, ed. Bartram Bernstein, 322–59. New York: Pantheon Books.

Lauter, Paul (1983) 'Race and Gender in the Shaping of the American Literary Canon: A Case Study from the Twenties.' *Feminist Studies* 9: 435–63.

Lawrence, D. H. (1961) *Studies in Classic American Literature*. New York: Viking Press.

Lentricchia, Frank (1980) *After the New Criticism*. Chicago: University of Chicago Press.

—— (1984) *Criticism and Social Change*. Chicago: University of Chicago Press.

Levin, David (1978) *Cotton Mather: The Young Life of the Lord's Remembrancer, 1663–1703*. Cambridge, MA: Harvard University Press.

Levin, Harry (1958) *The Power of Blackness*. New York: Alfred A. Knopf.

Lewis, R. W. B. (1955) *The American Adam: Innocence, Tragedy, and Tradition in the Nineteenth Century*. Chicago: University of Chicago Press.

—— (1959) *The Picaresque Saint: Representative Figures in Contemporary Fiction*. Philadelphia: Lippincott.

Lewis, Thomas E. (1979) 'Notes toward a Theory of the Referent.' *PMLA* 94 (May): 459–75.

Lewisohn, Ludwig (1932) *Expression in America*. New York: Harper.

Lovelace, Richard (1979) *The American Pietism of Cotton Mather: Origins of American Evangelicalism*. Grand Rapids: Christian University Press.

Machor, James L. (1980) 'Tradition, Holism, and the Dilemmas of American Literary Studies.' *Texas Studies in Literature and Language* 22: 99–121.

Marx, Leo (1953) 'Mr. Eliot, Mr. Trilling, and *Huckleberry Finn*.' *American Scholar* 22 (Autumn): 423–40.

—— (1964) *The Machine in the Garden*. New York: Oxford University Press.

Matthiessen, F. O. (1935) *The Achievement of T. S. Eliot*. Boston: Houghton Mifflin.

—— (1941) *American Renaissance: Art and Expression in the Age of Emerson and Whitman*. New York: Oxford University Press.

—— (1952) 'The Responsibilities of the Critic.' In *The Responsibilities of the Critic*, ed. John Rackliffe, 3–18. New York: Oxford University Press.

May, Henry (1957) *The End of American Innocence*. New York: Alfred A. Knopf.

Mencken, H. L. (1917) *A Book of Prefaces*. New York: Alfred A. Knopf.

Metscher, Thomas (1979) 'Literature and Art as Ideological Form.' *New Literary History* 10: 21–39.

Metzger, Walter P. (1955) 'Academic Freedom and Big Business.' In *The Development of Academic Freedom in the United States*, ed. Richard Hofstadter, 413–20. New York: Columbia University Press.

Michaels, Walter Benn (1977) *'Walden*'s False Bottoms.' *Glyph* 1: 132–49.

Miller, Perry (1933) *Orthodoxy in Massachusetts, 1630–1650*. Boston: Beacon Press.

—— (1939) *The New England Mind: The Seventeenth Century*. New York: Macmillan.

—— (1953) 'The Doctrine of the Symbol.' *Virginia Quarterly Review* 29: 303–5.

—— (1956) *Errand Into the Wilderness*. Cambridge, MA: Harvard University Press.

—— and Johnson, Thomas H. (eds) (1963) *The Puritans*. Vol. 1. New York: Harper and Row.

Mills, Nicolaus (1973) *American and English Fiction in the Nineteenth Century*. Bloomington: Indiana University Press.

Morgan, Edmund (1944) *The Puritan Family: Religion and Domestic Relations in Seventeenth-Century New England*. New York: Harper and Row.

—— (1958) *The Puritan Dilemma*. Boston and Toronto: Little, Brown.

Morris, Wesley (1972) *Towards a New Historicism*. Princeton: Princeton University Press.

Morsberger, Robert E. (1970) 'Segregated Surveys: American Literature.' *Negro American Literature Forum* 4: 3–8.

Nikolyukin, A. N. (1973) 'Past and Present Discussions of American National Literature.' *New Literary History* 4: 575–90.

Parker, Hershel (1985) *Flawed Texts and Verbal Icons*. Evanston: Northwestern University Press.

Paul, Sherman (1953) 'Resolution at Walden.' *Accent* 13: 101–13.

Pearce, Roy Harvey (1965) *The Continuity of American Poetry*. Princeton: Princeton University Press.

Pizer, Donald (1963) 'Synthetic Criticism and Frank Norris; or, Mr. Marx, Mr. Taylor, and *The Octopus*.' *American Literature* 34 (January): 532–41.

Poirier, Richard (1966) *A World Elsewhere: The Place of Style in American Literature*. New York: Oxford University Press.

—— (1971) *The Performing Self: Compositions and Decompositions in the Languages of Contemporary Life*. New York: Oxford University Press.

—— and Vance, William L. (eds) (1970) *American Literature*. 2 vols. Boston: Little, Brown.

Porte, Joel (1969) *The Romance in America: Studies in Cooper, Poe, Haw-*

thorne, Melville, and James. Middletown: Wesleyan University Press.

Porter, Carolyn (1981) *Seeing and Being: The Plight of the Participant Observer in Emerson, James, Adams, and Faulkner*. Middletown: Wesleyan University Press.

Rahv, Philip (1956) 'Fiction and the Criticism of Fiction.' *Kenyon Review* 18: 276–99.

—— (1957) *Image and Idea*. New York: New Directions.

Ransom, John Crowe (1938) *The World's Body*. New York: Scribner's.

—— (1941) 'Criticism as Pure Speculation.' In *The Intent of the Critic*, ed. Donald Stauffer, 91–124. Princeton: Princeton University Press.

—— (1943) 'The Inorganic Muses.' *Kenyon Review* 5: 278–300.

Reynolds, David (1981) *Faith in Fiction: The Emergence of Religious Literature in America*. Cambridge, MA: Harvard University Press.

Riddel, Joseph N. (1981) 'Emerson and the American "Signature."' School of Criticism and Theory. Summer.

Ruland, Richard (1967) *The Rediscovery of American Literature: Premises of Critical Taste, 1900–1940*. Cambridge, MA: Harvard University Press.

Rutman, Darrett B. (1970) *American Puritanism*. New York: W. W. Norton.

Schwartz, Delmore (1953) 'The Duchess' Red Shoes.' *Partisan Review* 20 (January): 55–73.

Shechner, Mark (1978) 'Psychoanalysis and Liberalism: The Case of Lionel Trilling.' *Salmagundi* 41 (Spring): 3–32.

Sherman, Stuart P. (1918) *American and Allied Ideals: An Appeal to Those Who Are Neither Hot Nor Cold*. War Information Series, No. 12. Washington, DC.

—— (1923) *The Genius of America*. New York: Scribner's.

Smith, Henry Nash (1950) *Virgin Land*. New York: Vintage.

Spengemann, William C. (1978) "What Is American Literature?" *Centennial Review* 22: 119–38.

Sprague, Claire (ed.) (1968) *Van Wyck Brooks: The Early Years*. New York: Harper and Row.

Steiner, George (1972) 'Whorf, Chomsky, and the Student of Literature.' *New Literary History* 4: 15–34.

Stonum, Gary Lee (1981) 'Undoing American Literary History.' *Diacritics* 11: 2–12.

Stovall, Floyd (ed.) (1963) *Eight American Authors*. New York: W. W. Norton.

Sundquist, Eric J. (1981) 'Suspense and Tautology in *Benito Cereno*.' *Glyph* 8: 103–26.

Tabachnick, Stephen E. (1981) 'The Problem of Neglected Literature.' *College English* 43 (January): 32–44.

Tate, Allen (1955) *The Man of Letters in the Modern World*. New York: Merridien Books.

Taylor, Benjamin (1981) 'Negotiations: A Conversation with Richard Poirier.' *Salmagundi* 52: 107–18.

Taylor, W. F. (1942) *The Economic Novel in America*. Chapel Hill: University of North Carolina Press.

Thomas, Vincent (1952) 'The Modernity of Jonathan Edwards.' *New England Quarterly* 25: 60–84.

Tocqueville, Alexis de (1945) *Democracy in America*. 2 vols. New York: Vintage Books.

Todorov, Tzvetan (1973) 'The Notion of Literature.' *New Literary History* 5 (Autumn): 5–16.

—— (1981) *Introduction to Poetics*. Minneapolis: University of Minnesota Press.

Tompkins, Jane (1981) 'Sentimental Power: *Uncle Tom's Cabin* and the Politics of Literary History.' *Glyph* 8: 79–103.

—— (1984) 'Masterpiece Theater: The Politics of Hawthorne's Literary Reputation.' *American Quarterly* 36: 617–42.

Trachtenberg, Alan (1965) 'The American View of Life.' *Nation* (5 July): 42–5.

—— (1967) 'Mind-Expanding Verbs.' *Nation* (3 July): 58–9.

—— (1977) 'The Writer as America.' *Partisan Review* 44: 466–75.

Trilling, Lionel (1950) *The Liberal Imagination*. New York: Doubleday.

—— (1965) *Beyond Culture*. New York: Viking Press.

Weimann, Robert (1976) *Structure and Society in Literary History*. Charlottesville: University of Virginia Press.

Wellek, René (1979) 'A Rejoinder to Gerald Graff.' *Critical Inquiry* 5 (Spring): 576–9.

Wendell, Barrett (1891) *Cotton Mather*. New York: Dodd and Mead.

Williams, Raymond (1977) *Marxism and Literature*. Oxford: Oxford University Press.

Williams, William Carlos (1925) *In the American Grain*. New York: New Directions.

Winters, Yvor (1938) *Maule's Curse: Seven Studies in the History of American Obscurantism*. New York: New Directions.

—— (1947) 'The Anatomy of Nonsense.' In his *In Defense of Reason*. Chicago: Swallow Press.

Wise, Gene (1973) *American Historical Explanations*. Homewood, IL: Dorsey Press.

Ziff, Larzer (1973) *Puritanism in America: New Culture in a New World*. New York: Viking Press.

Index